PUTTING ON PANTO TO PAY FOR THE PINTER

Henry Marshall pantomimes at Salisbury Playhouse 1955 to 1985

CHRIS ABBOTT

First published in the United Kingdom in 2012
by The Hobnob Press, PO Box 1838, East Knoyle, Salisbury, SP3 6FA
www.hobnobpress.co.uk

British Library Cataloguing in Publication Data
A catalogue record for this book is available from the British Library

ISBN 978-1-906978-26-6

Typeset in Minion Pro 12/16 pt. Typesetting and origination by John Chandler
Printed by Lightning Source

Cover design by Tim Abbott (Mulberry Interactive).
Cover image: Babes in the Wood 1968: Roger Hume (Friar Tuck), Oliver Gordon (Daisy Dimple) and Frank Ellis (Willie Whiskers).

Contents

Acknowledgements

Christine Absalom
Doreen Andrew
Frank Barrie
David Beames
Jessica Benton
Christopher Biggins
Olivia Breeze
Jack Chissick
Stephanie Cole
Sara Coward
Peter Cregeen
Helen Dorward
Christopher Dunham
Christine Edmonds
Frank Ellis
Brigit Forsyth
Richard Frost
Kim Grant
Lionel Guyett
Paul Haley
Chris Harris
Emlyn Harris
Janet Hargreaves
Ronald Harwood
Maria Heidler
Vivien Heilbron
Elwyn Johnson

Barbara Lawton
Christopher Littlewood
Knight Mantell
Arthur Millie
Ian Mullins
Donald Pelmear
Jeffrey Perry
Brian Protheroe
Jane Quy
Graham Richards
David Ryall
Kate Salberg
Jane Salberg
Peter Robert Scott
Simon Sladen
Mike Starke
Sue Starke
Michael Stroud
Josephine Tewson
Charlie Waite
Jane Ware
June Watson
Timothy West
Marcia Wheeler
Sonia Woolley
Gilbert Wynne

Particular thanks to Emma Battcock for giving permission to quote from Henry Marshall's scripts and gag book, all now found in the Henry Marshall Collection at the University of Bristol.

Many thanks to all those who searched their archives to share photographs, only some of which could be included in this book: Emma Battcock, Jessica Benton, Stephanie Cole, Frank Ellis, Lionel Guyett, Emlyn Harris, Vivien Heilbron, Ian Mullins, Donald Pelmear, Brian Protheroe, Michael Stroud, Charles Waite, Marcia Wheeler, Sonia Woolley. Particular thanks to Peter Brown (Playhouse production photographer 1966-96) and Salisbury Newspapers for kindly granting permission to use photographs from their archives.

Archivists and librarians at Salisbury Playhouse, Salisbury Library, Hayley Abbott, University of Bristol Theatre Collection (Jo Elsworth, Bex Carrington and Heather Romaine) and the British Library. Items from *The Stage* reprinted by permission.

Picture credits: Peter Brown (front cover, pages 93, 102, 104, 106, 107, 110, 111, 112, 115, 124, 127, 134, 150, 151, 153, 155, 157, 158), Salisbury Newspapers (36, 38, 39, 41, 42, 49, 55, 67, 72, 73, 75, 76, 78, 80), Vivien Heilbron (84, 90, 92, back cover), Donald Pelmear (62, 63), Marcia Wheeler (68), Chris Abbott (9, 128, 202, 203), Rowland Adams (46), Danny Taylor (vii). The author and publisher have tried to establish and credit copyright owners of all photographs, where known, but will be happy to add to future printings any whose names they have failed to trace.

The Henry Marshall pantomimes still seem to me to be the blueprint for how pantomimes ought to be. I'm so glad you're writing about them.

Timothy West

(in an email to the author, 26th Oct 2010)

Foreword
by Stephanie Cole

Stephanie Cole is a stage, television and film actress. Her long and varied career includes a formidable list of theatre credits and popular TV series such as Tenko and Waiting For God, and more recently Coronation Street. She has an honorary MA from the University of Bristol and an OBE for services to Drama, Mental Health and the Elderly.

THIS IS A book for anyone who loves panto: its main theme may be Henry Marshall's pantos at Salisbury but we learn so much of panto history along the way and, perhaps more importantly, what makes a great or good pantomime. Henry's writing was based in historical fact or legend, so the pantos are rooted in our past and our myths. The story is all-important and, a rarity this, in all the songs the story is moved forward – even in the case of the Principal Boy/Girl duets. Henry and Oli always referred to them as 'lavatory numbers' because the children always chose that moment to clamour for the loo!

Henry and I were married for some years, and while he was still writing the pantos we spent much of the winter going to other productions (10 or 12 was the norm) so that he could pick some of the best gags for next year. The routines in Henry's pantomimes, based as they are on centuries of knowledge, are fool-proof if all the instructions are followed.

Indeed, panto is a very disciplined art-form – not a free-for-all as some imagine. And Henry and Oli made sure the running time was about two hours including an interval – vital!

I did some six or seven pantos in the early years of my career. The first was a Clinton-Baddeley with Jessie Matthews as the Fairy Queen, but four of them were by Henry and there is no doubt that they were the very best; written and directed by a master.

This book is a fitting and entertaining tribute to Henry and the whole team.

Prologue – Here We Are Again

THE ORIGINS OF pantomime are much discussed, written about and sometimes disputed, but about one thing all are paradoxically agreed: 'the modern English pantomime is not a pantomime.'[1] Continuing his description of the generally-agreed account of the origins, Clinton-Baddeley goes on to recognise the combination of factors that created this essentially British art-form (for he seems unaware of the long history and continuing survival of Scottish pantomime).

It is descended from the Regency spectacles, the early Victorian extravaganzas, and the mid-Victorian burlesques. ...for a long time it carried the remnants of the harlequinade attached to its tail. The great success of the burlesques induced managements to put them on at Christmas – taking the place of the old opening but keeping the harlequinade as an unexplained second part of the performance. ...[By the 1880s] things had gone a stage further. Burlesque had knocked out the old pantomime, only to be knocked out by its own offspring, the new pantomime, which somehow in the process of doing so had re-absorbed a quantity of traditions derived from the old pantomime. ...Nobody wilfully throws away a good thing. ... Fairy Queens are not likely to abjure their inheritance merely because they are appearing in a different sort of play. Devils do not forget the etiquette of their ancient calling. And comedians are not going to renounce their favourite gags simply because they find themselves in a new entertainment.[2]

On the face of it, there would seem to be little connection between a south of England repertory theatre in the 1950s and a great Regency and Victorian tradition, but in fact the link is not ephemeral or tenuous. It can be traced back from producer Oliver Gordon and writer Henry Marshall to a late Victorian Harlequinade performer. By the 1930s, painter and decorator Harry Ewins was settled in to his second profession, quite different though it was to his early years in the family trade of Harlequinade performer. Harry had played Clown, one of the stock characters that appeared alongside the acrobatic Harlequin, his pretty lover Columbine, the aged Pantaloon and the Policeman. The cry of 'Here we are again' rang out each year as the performers appeared to announce the final part of the evening's pantomime; although not at Boxing Day or the other early performances, where the performance would be over-running. Only when the running length had been trimmed would the Harlequinade take its rightful place.

Carried on to the stage as a baby, Harry took the role of Clown in the Harlequinades at the Marylebone (later West London) Theatre. He learned the part from his Uncle, also called Harry Ewins, and whose appearances included *Sinbad* starring Dan Leno at the Surrey Theatre in 1887 ('Magnificent Scenery. Grand Ballets. Wonderful Novel Effects – Seats can be booked at all West-End libraries')[3]. In this way, both were part of a line of Clowns stretching back to Joseph Grimaldi, who had played the part in the same theatre. In 1894 the first Harry Ewins was appearing in *Dick Whittington* at the Elephant and Castle Theatre where he also presented his speciality trap scene. By 1897 this had become the Demon Trap Scene, a speciality alongside a troupe of performing dogs in *Dick Whittington* at the West London. However, it was in this pantomime at the Elephant and

Castle Theatre that Harry had the tragic experience of his wife, Kitty Tyrell, playing King Rat, coming off stage and dying in his arms. Kitty Tyrell had a daughter in 1888 when she was living with Harry at 54 Gurney Street, New Kent Road, so she left a six year old child. The doctors decided that her death was caused by over-tight lacing of her costume. It seems incredible that Harry continued his pantomime career – but he did. The description in *The Stage* is desperately sad and yet also evocative of its day.

1870 photo of the Payne brothers as Clown and Harlequin

It is not often that a tragedy occurs in the course of a Boxing Night pantomime production, and the death of Miss Kitty Tyrell (Mrs Harry Ewins) at the Elephant and Castle, is inexpressibly sad and painful. Miss Tyrell was playing King Rat in Dick Whittington and, after singing a duet with Mrs Daisy Gertrude (Silver Star) in the second scene, danced off and was suddenly taken ill at the wings. She was removed to her dressing-room and died in the presence of her husband, Mr Harry Ewins, who besides appearing as Johnny Nod in the pantomime was also, by the grim irony of fate, cast for the part of the clown in the harlequinade. Syncope, brought on by too tight lacing and accompanying excitement, was considered by Dr Boan to be the cause of the unhappy lady's death. Miss Tyrell, who was very popular on the South side, was buried on Tuesday at Willesden Cemetery, in the presence of many of her pantomime colleagues. The inscription on the coffin was: Kathleen Ewins, died December 26th

1894 in her 35th year.' This deplorable event naturally cast a gloom over the company now appearing at Mr. D'Esterre's theatre.[4]

Pantomime titles were longer in those days; in 1900 the Royal West London, as it now styled itself, offered Harry and company in *Pearl of the East; or the Beautiful Slave, the Maudlin Monarch and the Tricky Old Man in the Moon.* In 1901, probably worn out at an early age after the rigours of performing and from personal sadness, Harry Ewins died at the age of 39 years. His nephew, also named Harry, took over the performances at the Marylebone Theatre. In 1902 the pantomime was *Robinson Crusoe* and the younger Harry was playing Friday, and in 1907 he was in *Puss in Boots*, playing the Ogre as well as his Clown role. Transformations and trap scenes were a special feature at the West London which proudly advertised that it had the deepest stage in London. Times were changing however and by 1911 Harry was playing Old Man of the Sea in a touring south London production of *Sinbad*, and *The Stage* review notes that 'he appears and disappears through the traps in the old-fashioned way with startling suddenness'.[5]

Harlequinades evolved from the classic Commedia characters, with the beautiful Columbine pursued by a variety of suitors but won by the acrobatic Harlequin just in time. The central characters are surrounded by foolish older men, rascally knaves, gossiping servants and the ever popular Clown, in addition to singers and dancers.[6] Harlequinade performers often worked only part of the year on stage, and it became a tradition for them to also work as stage carpenters, so it is not surprising that Harry Ewins took up painting or decorating after what he thought would be his last Clown appearance in 1914. The Harlequinade largely disappeared over the next twenty years or so and survives today only in a few unlikely places like the Peacock Theatre at Tivoli Gardens, Copenhagen, where each summer the stock characters appear and go through their routines like ghosts from the distant past[7].

Harry Ewins, then, thought his performing days were over; until 1938 when pantomime writer A. E. Wilson tracked him down, and introduced him to John Counsell at the Theatre Royal Windsor, where one last Harlequinade was planned as part of a pantomime. Harry agreed to take on the role, with himself as Clown, his son as Pantaloon... and Oliver Gordon as Policeman. It is through that performance in Windsor that the Salisbury Playhouse productions written by Henry Marshall and produced by Oliver Gordon are linked to a historic tradition of English pantomime. But we are getting ahead of ourselves, for we have not yet met the four men of theatre who take the major roles in this story: author and fight director Henry Marshall, his brother the actor/producer Oliver Gordon, theatre manager Reggie Salberg and Roger Clissold, director.

Scene 1
Enter the Immortals

OUR STORY BEGINS in 1955 but its roots lie much earlier, in the medieval mystery plays. It is traditional for a pantomime to begin with opposing speeches from the forces of good and evil, the immortal figures who re-appear in each production and create the magical world inhabited by pantomime characters. These forces of good and evil pre-date pantomime by many years.

> The Fairy has never lost her connection with the doctrine of Good and Evil which belonged to medieval theatre. It is traditional that she should enter from the right, or good, side of the stage – the OP side – and she always used to transfer her wand from her right hand to her left when dealing with the infernal powers. This was to 'protect the heart' and is no doubt a gesture of some antiquity... The Demon King is a particularly good example of the new entertainment re-introducing the delights of the old. The Spirit of Evil was a familiar figure in medieval plays and old pantomime... ...[and] always enters from Stage Left, the bad side, and so certain a tradition is this that in all old theatres the star-trap will be found by the left wing. Until recently a Demon was expected to be an acrobat, and the natural egress from the infernal regions was through the floor. In this less skilful age the Demon may enter more slowly through an ordinary trap, or less happily from the wings. But it will always be from the left...[8]

We begin this story not with a dialogue between Fairy and Demon, but by introducing the four theatrical luminaries without whom the Salisbury pantomimes could not have achieved their legendary eminence. And it is Henry Marshall – real name Marshall King Battcock – who is at the centre of this story, as inheritor of a long-standing pantomime tradition and author of all the pantomimes at Salisbury Playhouse from 1955 to 1985. His pantomime pedigree, however, goes back much earlier than his arrival at Salisbury. As far as we know, he was not named for the Harlequinade clown Henry Marshall, known as Marshalino, at the Surrey Theatre, and who died destitute in the 1850s, but it is tempting to wonder whether he knew about that performer.

The Henry Marshall with whom we are concerned was born at Eton on 19th February 1920. As a young man, Henry acted for a while and worked as a Stage Manager, but he soon found himself writing for the stage. In 1942, the Bromley School of Art produced a dramatic revue for one week with music by Henry Marshall. He wrote *Drake's Drum* for the Theatre Royal York and (with his brother Oliver co-writing, playing the lead and directing) *Dead Men's Shoes* in 1944 at Windsor. *The Stage* review noted drily that 'Henry Marshall's previous plays have been in rather serious historical

Henry Marshall in the 1940s

vein, but in collaboration with his brother he has produced a comedy thriller which has distinct possibilities'.[9] The same team produced *Spanish Incident* at the Embassy, Swiss Cottage in 1947. It was his brother's suggestion that he change his name to Henry Marshall, and drop Battcock. Henry's play *Silver Trumpets*, without Oliver's involvement this time and dealing with the life of Johann Sebastian Bach, had been premiered at Windsor in 1944, as was *Give Me the Sun*, a play set in a bombed-out house, at the Boltons in 1947. *The Silver Trumpets* later opened in London at the New Lindsey Theatre in Kensington and *Drake's Drum* was at the Embassy in Swiss Cottage in 1946. Once again, *The Stage* was less than enthusiastic: 'If one is prepared to forget that the play is artificially contrived, the characters merely pure black or pure white, and the sentiment of the kind one enjoyed in adolescence, one may have a jolly good evening.'[10] This was, of course, a young man's play; one cannot but assume that these were the words of an elderly reviewer. The Spanish Civil War was the setting for *Spanish Incident*, seen at the Croydon Grand in 1947. By 1952, Henry Marshall was writing for BBC Radio, with *The Green Apron* on the Home Service. Henry continued to write plays in his later years and these included *A Man Like Me*, premiered in 1961 at Salisbury, and for Perth Theatre *The Three Musketeers* in 1967.

It was when his brother Oliver was running the Theatre Royal Windsor during the Second World War, however, that Henry Marshall had begun writing the pantomimes for which he was to become most well-known. It was also at this time that Henry met the Lupino Lane family, including Wallace Lupino and Lauri Lupino Lane, whose routines he was to include in many of his pantos, and echoes of which appear throughout the routines in his gag book.[11] He was also delighted to be invited to write a script for Laurel and Hardy. Henry wrote the music for his pantos as well, having studied composition at Cambridge. The Windsor panto scripts were written by Henry with 'suggestions' added by Oliver Gordon, and many of the

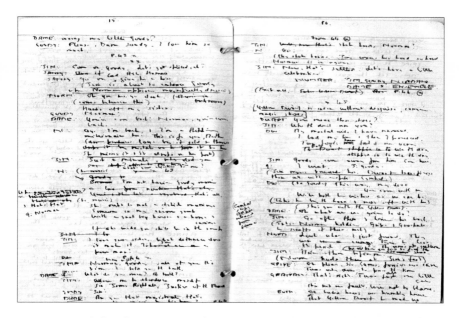

An early hand-written script by Henry Marshall for Goody Two-Shoes

routines and character names later seen in Salisbury were created in those years, with Oliver already playing Silly Sammy in *Jack and the Beanstalk*, for example, at Windsor in 1944. In 1947, Henry's script for *Babes in the Wood* was seen at the Alexandra, Birmingham. In the following year, Henry wrote *Robinson Crusoe* for the same theatre, with Oliver Gordon producing and Norman Wisdom as Billy. Henry Marshall wrote the Tiddler Song for Norman Wisdom at about this time, a song that was to reappear over the years in many future scripts.

In 1949 Lauri Lupino Lane appeared in *Queen of Hearts* and it is from around this time that Henry Marshall's gag book dates, with many of the front cloth gags in it inherited from the Lupino Lane family. The Lupino family origins lie in Italy like those of other famous theatrical families such as the Grimaldis and the Bolognas, and the family seem to have been descended from a puppet-master named Luppino who is recorded to have appeared at Bartholomew Fair in 1642. The family developed many skills and became known in theatre, circus and at outdoor entertainments, but it is for their acrobatic skills in routines such as those in the gag-book for which they are best known.

> There have been Lupino puppet-makers, tight-rope performers, acrobats, dancers, singers, comedians, costume designers, musicians, managers, wig-makers and what-not, but above all they have shone in pantomime generally and in the Harlequinade in particular. ...In the Drury Lane pantomime of 1889 [George Lupino] turned a triple pirouette out of a star trap, winning a wager of £50. This trap work subsequently became one of the great assets of the family... It was said that [Edward VII] used to stand underneath the stage and watch Lupino as he disappeared down one trap and was shot up ten feet into the air from another.[12]

In addition to Salisbury, Henry Marshall wrote pantomimes that were performed in Cheltenham, Colchester, Northampton, Canterbury, Ipswich, Chesterfield, Torquay, Hull, Belfast, Harrogate, Derby, Dundee, Westcliff, Hornchurch, Lewisham and many other venues, including RADA's first pantomime in 1978. The productions were always tweaked to suit the particular casts and theatres of course; for example, when Roger Clissold directed *Jack and the Beanstalk* at the Derby Playhouse in 1969, Queen Iodine had become King Engelbert and the band was rather larger than could be afforded at Salisbury. Henry Marshall also had a script produced at Georgetown, Ontario in Canada, as well as writing extra scenes for the London Palladium *Babes in the Wood* starring Frank Ifield and Arthur Askey in 1965. The book for that pantomime was by David Croft, but there was a need to fit in a range of changing guest stars, including a Risley artist (foot juggler) and The Herculeans, one guise in many over the years for Johnny Hutch and his team of apparently ageing acrobats. The production travelled around the number one houses for the next few years: Henry kept his script credit and presumably worked on the changes needed for each group of star names and speciality acts. He had learned the craft of inserting speciality acts into a pantomime script at the Alexandra Theatre in Birmingham.

Jane Quy, a regular in Henry's Salisbury pantomimes, remembers him as a little man with a beard and a grey hat and coat, always around but in the background during rehearsals. Most of all, however, he should be remembered by the profession as the prime exponent of repertory pantomime, despite his considerable experience in the commercial sector. He celebrated the focus on the story which can survive in panto when there is no star or speciality act to intrude. In 1971 Henry caused something of a stir in a letter to *The Stage* suggesting that repertory pantomimes did not exist before 1941, apart from the 1938/89 Windsor production and some a few years later in Watford[13]. Letter writers in following weeks suggested such productions began much earlier, in Northampton in the 1930s and at the Elephant and Castle theatre in the 1920s, though some of the disagreement may be due to different understandings of the term repertory. By the time of his letter to *The Stage*, Henry was much better known as an eminent Fight Director, and he continued to teach stage fighting at RADA until he retired in 1995. Henry's yearly ads in *The Stage* provide a listing of the many productions of his pantomime scripts by professionals and amateurs. He wrote for television and radio too, and was one of those involved in setting up the Society of British Fight Directors in 1969.

The second of the four theatrical luminaries responsible for this enduring pantomime tradition was Henry Marshall's older brother Oliver (there was also a third brother, Roy Dingwall Battcock, who had a military career as a Major and was later a tour guide at Highgate Cemetery and the Houses of Parliament[14]). Oliver Gordon – born Oliver Gordon Battcock on 16th September 1903 - had a long and impressive theatrical career before coming to Salisbury,

Oliver Gordon in the early years of his career

having appeared widely from the West End to Preston. He began in Basil Foster's production of *The Midshipmaid* at the King's Theatre Southsea in the early 1930s, which later moved to the Shaftesbury. Other West End appearances followed, including *Diplomacy* with Gerald du Maurier and *Vintage Wine* with Seymour Hicks at the Victoria Palace, and several productions at the Players Theatre. Many small parts followed, and in the words of one *Stage* reviewer in 1937 '*he was fully adequate to meet the slight demands made upon him*'[15] although at the Glasgow Alhambra in 1940 he was said to have offered '*a neat little cameo as the Curate*[16].' He also made a speciality of playing the Butler, and did so in a wide range of plays, and was an expert farceur, his skills in that direction honed by his experience of working with Ralph Lynn on the Ben Travers farces.

Oliver appeared several times in the company at the Theatre Royal Windsor in the nineteen-thirties and forties, after John Counsell took over the theatre and set up the Windsor Repertory Company. Reviewing his performance in his brother's play *Dead Mens Shoes*, *The Stage* said '*Oliver Gordon is a comedian with a perfect sense of timing, and it is apparent that he knows exactly the kind of material which suits him best'.*[17] At Christmas 1938, the Windsor company put on their first pantomime, *Aladdin* – and it was then that it was decided to revive a Harlequinade as part of the performance.[18] Oliver Gordon had appeared in the Christmas production *Alice and Thomas and Jane* at the Westminster Theatre in 1933 that was followed by a Harlequinade, but he appeared only in the play on that occasion.

For the Windsor Harlequinade then, the elderly perfomer we have already met, Harry Ewins, was engaged to give guidance and advice. Having played Clown – Grimaldi's role – in many Harlequinades in his youth, he now took on in addition the role of Producer, cast his son as Pantaloon and Oliver Gordon as the Policeman. Harlequin was cast from the resident company and a local ballet dancer played Columbine. John Counsell has described in his memoirs how the good-natured cockney Ewins – by now in his sixties and working mainly as a house painter – was very approximate in his descriptions of what would happen[19]. He did, however, hand in a long list of the props that would be needed, although the efforts of the in-house team failed to make the grade and Ewins and his son ended up making their own. The dress rehearsal was predictably chaotic apart from the appearance through the curtain of the fully made-up and traditionally costumed Ewins and son as Clown and Pantaloon, as if reappearing from the past. In the end the Harlequinade was so successful that a whole show was built around it the following year. By his participation in this interlude, Oliver Gordon was a living link between the old Harlequinade performers and the actors with whom he was to work in the 1950s and 1960s.

Windsor was to be Oliver's base throughout the war, after John Counsell joined the services in 1941. Counsell left Oliver Gordon in charge of the productions on the advice of colleague Rule Pyott, who described Ollie to him as having 'complete integrity, a natural authority and a knack of getting on well with everybody. He's acted here often enough to know your methods, is a glutton for work and would, I am sure, drive things along on the lines you have laid down'.[20] Sure enough, all went well and Oliver made a success of the theatre during the five years when Counsell was in the forces, running it jointly with Arnold Pilbeam, who looked after the administrative side. In 1942, his Brighton production of *Tinker's Hatch* came into town at the Ambassadors. He also produced Shaw's *You Never Can Tell*, his favourite play according to a *Stage* review of the 1962 Salisbury production. When the war was over, John Counsell returned and Oliver Gordon moved on, as agreed between them; but Counsell is fulsome in his praise of his producer and the ways in which he met the challenges of weekly repertory theatre.

> His energy was prodigious and, keeping unswervingly to the general lines of policy laid down for him he pursued relentlessly his task of making sure that, whatever monumental difficulties cropped up, the curtain would rise at seven-thirty every Monday night on a different play[21].

Although Oliver had appeared in Windsor pantomimes previously, the 1947 *Cinderella*, in which he also played Buttons, was the first he produced. With his brother Henry Marshall among the writers, the team that were to be so successful at Salisbury was beginning to be assembled. It was a team that did not stay together for long after the War however when John Counsell returned from military service. He missed the expertise of Oliver Gordon when he tried to take over the Windsor pantomimes even though he continued to use Henry Marshall as writer. Oliver had built the pantos up during the war through his personal enthusiasm for the art form and they had become very profitable; without him, it took a long time for the new team to find their way forward. Counsell admitted himself that it was only after he became more enthusiastic about pantomime that the productions started to improve. By this time, however, Oliver Gordon was mostly working elsewhere.

The pantomime partnership with his brother, Henry Marshall, as librettist, which started at the Theatre Royal Windsor, continued at the Alexandra Theatre, Birmingham under Derek Salberg and then moved to the Salisbury Playhouse with Reggie Salberg. Salisbury, however, was in the future and over the next few years Oliver Gordon produced at

Oliver Gordon as Idle Jack in Dick Whittington

many other theatres, including Wolverhampton from 1947 to 1951. He married Barbara Shotter, a young actress who had been in the Windsor company and who later appeared in the West End, often with the Lupino Lane company, and she then played the lead in Emile Littler's very successful touring production of *Annie Get Your Gun*. She also appeared on ATV with the Lupino Lane family during the early years of independent television.

Oliver's other great enthusiasm – cricket – was coming to the fore, and in 1947 he played alongside Lauri Lupino Lane and others in *The Stage* vs. Old England match at the Oval and in aid of the Actors' Orphanage (for which organisation he served on the Executive Committee 1939-1940). This was a match with a fine tradition, with Dan Leno having arrived for it on a camel and George Robey once turning up with a bat with a hole in it. Oliver had also been an active – and successful – member of The Stage Golfing Society in the 1930s. He was known in his cricketing guise as O. G. Battcock, made his debut for Buckinghamshire in 1925, and played minor counties cricket from 1925 to 1939 and from 1946 to 1951, making 115 appearances. In 1937 at Hampstead for Actors vs. Musicians, *The Stage* reports '*Oliver Gordon knocking up another six 4's in his total of fifty (not out) in the nicest style.*[22]' Indeed, his Wikipedia entry mentions only his cricketing prowess, including two appearances for the MCC against Cambridge in 1938.

By 1949 he was producing *Queen of Hearts* at the Alexandra Theatre Birmingham, with music and lyrics by Henry Marshall, although this was not a title Henry was to repeat at Salisbury. *The Stage* review gives a taste of panto of the period:

> There are qualities one always expects in an Alexandra pantomime and always finds. One can confidently look for a lavish display of colour, and a competent ensemble of dancers, for an upstanding hero and a very feminine heroine, and, above all, for an excellent selection of specialities.[23]

The cast on that occasion included Lauri Lupino Lane and Wallace Lupino, and we know it was from the Lupino family, among others, that Henry Marshall and Oliver Gordon acquired much traditional pantomime business, a great deal of it carefully written down in the surviving Gag Book[24]. The colour and dancing could be re-created at Salisbury – and perhaps the pantomime horse - but there would be no room for speciality acts. *The Queen of Hearts* at the Alex, by comparison, included the Cooper Twins as the Court Tumblers, the musical items of the Maple Leaf Four, the dancing Lehmiski Ladies (regulars at the Alex) and the Skating Dexters.

The scripts Henry Marshall wrote for the Alex and for

Windsor after the War give a flavour of how the popular stories evolved. *Cinderella* – perhaps the most popular pantomime of all - was presented in Windsor in 1946, a suitable fairytale romance for a country just recovering from the War years. The script – licensed for performance by the Lord Chamberlain on 18th December – included Ugly Sisters called Olive Oil and Hydrophobia (later shortened to Olive and Hydro) and Oliver Gordon played the single Broker's Man, a representative of Pinch & Kissem. Perhaps in order to accommodate the speciality acts popular at the time, Henry's script also includes characters that would disappear in later versions, including Flirtella (Cinderella's cat) and – somewhat bizarrely – Buffalo Jill. Perhaps the biggest difference between this and the later Cinderellas was the prologue with the traditional battle between the immortals, the Demon King and the Fairy Queen, although this may also have been added to meet the style of traditional pantomime popular at the Theatre Royal Windsor.

Fairy Queen
All hail fair mortals, welcome to our scene,
Accept this greeting from your Fairy Queen;
A royal welcome from the Queen of Light
Who bids defiance to the powers of night.

Demon King
All hail vain mortals, a curse on Christmas time,
There's more than light and sweetness to this tale of Pantomime;
There are tears and sneers and sorrow, and the evil that I bring,
And all the blood and thunder that goes with the Demon King.

After this, we are into the hunting scene, which would be the beginning of *Cinderella* in all the later versions by Henry Marshall.

The story is already set in Florazel, Buttons sings the Tiddler song and does the cooking scene following the instructions on the radio – or wireless as it would have been described then. It's a long and sometimes confusing story, before ending up with a songsheet with plenty of scope for audience actions.

> Oh dum-a-dum-dum goes the big bass drum,
> And the trombone goes boohoo.
> Root-a-toot-toot goes the little old flute
> And the trumpet's playing too.
> Oh ding dong dell goes the great big bell
> And the cymbals all go clang.
> You can hear the feet, coming down the street,
> It's Baron Hardup's band.

In 1950, a smaller cast were involved in a version of the same script at the Alexandra Theatre, Birmingham, this time with Norman Wisdom as Buttons. The Ugly Sisters were still Olive and Hydro in the script, but had become Buttercup and Daisy by the time the programme was printed. The Broker's Men Lancelot and Adrian – two of them this time – were played by a contortionist act called the Aberdonians. The Three Monarchs, comedy harmonica act, also appeared, as did the Six Gotham Singers, the Lehmiski Ladies, the Alexandra Babes and the Douglas George Lilliput Ponies. It was all very different from what was to be presented from very similar Henry Marshall scripts in a small repertory theatre in Wiltshire, but the basic elements of the story and the style were all there.

Oliver Gordon ran his own company for a time in 1951 with Leslie Yeo in St Johns, Newfoundland, (although he had to fly back to produce *Sleeping Beauty* at the Alexandra). Included in the cast of British actors who went to Canada was Geoffrey Lumsden, who was later to appear many times at Salisbury. In 1953 they even took an Alexandra pantomime, *Robinson Crusoe*, across the Atlantic. A further tour to Newfoundland with the London Theatre Players in 1956 included Nancie Herrod and her husband, Scenic Designer Stanley Rixon, both later to be Salisbury panto stalwarts.

After he was based at Salisbury, Oliver Gordon also continued to work at many other theatres. In 1962, for example, he directed Dilys Laye in William Douglas Home's *The Cigarette Girl* which launched in Edinburgh and then came to the Duke of York's. It was at Salisbury, however, that Oliver Gordon spent most of his non-cricketing time for the rest of his life. He is remembered as a brisk, efficient if old-fashioned producer, who used, says Stage Manager Marcia Wheeler, shorthand direction such as 'Christ and upcentre' or 'last despairing spasm'.[25] Perhaps his most famous coinage, however, was the word still remembered by Stephanie Cole and many others who worked with him: 'If you said shall I move to the door now, he would say it's a matter of complete imbuggerance to me old cock. Ollie was the first person I knew of to use the word'.[26]

He was much loved by all who knew him, and Reggie Salberg and his wife were particularly supportive, often providing meals for him as well. Jack Chissick remembers hearing the story of Ollie turning up one day to find meat in gravy cooking on the stove, which he consumed with relish. It was only when Reggie and Noreen came home and he thanked them that he discovered that what he had eaten was a collection of lights from the butcher being boiled up for the dog.[27]

Ollie blocked fast in the rehearsal rooms at Lower Bemerton, and then worked within that, and he already knew the likely moves for many of the most popular plays. Michael Stroud was similarly impressed with his abilities.

> Oliver Gordon could put King Lear on in a week. He didn't know what to do when we went to three weeks, he said we had better go to

the cinema. He was a lovely man, Ollie, he really was a gentleman. He used to call everyone cock 'Just go down there cock.' There was no subtlety about him but he could get it on. [28]

When the company put on *A Streetcar Named Desire*, he handed a marked-up copy of the script to Marcia Wheeler with all the sound cues included; it turned out to be an original prompt script that had been owned by Elia Kazan. Oliver appeared in all the pantomimes during his time at Salisbury as principal comic and later Dame, and produced them too. He also produced many of the other repertory productions at the theatre and occasionally made appearances as well. Outside the theatre, he was known to speak mostly of cricket, which remained his first love. He died on 26th September 1970 at the early age of 67. His Wisden obituary makes only passing reference to his theatrical career.

> BATTCOCK, OLIVER GORDON, who died in Guy's Hospital, London, on September 26, ten days after his 67th birthday, was reputed to have taken around 6,000 wickets in club and minor county games, with bowling of medium pace, during a cricketing career spanning 50 years. Good length and late out-swing played a big part in his success. He assisted Buckinghamshire from 1923 to 1952, being captain in the last three seasons, and in Challenge Match of 1938 he dismissed twelve Lancashire batsmen for 65 runs, Buckinghamshire winning in a single innings. He captained Datchet for 25 years, taking over 2,000 wickets for them, and for a number of years led Incogniti on tours abroad. He was also a useful left-handed batsman. As Oliver Gordon, he gained distinction as an actor and producer. [29]

The Salisbury Playhouse, always known to an older generation of local theatregoers as the Arts Theatre, was a much-loved but tumbledown building which started life as a Primitive Methodist chapel in 1869 and was later The Picturehouse, one of the first cinemas in the city, and even a drill hall for a time. In 1943 it reopened as the Garrison Theatre under the control of ENSA, and many famous performers appeared there during the Second World War. Most performances were given for members of the services but occasionally productions were opened to civilians. When the War ended in 1945, ENSA gave up the theatre and it was taken over by the Arts Council following lobbying by the Salisbury and District Society of Arts. Productions toured widely after they were seen at Salisbury and the previous wooden seats in the theatre were replaced by plush ones from the Kidderminster Opera House. A number of different people including Barbara Burnham, Peter Potter, Michael Wide and Frank Hauser took on the challenge of running the Arts Theatre in that difficult post-war period, but business was not always good and the theatre-going habit had not yet been firmly established in the town. The Arts Council pulled out in 1951 and a local trust took over and worked hard to build up audiences, and renamed the theatre The Playhouse in 1953. It was only with the arrival of Reggie Salberg as General Manager in 1955 that the process began that was to create the reputation on which the current very successful theatre is built.

In Reggie Salberg we meet the third of the four individuals that created the Salisbury pantomime tradition and maintained the links with a glorious past. Reggie Salberg came from a famous theatrical family, and one still represented in the profession today. His father, Leon Salberg, ran the Alexandra Theatre, Birmingham and Reggie was born in that city in 1915. The Alex – still a working theatre today – was originally the Lyceum and was built in 1901, with scarlet and gold seats for two thousand. The pantomime tradition had started in 1902, and Leon Salberg bought the theatre in 1911, rebuilding it in 1935 to make the stage wider. Derek Salberg took over the management of the theatre when his father died in 1937 and continued to build

Reginald (Reggie) Salberg

the Alexandra pantomime tradition, as he described in the book he wrote about those productions.[30] He describes some of the inevitable traumas that arose, for example with the 1951 *Sleeping Beauty* when the sudden loss of one of the actors meant that he had to work with Oliver Gordon as producer and Henry Marshall as writer to reshape the book completely. Unfortunately, Derek felt the production did not really take off although 'scenically it was first class, particularly the Highland waterfall and glade scene.' This was the beginning of a longstanding link with Jimmie Currie and his Waltzing Waters, which closed many a pantomime first act in the 1950s and 1960s. Ambitious though the Salisbury pantomimes were, they did not aspire to water effects... After the 1952 *Dick Whittington*, Derek Salberg changed producers and later took over the production of the pantomimes, freeing Oliver Gordon to work elsewhere and then to move to Salisbury, where he would work with Derek's brother: Reggie. Writing in a 1983 pantomime programme, Reggie recalled the pantomimes the brothers saw as children.

> The Alexandra Theatre, Birmingham, of which my father was Managing Director, had a long pantomime tradition and each year vied with The Grand, Leeds, to boast of the country's longest run. Both ran until Easter and one year The Grand celebrated Whitsun with its pantomime still running. Thus, like many children, it was at Christmas that I got my first taste of theatre. In addition, my father used to invite members of the cast home to a meal and I developed a taste for theatre people which has never left me. One vivid memory is of being asked to take morning tea (after knocking hard) to Wee Georgie Wood and his bride who were spending their wedding night at our house; when I entered it was rather like seeing a young mother in bed with her prematurely aged child![31]

Reggie was among the many who remember those Alexandra Theatre productions: Richard Frost, later to appear in Henry Marshall pantomimes at Salisbury and Westcliff, and now a pantomime director, grew up seeing them each year when he was taken for a day out by his Aunt.

> The first pantomime I saw in Birmingham when I was 9 was at the Alex, written by Henry. I recognise a lot. What's that song from Robinson Crusoe? The sea, the sea – Robinson's solo. When I went to see Robinson Crusoe at Salisbury I remembered that as a child, that number.[32]

Reggie Salberg went to Clifton College, read Law at Oxford and then served in the Middle East during the Second World War. He actually acted during his time in the Forces, remembering in later years his 'triumph as Fairy Jewboy in my Unit's somewhat unusual version of *Cinderella*.' On leaving the forces, he set up a repertory company at Kettering in 1946, where he married one of the company, the Hon. Noreen Craven. He ran the company with his cousin, Basil Thomas. In 1947 he set up a second company at the Preston Hippodrome and soon added the New, Hull and the Penge Empire to his portfolio. It must have taken all Reggie's undoubted entrepreneurial skills to try to fill those theatres; the Preston Hippodrome, for example, was a variety theatre built in 1904 with 1,266 seats. The Salberg players charged from 1/- to 3/6d for a ticket and there was a tea and coffee lounge as well as the licensed bars. It was Reggie's practice at the start of each season to publish a list of possible plays to be put on and to let the audience choose the ones that they wanted to see.

Oliver Gordon was one of the Producers working for him at these theatres, and actors such as Derek Smee, Doreen Andrew and Kenneth Keeling, later to be Salisbury stalwarts, first worked for Reggie in those days. Stanley Rixon, later the designer at Salisbury, worked at the New Theatre Hull, where Reggie introduced a repertory season from 1952 that ran for three-quarters of the year. At Salisbury, Reggie soon began exchanging productions with the theatre at Hull and he set up the Junior Theatregoer's Club which enabled the youth of the town to buy tickets on the door at a reduced price – and in the process develop a lifetime theatre-going habit.

All this was achieved in the Salisbury Playhouse, a 400 seat theatre. The official capacity was around 395, as anything over 400 would have required the theatre to be equipped with a Safety Curtain. The former cinema projection box at the back of the stalls was opened up to become the only box, and a particularly palatial and well-sited one, which is remembered by some as being full of children at pantomime time, bringing the capacity to well over 400. Reggie was something of an expert at publicity and managed to build a great deal of local support for the theatre. He regularly invited nuns from a local closed order to form the audience at Dress Rehearsals, an interesting experience on one occasion when the play performed was Brendan Behan's *The Hostage*. However, the nuns stayed to the end and appeared to enjoy the performance and to recognise all the references.

Before the panto there was sometimes a short run of a new play, often by local author John Creasey. This was usually in the hope that he might give a donation to the theatre. Several actors remember those Creasey plays as containing dialogue that was very difficult to deliver convincingly, although maybe it was all part of a rounded training. After the panto each year, Reggie had to lay off quite a few of the actors, but it was the income from the pantomime that paid for the more challenging work that did not bring in as large an audience. On Monday evenings, the theatre put on more challenging fare such as one act plays by Harold Pinter, and Beckett's *Waiting for Godot*. 'We put on the panto to pay for the Pinter',[33] as Chris Harris remembers him saying. Reggie also took risks, as Lionel Guyett found when he joined the company in the 1960s.

> Reggie was a very clever man. He would throw parts at you to see what happened, you don't get that now. You made lifelong friends that you kept in touch with. You kept in touch and went to see them – Reggie had a knack of choosing the right people. If he chose the wrong people they left, they didn't survive the family. Many of us stayed on and went through the season.[34]

Mention of Reggie's comments immediately summons up a memory of his unmistakeable voice, still to be imitated fondly when Salbergians get together. Mike Starke sums up his character in an affectionate portrait of the man.

> Reggie's appearance belied the passion and expertise that were the hallmarks of his success. Had he staged a dramatisation of Winnie

the Pooh, he could easily have cast himself as Eeyore. He spoke in a slow and seemingly lugubrious drawl. No word was wasted and, while he could be ruthlessly honest in his opinions, there was never a hint of unkindness. Anyone reminiscing about Reggie slides, always affectionately, into their own imitation of his measured monotone. When Reggie laughed, which was not infrequently, it had the same slow deliberation as his speech. It rumbled up from the dark recesses of his chest to emerge almost like a wheezy cough. In moments of relaxation, he would chew on an arm of his glasses, gaze into the middle distance and quietly regale you with hilarious anecdotes about plays and players. Reggie's clothes never seemed altogether happy in their work. It was almost as if they were trying to escape by the shortest route; following the pull of gravity, downwards. One accessory was never far from its owner. Draughty theatres had left Reggie with a propensity for a runny nose, it seemed, and when this occurred, his cure for it was to grip his handkerchief in his teeth to stem the drips and carry on with what he was doing, oblivious to the quizzical looks from those around him. The affection in which Reggie was held spread across the footlights to his audience. His eclectic choice of productions was always geared to offer audiences quality, with the impresario's eye for achieving quantity, in terms of bottoms on seats. Not that Reggie was afraid to stage what we might call 'challenging' work nowadays. With his characteristic honesty, he would warn audiences they might not like a forthcoming 'modern' attraction. I recall some of the most formidable county-set matrons emerging from such performances to make a bee-line for Reggie in the theatre foyer and thank him for his warning, but add that they didn't find it all that bad after all. He quite simply gained and held their trust, giving them a rich and varied fare of theatrical experiences.[35]

After a great deal of fund-raising, the new Salisbury Playhouse opened on a nearby site in the Maltings in 1976 and the old building was demolished. The new building used the same design as that of the Mercury Theatre in Colchester. At this point, Reggie retired as General Manager of the theatre and the Studio Theatre in the new building was named after him. Many memories of Reggie will follow, since he lives on in the memory of so many who are grateful to him for giving them the chance to begin a theatrical career. The essence of the man, however, is made clear in the words of Maria Heidler, who joined the company in the 1970s and remembered Reggie's Christmas bonus ceremony when, years later, she was at a writing workshop in Canada.

> We had to imagine we were travelling back in time with the Ghost of Christmas Past. And now the air is damp, I wrote, I can hear glasses clinking and excited chatter. Oh, Spirit! I am in Salisbury! My first professional job. Here is the Theatre Bar, and we've just finished the Christmas Eve matinee of the Pantomime. The next show will be the Boxing Day matinee, so everyone is saying 'Happy Christmas' before we make a dash for the train that will take us back to London. Everyone has their parcels for home piled up behind the piano - and there by the bar is Reggie Salberg, the Big Boss of the Theatre, beaming like Mr. Fezziwig. One by one he calls us over and hands us a small brown envelope. The others tell me it is our Christmas Bonus. Reggie takes the time to speak with everyone. At last it's my turn. He smiles at me. He says, 'Well done. We look forward to having you back for the rest of the Season.' I remember thinking then, that one day, I wanted to do just that. To share the profits of joy with my team.' To this day I don't know how he did it. That might even have been the last year that this tradition happened. Plans for the new Playhouse were in the works and change was on the horizon.[36]

When Oliver Gordon died in 1970 there was no obvious successor as pantomime director, and choreographer and actor

Christopher Dunham produced the 1970 show. By 1971, however, Roger Clissold took on the Director role. Roger Clissold had joined the theatre as ATV Trainee Director in 1965 and had been closely involved with the annual pantomimes, working with Oliver Gordon and also appearing from time to time in cameo parts such as Richard the Lionheart or, memorably, Miles the Crocodile. When he became Director of Productions in 1970, he continued the Salisbury pantomime tradition, very much in the style and ethos that had proved so successful. In this way, Roger Clissold took on the mantle of Oliver Gordon and, with Henry Marshall's scripts and Reggie Salberg's support, continued the pantomime tradition for many years and indeed took it with him to Derby Playhouse when he ran that theatre.

Roger Clissold was born in 1939 and began his acting career playing walk-ons and carrying spears at the Old Vic in the early 1960s. He then joined Nottingham Playhouse, where he met his

Roger Clissold in 1963

wife Sonia Woolley, when Ian McKellen was a member of the company and John Neville was directing. He also acted at the Liverpool Everyman and at the Chester Playhouse. He moved to Salisbury after he was awarded an ABC television trainee directorship, an enterprising scheme by which television was seen to support live theatre at a time when it was more often seen as a threat. Sonia Woolley remembers her arrival at the theatre with Roger.

Oliver was sort of Resident Producer and did some of the plays but not all of them and Reggie very much wanted to get younger blood in. So Roger was given quite a few productions, but Ollie always did pantomime. He nearly always did musicals but again Reggie would occasionally get somebody else in. I'd been at Nottingham Playhouse doing a certain amount of walking on and things and working with the PR department; that was where I met Roger. And Reggie said 'Oh we could do with somebody to do that sort of thing.' He used to pay me a bit of money but it was also kindness: he was very loyal to his staff, people who worked for him. So I did a certain amount of work in the office, and I shared an office with Oliver Gordon. I did some parts and some walk-ons and things. It was cheaper if you could use people who were on minimum wage, and it also meant that I was doing the same hours as Roger. [37]

After going freelance as a director in 1968 Roger Clissold was appointed Resident Producer at Derby Playhouse. It was at Derby in 1969 that he directed his first pantomime: *Jack and the Beanstalk*, and a Henry Marshall script of course. *The Stage* found it to be a most impressive production which broke new ground for Derby with a male principal boy, Elwyn Johnson, and no imported names to break up the story: very much in the tradition of the Salisbury pantomimes, in fact. He then returned to Salisbury and, when the new theatre opened in 1976 he took over from Reggie Salberg as Artistic Director. In 1981 he moved to Leatherhead as Artistic Director of the Thorndike Theatre.

Scene 2
Market Day in a Small Village

SALISBURY IN THE mid 1950s was a market town – rather than the village which seems to be the setting for many pantomime opening scenes – and for those living there it seemed far from theatrical centres like London or Bristol. Most families were unlikely to travel far for entertainment anyway, and when they did so it was likely to be to the cinema, by then near to its zenith as a popular art-form. Salisbury had three cinemas at the time: the Regal in Endless Street, the Odeon in Fisherton Street and the Gaumont (still surviving but now the Odeon) in the New Canal. Cinema fare of the time was often still in black and white, and for many looking back who lived through those years as children, it seems as though the city broke through into colour (rather like the later sections of the film of *Wizard of Oz*) on three yearly occasions: when one of the Chipperfield's, Billy Smart's or Bertram Mills' circuses came to Hudson's Field in the summer, when the Charter Fair came to the market place in October… and when the pantomime opened each December.

Like many provincial towns, Salisbury had lost most of its theatres by the 1940s. The Palace Theatre (previously the County Hall) in Chipper Lane had been the grandest, a music hall which was eventually turned into a garage, though with the ghostly outline of circle and balcony still visible on the walls as late as the 1960s. The Palace opened as the County Hall in 1899 but by 1910 it was mostly showing films and was known as the Electric Palace. Touring productions still appeared on stage from time to time however, and there were often professional pantomimes at Christmas, each one usually lasting a week. In 1931, however, the Palace Theatre closed. The first pantomime in the Playhouse building was *Cinderella* during Peter Potter's time. There were sometimes two pantomimes in the 1940s, since the theatre had a resident and a touring company at the time. When Michael Wide was General Manager he wrote the pantomimes himself, including a production of *Mother Goose* with Gerald Flood in the title role.

By 1955, Reggie Salberg had arrived and actor John Barron directed the first Henry Marshall panto there, which was *Robinson Crusoe*. The theatre's Board of Directors agreed to the engagement of a five piece orchestra, and hoped that the show would make around £300 profit, provided that Customs and Excise agreed to exempt the performances from tax, which they duly did. At the same meeting,[38] the Board agreed salaries which varied from £16 a week for a leading performer to £6 a week each for the dancers – reduced by 10/- during the rehearsal period. The previous manager's wife, Ann Wide, was paid £25 for choreographing the show, and a sky cloth was purchased for the stage at a cost of £22.

Although the production was later looked back on as something of a false start by some of those involved, *The Stage* declared Henry's book to be excellent. Additional local material was by writer and cartoonist Daniel Pettiward, who was to be a firm supporter of the Playhouse for many years to come and had appeared in earlier pantomimes under Michael Wide. Many traditional routines were included: the mop drill, *There's a hole in my bucket* and not forgetting Helen Jessop's snake dance which got a special mention in the programme. The songsheet was about *Shutting shoe-shops sharply at six* and led by Ronald Harwood as Billy Crusoe – surely a songsheet worth resurrecting if anyone has the music. The *Salisbury Times* described it as a bright and tuneful entertainment and particularly commended the lighting. At this stage, the productions were still using popular songs of the day with Robinson and Polly singing *No Two People* and *I'm in Love for the Very First Time*. The chorus appeared as animals on the island, an effect, noted the *Salisbury Times*, that would delight the children. [39]

Doreen Andrew was Robinson Crusoe, with her husband Kenneth Keeling as Will Atkins. She remembers that he adored pantomime although she was always much more comfortable in revue. 'But I was very happy to be cast as Principal Boy and thoroughly enjoyed the period of rehearsal, especially being directed by John Barron, whose work I'd much admired.' However, one aspect of the production was to have a lasting effect of a different kind on Doreen.

> The very talented Wardrobe Mistress Kate Servian had found in the depths of the wardrobe a large bag of feathers, and we agreed they would make a rather fun costume and they did, as well as covering a large sunshade. After the first night I developed a sore throat and thought that the very concentrated rehearsals and the anxiety of the dress rehearsal had made me more tired than I realised: I never considered it could be an allergy to the dreaded feathers! The result was that I spent the run not feeling on top form physically and worrying that something was preventing my performance from being up to scratch. As soon as the run finished, I seemed to shake off all feeling of being under par. Several years later, after another run-in with feathers, I became rather ill and had to call in a doctor who promptly diagnosed asthma and put me on proper medication...[40]

Doreen remembers that Henry Marshall was around for some of the rehearsals, and she found him to be very approachable and encouraging, apart from when any of the actors playing comic parts queried his script; the rest of the cast recognised that the work was tried and tested, and that Henry knew his audience.

Kim Grant played King Neptune in Act I ('regal but perhaps over-green' according to the local paper) and the Cannibal King in Act II, as well as a variety of other small parts. He remembers walking from his digs to the theatre for the first rehearsal in that very wet, cold winter. It was a freezing cold morning, and when he remarked on this to John Barron he was peremptorily told it would get worse. As King Neptune, he wore a lot of fabric seaweed and a liberal coating of green face paint and glued-on sequins. In the interval – and with only a single cold water tap – he had to wash all that off and then black up as the Cannibal King. As if that wasn't enough, John Barron insisted that he then change back again to green as King Neptune for the walk-down, so that he could appear opposite the Fairy. His props were collected from a small bench SL, the side of the theatre open to the elements, so that they were often covered in snow or ice. 'Apart from fit-up theatres,' he says now, 'I don't remember anything being quite so primitive.'[41] He also had to contend with Ronald Harwood as Billy Crusoe doing his best to make him corpse at various moments during the show, although the *Salisbury Times* review commended his singing of *Fishermen of England*. Although he did not appear at Salisbury again, Kim did play the title role in a Henry Marshall *Robinson Crusoe* at Northampton in 1963-64, and worked for Derek Salberg at the Alexandra Theatre in Birmingham and in Hereford.

Ronald Harwood – when he was an actor rather than the playwright he later became – was comic lead in the production. He remembers an incident at the dress rehearsal when an effect required glitter to fall from the flies, but it went wrong and landed on Kim Grant.

Someone said to him, 'Kim, you're covered in star dust' and he said, 'I know my dear, and the money it cost me!' The line has become one of our family sayings.[42]

Another memory from the production has been long-lasting in its effects as well; it was not only Doreen Andrew who was to have later health problems as a result of the 1955 *Robinson Crusoe*. In one scene, Ronald Harwood was on roller skates and he slipped and fell badly on his back. 'No damage was found but the injury plagued me for the rest of my life, until November 2010 in fact, when I had a laminectomy on my spine with miraculous results.' Writing almost

Babes in the Wood 1956: Robin Hood (Josephine Tewson) and Maid Marion (Hermione Gregory) face up to the Sheriff (Ian Mullins) and the Robbers (Kenneth Firth and Leonard Rossiter)

twenty years later in a pantomime programme, Reggie Salberg remembered that the 1955 *Robinson Crusoe* at Salisbury played for three weeks and parties were rare. By the third week the cast were playing to half empty houses and, says Reggie, 'Frankly, the show was not very good.'

By the following year, there was a new air of confidence for *Babes in the Wood*, with Josephine Tewson's Principal Boy well matched against Leonard Rossiter as one of the Robbers. His performance was remembered for many years, and *The Stage* commented that 'there are so many good things in this show [but] nothing better than Leonard Rossiter's performance. It is a real gem.'[43] Reggie, too, remembered Rossiter's wonderful comedy performance and from then on, he said, the pantomimes never looked back. Josephine Tewson was Robin Hood in the production, and was seen by West End producers who then cast her as Ivy Crush in *Free as Air* at the Savoy Theatre with Leonard Rossiter, who she later married, also in the cast as an understudy. This was the first of Josephine's two pantos at Salisbury, and she remembers them both, she says, as 'great fun if hard work. They worked very well having a strong story line and some very funny set pieces. Len Rossiter and Ken Firth (bad and not so bad robbers) had a wonderful duel using every sort of weapon which I used to watch and enjoy every night.'[44] Many other actors were impressed with the seriousness of the approach to the fights in the Salisbury pantomimes over the years, which can be ascribed to Henry Marshall's interest and expertise in stage fighting. Stephanie Cole, playing Dandini in the 1960s, still remembers the authentic small sword fight she had with Brigit Forsyth as Prince Charming in *Cinderella*.

In the 1956 *Babes in the Wood*, Ian Mullins was the Sheriff of Nottingham, and even today finds himself sometimes wandering round the house singing:

Good Prince John has kindly taken on the duties of being a king,
And while I'm here I'd like to make it clear that I insist upon just one thing…

Ian Mullins has many happy and often hilarious memories of the four pantomimes he went on to appear in at Salisbury. In his first year, Ian had worked under producer Terence Dudley and appeared in his productions of *The Glass Menagerie* and *Lady Audley's Secret* as well as *Babes in the Wood*. One of Ian's strongest memories is, not surprisingly, of Leonard Rossiter.

Babes in the Wood 1956: The Sheriff (Ian Mullins) threatens Maid Marian (Hermione Gregory)

I recall Len so well in that. One night his wig fell off and he put it back on back to front and then parted it so he looked out between the long hair; the audience was in hysterics. I had a huge S on the front of my costume which Len used to encourage the audience to hiss at me.[45]

The *Salisbury Times* was most impressed with the production, stating that it was the best Christmas offering the theatre had staged for many years, and the anonymous reviewer also noted the success of Leonard Rossiter and Kenneth Firth as the Robbers, saying that they were 'beautifully unwicked and dumb' and that Rossiter gave 'a magnificent performance; he is an absolute natural and quite steals the show'. The review also gives something of a picture of how that production must have looked.

The transformation scene and ChristmasLand, on which the curtain to the first half falls, is quite beautiful. The Babes see before their very eyes all the toys they would love. There are the Dutch dollies, the golliwog, the baby doll and, finally, the tin soldiers drilling with splendid precision.[46]

The campfire scene in Sherwood Forest included a medley of traditional songs such as *The Lincolnshire Poacher* and *A Hunting We Will Go*, led by Sidney Burchall's Friar Tuck; in Henry's version of this script it was usually Friar Tuck or Little John who led the songs. The song sheet was written by musical director Sydney Carmen, and posed the question *'What do they do when the bulb blows out on the tall Cathedral spire?'*

Playing Fairy Starlight was Janet Hargreaves, in her first job after training at RADA and just taken on at the theatre as Acting ASM.

The Fairy always fell to the Acting ASM then (if female) whether she was good casting or not. I was not. Kate Servian, the mightily gifted and patient wardrobe mistress, made me a frock of layers of pale blue net with much glitter (cheaper than sequins but my, did it scatter like measles all over the stage..) topped with a large glitter star (I was Fairy Starlight after all) which was clamped to my forehead by a circlet of wire; this was extremely painful as it pressed so tightly to my brow to keep the ruddy star in place. So, between entrances, I'd push a pad of Kleenex under it to keep it from cutting into my head. Well of course one performance I forgot to remove it, didn't I? On I came, to dance (very badly) to Delibes with half a dozen local chorus kiddies half my size (I was 5'7' and a good 9 stone with size 7½ feet) with said Kleenex still in place .. chaos! - corpsing all round especially Jo Tewson as Robin Hood, with me blissfully unaware that anything was amiss.

I was also expected to help in the scene changes of which there were many, and these included un-cleating flats and re-setting them - not easy to carry 12' flats in wings (Fairy Starlight's that is, not the theatre's.) We also had to get from stage left to right (and vice versa) via a covered (just) passageway behind the stage which was open to the elements at each end: not only did we then leave wet footprints on stage, but it made it lethally slippy.

Aladdin 1957: Helen Dorward as Aladdin

I treasure these memories, over fifty-six years ago . . . and the gifted and supportive company who put up with a callow kid sticking her nose into the professional theatre for the first time. [47]

Another early Principal Girl was Ian Mullins' wife Helen Dorward, who Reggie remembers as the only Principal Boy who didn't sing – 'because she can't' according to one of his programme pieces. She appeared as Aladdin in 1957, in a production that marked the first panto at Salisbury to be produced by, and to feature, Oliver Gordon. The Geni of the Lamp for this *Aladdin* was Timothy West, in the first of his two pantomimes at Salisbury during his time there as an ASM. He admits:

I have no stories apart from the shameful admission of having been off one night as the Geni. Poor Helen Dorward rubbed her lamp until it dazzled the audience. I can't remember what excuse I made in verse for failing to appear, but nobody was fooled...[48]

Aladdin 1957: Ian Mullins as Abanazer with the chorus

Ian Mullins was again cast as the embodiment of evil, this time Abanazer, and at the beginning of the show he appeared through the front curtain and proceeded to frighten most of the audience, perhaps a little too much for some of them, as he remembers.

The story goes that when some children were about to be turned away because there were no seats, Reggie told them to wait a couple of minutes and there may be some available. Sure enough, after my frightening delivery, a few children had to be taken out – whereupon Reggie re-sold the seats!

The story might sound apocryphal were it not for the similar tales told over the years about Reggie's ability to sell more than 100% of the house in this way, and by inflating the occupancy of the stalls box. Peter Cregeen remembers the same thing happening in 1961, with Reggie standing by the exit doors about five minutes after the show started and reselling seats using exactly the same system.

The *Salisbury Times* Dramatic Critic had his own favourite sections of the 1957 *Aladdin*.

> The highlights, to my mind, are the transformation scene wherein the horrible cave in which Aladdin finds himself trapped whilst in quest of the lamp is changed to a veritable treasure-house; the bath-house sequence in which Wishee Washee is stripped and given a bath himself; the courtroom scene wherein the music of a collection of well-known tunes is used to fit the occasion; and the kitchen capers when Abanazer works his magic.[49]

Ronald Magill's Dame, the first of four in a row at Salisbury, sang *Mighty Like a Rose*: not perhaps first choice for a Widow Twankey today. The local paper also noted approvingly that it was 'seen on Christmas Eve by old folk and deserving children.'

The first *Cinderella* of the Henry Marshall years followed in 1958, though using a script which bore many similarities to those by the same author for the Alexandra in Birmingham and the Theatre Royal Windsor. Although the precise Salisbury version for that year has not survived, the earlier scripts have similar plot elements and characters, sometimes expanded for the extra facilities of bigger theatres and casts to match. In 1947 at Birmingham, for example, there was a much larger cast but, as at Salisbury, the Babes came from the Bellairs School of Dancing. The Birmingham programme, which includes the full script, also features photographs not just of

Aladdin 1957: Abanazer (Ian Mullins) Widow Twankey (Ronald Magill) & Aladdin (Helen Dorward)

the cast but of Oliver Gordon and even Henry Marshall. The adult dancers, as usual at the Alex, were the Lehmiski Ladies, with the show's choreography under the control of Helena Lehmiski, who ran a dancing school in Edgbaston.

Timothy West's first wife, Jacqueline Boyer, arranged the dances for *Cinderella* at Salisbury, with Timothy playing Major Domo as well as fulfilling his off-stage duties. The couple lived in a caravan outside the Old Castle Inn on the edge of Salisbury and Timothy writes in his autobiography of his admiration that the theatre was then run by a total of nine people: Reggie Salberg and his Secretary; Stan Astin as electrician with his wife Pauline in the Box Office; Roberto Petrarca the carpenter and Jean Adams the scenic artist; Kate Servian for wardrobe and a total of one Stage Manager and two ASMs. The only other staff consisted of the Front of House

Manager and a book-keeper who came in twice a week to keep up the accounts.[50]

Pauline Astin, a fiercely protective Box Office manager, is well remembered by those who appeared at the theatre as well as the audience. She was still there in the 1960s when Christopher Biggins joined the company as a Student ASM, and was instantly renamed Sunshine by Oliver Gordon. Pauline Astin was, he says, 'a big, imposing lady with heavily dyed hair piled up high on top of her head. To me she was a dragon, but like most people who have scared me throughout my life, she ended up a close friend and a wonderful person.' [51] She was a woman of strong views too; Chris Dunham remembers her saying to an audience member 'I don't know why you're coming to see this, everybody says it's terrible.' [52]

Cinderella 1958: Olive (Ronald Magill), Baron Hardup (Geoffrey Lumsden) & Hydro (Ian Mullins)

The *Salisbury Times* anonymous review of Cinderella[53] notes that the show 'makes no pretence at being lavish or opulent, but I stake what little my reputation is worth in saying that it would be hard indeed to find a nicer pantomime.' The review notes approvingly the lack of 'incongruous episodes' sometimes to be found in other pantos, and that the many local references included one

to the 'new civic hall site.' The review ends with the reassuring note
that 'in case you are worried about what time the children should get
to bed, you are out by 9.40pm.' The same critic, writing in another
part of the paper, reminds readers that seats are available for later in
the run, but admonishes those who caused problems for the theatre
in those days before credit cards.

> I am told there are still some people who have no conscience about
> booking seats by telephone, and then not turning up. What selfishness!
> They not only prevent other people from seeing the show, but they
> also lose the theatre the money.[54]

In 1959, Josephine Tewson was back as Principal Boy for *Dick
Whittington* and has strong memories of the production. 'I remember
a hideously long front cloth for me and Tiddles while they changed
scenery into Morocco from the ship. It entailed me singing *'The
Lights of Home'* and if the scene change still hadn't been completed,
launching into John of Gaunt's speech about England!' First night
nerves took their toll, and on that occasion Josephine found herself
sailing straight on into Henry V's Band of Brothers speech before
Harfleur and not being sure how to get out of it: as she remembers,
'Nancie Herrod nearly suffocated trying not to laugh in the cat skin.'[55]
The local paper was most impressed with Josephine Tewson however,
remarking on her 'fine stage presence and all the dash and daring
which we love to see; she acts and sings well.' The toad-in-the-hole
appeared in the kitchen scene and this was also an early appearance
of a wall-papering scene, seldom seen now outside the circus. Playing
Mate was Raymond Bowers, making his first pantomime appearance
at Salisbury. He would become a regular at the Playhouse for many
years, and several company members remember the house he shared
in The Close, with its yellow room containing only a grand piano. The
songsheet was 'How can a guinea pig wag his tail,' described as well-

known by the *Salisbury Times* but which has obviously not maintained its fame over the years,[56] although Stephanie Cole remembers almost all of it:

> How can a guinea pig show he's pleased
> When he hasn't got a tail to wag?
> All other animals you will find
> Have got a little tail stuck on behind.
> Why don't they put a tail on a guinea pig
> And finish off a decent job?
> …The price of a guinea pig would go right up
> From a guinea up to thirty bob.

The production was a financial success too, setting a trend that was to continue for many years; the Directors noted with approval the profit of £903 15s 5d.[57]

Scene 3
Another Part of the Forest

I T HAD BEEN as a result of the arrival of Oliver Gordon as producer in 1957 that the initial Salisbury panto team was completed. In addition to Henry Marshall as writer, Oliver Gordon (and later Roger Clissold) as producer, and Reggie Salberg in overall control, there were other long-standing members of that creative team. Stanley Rixon, who had worked at the Opera House, Scarborough with the York and Scarborough Repertory Company and with Reggie Salberg at the New, Hull designed the pantomimes – and most of the plays at Salisbury – from 1958 to 1967, and he was joined from 1964 by Barbara Wilson, who was responsible for costumes every year from then and was still in post at the time of the last Henry Marshall panto in 1985 – and she is thus the person with the longest continuous involvement with the productions. Stanley Rixon – Rick – was known for his colourful and skilfully-painted sets in a traditional style. He worked at the Nuffield Theatre Southampton after Salisbury and died in 1993.

Peter Cregeen, whose later career was in television, appeared in the 1960 *Jack and the Beanstalk* as Giant Thunderclub ('terrific in more ways than one' according to the local paper[58]), with Ollie Gordon producing and playing Silly Sammy – a sort of Idle Jack for the more mature actor. Peter was immediately impressed by Oliver Gordon's understanding of pantomime.

*A first night photo: Reggie Salberg, Peter Cregeen and
Oliver Gordon*

He was the mastermind of the panto. He directed plays during the winter as well but the panto was his true love, and there was nothing he didn't know about it, having directed many of them elsewhere at the Alex Birmingham, Wolverhampton and Windsor. In those productions he had big stars like Norman Wisdom, unlike Salisbury where the cast was mainly made up of the resident company. I treasure the memories of Oliver controlling the latter days of rehearsal with a referee's whistle, not the usual practice for a director, but effective – while Henry sat in the stalls smoking his pipe and looking enigmatic...[59]

There was a record profit for this pantomime, too: £1016 4s 7d, and attendance was 97.5%, an attendance very few theatres at the time could match. The Directors not only noted the profit, but the fact that the repertory season as a whole was running at a loss of £4673 that year. Such losses were made good by the addition of the Arts Council grant, other fund-raising activities, and personal cheques from supporters such as Chair of the Directors Sir Reginald

Kennedy-Cox. Individual items of expenditure varied from year to year, although some recurred: the royalty to Henry Marshall for the script was £60 and the orchestra cost £225. Tights – essential for a show set in the medieval period – ran up a bill of £2 7s 0d, and the hire of wigs cost £20 2s 6d. More specific expenses for *Jack and the Beanstalk* included hire costs for a cloud machine (£15 6s 8d) and a cow skin for the actors playing Tallulah (£10 17s 6d).

The *Salisbury Times* reviewer was, as ever, most impressed; perhaps even more so since he (or she – the review is anonymous) was selected to win the prize as best participant in the communal singing – perhaps not an accident if the reviewer's identity was known to the theatre management. The review[60] gives a real flavour of the style of performance, at this stage still firmly rooted in an acrobatic tradition.

> It is fun all the way, and I vote it the best pantomime we have had for a long time, with the second half particularly good… The scenes which raise the roof include the Dame's (Christopher Benjamin) kitchen, where a duck cooking attempt is interfered with by a number of tricks that don't come off, and which ends with a snowball fight, with the audience joining in. Then there is the giant's kitchen, wherein Slosh and Wallop (Bryon O'Leary and Victor Carin) have a fine old chase after Silly Sammy (Oliver Gordon). They dive through 'brick' walls and disappear and re-appear from sliding panels and revolving doors. Thirdly, there is the band rehearsal, with King Bertram (Raymond Bowers) conducting and with the Dame playing her 'slush pump…' The battle to the death with sword and dagger against the giant's club is a real thriller and has the children out of their seats. My, how they enjoy it, and they don't want much prompting to join in telling Silly Sammy his name, shouting to warn of the giant's presence and in singing the songs. The dancing is very pretty, especially the transformation scene to close the first act, when Nature's trees, flowers

and the like come to life. Wonderfully effective, too, is Cloudland…
See this show and give yourself and the children a break.

With the cycle of six pantomimes now about to be complete,
the following year saw a return to *Robinson Crusoe*, and this time much
more successfully. The number of pirates increased and they gained the
names and descriptions that were to be theirs in successive productions
until this particular pantomime went out of fashion: 'One Eye wears
a patch over his right eye. Gash is heavily scarred. Barmy is small and
a bit daft.' The Bow Street Runners had appeared as a double act, and
Nellie the Elephant makes her first appearance. Since this was before
the demise of the Lord Chamberlain, the script can still be found in the
British Library, with a notice that it was licensed on 25th October 1961.
It is perhaps surprising that some of the material did not cause problems
in those simpler days: for example the gag about Grannie, Annie and
Fanny going missing, only the first two being found and no sign of the
third. Presumably there may have been other additions during the run
that were not officially sanctioned by the Lord Chamberlain.

After a rather surprising prologue in Puerto Rico, where the
pirates decide to return home to get their treasure, we begin as is
more traditional in the port of Hull, where it is apparently Pancake
Day and the pirates are singing *Hearts of Oak*. Many of the regular
routines such as the mop drill and the UV underwater scene with
fluorescent fish are already in place, though some of these will
migrate in later years to the other sea voyage panto, *Dick Whittington*.
An animal ballet included the snake dance from 1955 and the first
half ended traditionally with a tableau. In the second act, the script
includes a very detailed description of the battle with muskets at the
stockade, as is only fitting with a writer who was also a fight director.
The porthole and water scene – also often seen in *Dick Whittington* –
made an appearance during the voyage home, and the audience song
was *Nellie the Elephant*.

Oliver Gordon (Silly Sammy) and Henry Marshall during rehearsals for Jack and the Beanstalk in 1960

In those days, there were only six different pantomimes produced and they were presented in rotation. Sonia Woolley once asked Henry and Oliver why they didn't then do any of the other stories like *Little Red Riding Hood* or *Puss in Boots* but they were insistent that those were not really traditional pantomimes. That was to change however when the new theatre opened in the 1970s, as we shall see. By the early 1960s the regular cycle had been established, with *Robinson Crusoe*; *Babes in the Wood*; *Aladdin*; *Cinderella*; *Dick Whittington* and *Jack and the Beanstalk* forming the only titles performed throughout the Henry Marshall years, apart from the single *Mother Goose* and *Puss in Boots* in the 1980s.

Henry was not alone in considering these six pantomimes to be the canon to be cycled through for audiences who would peak in their approval at around the age of 7 and so be too old to be seen to enjoy the same title the next time it came around. Of course, by the time after that they would be ready to enjoy nostalgically hearing once more the familiar story (and jokes) and thus pantomime weaves its spell. The titles chosen by Henry were among the oldest and most firmly established. *Robinson Crusoe* is first recorded on stage in 1781 and *Aladdin* in 1788. These were followed by *Cinderella* in 1804, *Mother Goose* in 1805, *Dick Whittington* in 1814 and *Jack and the Beanstalk* in 1819.[61] *Babes in the Wood*, sometimes but not always featuring Robin Hood, came along a little later in 1857. [62]

Even in the 1960s, the Salisbury audience were becoming a part of the show, with many of them already making it their practice to come year after year, and the combination of men of the theatre like Reggie, Ollie and Henry with talented and carefully picked young actors was to hold the theatre in good stead for years to come. A unique and much-loved producer, Oliver Gordon knew exactly what he wanted and did not allow the restrictions of the theatre's meagre resources to hold him back, as Sonia Woolley discovered when she joined the company in the 1960s.

He had one way of doing it; he had one way of doing everything. There were certain things which were always done the same way, they were sort of rituals. I think he learnt it working on the Aldwych farces. There were certain routines that Robertson Hare and company always did the same way. You come through the door, you stop, you turn, you take that, you go back again: and so on. It was absolutely mechanically sorted. He wanted to teach these things, he'd say 'Come here cock!' 'You don't come through that door like that, you stop, look…' He timed things exactly and taught this to anyone else who was in the panto. He'd done it for years and years and there were certain routines like the one called the ziz routine where they went in and out of doors. There were lots of people on the stage with various doors, some of which swung automatically, and some which didn't. Getting them constructed was quite a palaver in that little theatre as you can imagine. It was again choreographed so that one person comes through one door and one goes back through the other door. Of course the audience find it hysterical because they don't see all the palaver that's going on backstage; they don't see the joins, it's a bit like *Noises Off*. So he would teach all these routines and he would say to the set builders 'I've got to have one door that does that' and 'I've got to have a trapdoor that does that' and they were able to dive through there head-first. He knew exactly what he wanted and these set-pieces could be incorporated in any pantomime, you just paint the set differently. [63]

Rehearsals were efficient and orderly, with a lot to do in a very limited time. Henry Marshall was around much of the time and didn't approve of actors ad-libbing or, says Michael Stroud, 'wandering about too much'. Michael Stroud had joined the company after his school-friend Chris Dunham arranged an audition with Reggie, whose response was 'I'll hire you for one play and see if we like you and you like us.' The company were always well looked after, as Michael remembers.

In the old days it was a set routine, 10 o'clock rehearsal, 5 o'clock tea. They were good days. For me, those early days were what it is all about. Get your make-up on, do the show – sometimes you were good, sometimes not – then to the pub and then home and learn 18 pages or more of the next play. I had to sing *Ooly Ooly Golly Stonga* on the drums as the Cannibal King once and I used to sing other things and Oliver got very cross. I could see him actually wince when I changed the words to something silly... They were very close, Ollie and Henry.

There was always a Christmas party for the company at Reggie and Noreen's house at Bemerton. They really put on a spread, very good to keep the company together, he wouldn't let anyone be left alone, he would always check. I learnt everything – if I know anything at all – at Salisbury, as I didn't go to drama school.[64]

The timing of the shows was quite rigid. Reggie insisted that the evening should be over by 9.15pm so that people bringing small children could get their buses home. It was also Reggie's role to watch the finances; he could, says Sonia Woolley, 'cost things down to the last wig and the last costume hire.' By 1963, the shows were playing to almost 100% capacity, thanks also to what Mike Starke describes as 'its talented and tireless company of actors, directors and stage staff, hand-picked by Reggie with his unerring skill.'[65]

The Salisbury Playhouse building was not only cramped and leaky; it had no fly tower for lifting scenery and one side of the stage had no easy access. The lighting board was Stage Right and up a ladder, with the prompt also on that side, and the actors were able to see the sparks coming from the panel as they looked into the wings. The theatre had the bastard prompt on Stage Right since Stage Left had only a small wing and the tiny muddy corridor. These cramped conditions could lead to problems, and Christopher Biggins remembers Jane Quy on the book one night and catching up with her knitting, only to see it swept out of her hand by the curtain. [66]

Audience members were sometimes aware of these difficulties too. I well remember an actor – it was probably Michael Stroud or Raymond Bowers - reclining on a chaise longue at the beginning of the second act of a thriller, phone in hand, only to watch in horror as the opening curtain snagged on a cocktail cabinet bringing the whole lot to the floor to the accompaniment of the sound of breaking glasses and bottles. With a level of sangfroid appropriate to his character, he improvised a request over the phone for someone to come and clear up the mess – and the actress playing the maid duly obliged.

Unfortunately, the next show, *Robin Hood and Babes in the Wood*, saw profits fall to a mere £203 as a result of the harsh 1962-

1963 winter, with snow on the ground in Salisbury from December to March. Local schools closed for weeks on end, travel was severely curtailed even around the town, and more than 1500 people who had paid for tickets for the pantomime were unable to get there. Advance bookings for the plays were low too, and Reggie got Board approval to give all those who were unable to get to the pantomime free tickets for any play in 1963. Chris Dunham (as Will Scarlet) and another company member who would become his wife, June Watson (Nurse Enos), were among the cast. Since that time Chris Dunham has been involved with pantomime every year apart from the two occasions when he was appearing in the West End, and he grew up already enjoying them. 'I come from Lympstone near Exeter. I had an aunt who took me to the Theatre Royal Exeter. There was a chorus of 12 and a chorus of Babes and we were still there three hours later...' [67] June Watson, on the other hand, was brought up on Scottish pantomimes, and saw Harry Gordon and Dave Willis at the Kings Edinburgh.

Although this production broke with tradition by having a female Dame – not a unique occurrence at Salisbury where the key aim was always to make the best of the current repertory company – there was a traditional female Principal Boy in the form of Jill Graham's Robin Hood. June Watson remembers she got the part of Nurse Enos because 'it was decided that I was the only one to play it, there was no suitable man. The trouble is you can't be as vulgar.' [68] She also remembers playing to only 25 people one night due to the snow, but Chris agrees that female Dames are very difficult to carry off. 'It doesn't work. There are things you can't do to a woman. You can hit a man but not a woman. And they're real breasts...' [69]

The Babes were as usual supplied by the Bellairs School of Dancing, in this case real twins: Tina and Judy Spooner. They were known as Tina and Judy in the story – and the Babes at Salisbury were still known as Tina and Judy in the very last Henry Marshall *Babes in the Wood* at Salisbury in 1985. Oliver Gordon was producing but not yet playing Dame. Instead, he was one half of the Robbers, alongside Stage Director David Daker. The care and detail of a classic Henry Marshall script is shown by the stage directions for the opening scenes. We begin with a prologue featuring not immortals in this most un-magical of pantomimes, but a historical prequel showing us how Robin became an outlaw. We note that even the armorial bearings are specified – as they continued to be in later versions of the scripts.

PRINCE JOHN is discovered, hands on hips, HIS PAGE beside him carrying a shield and a lance. The device on the shield is two gold lions reguardant on a red background. Timpani roll ending in cymbal crash as PRINCE JOHN raises his hand in a commanding gesture.

Robin then appears, kills a deer and is banished as an outlaw. The half-tabs open, the lighting changes and we find ourselves in a carefully-described Robin Hood's camp in Sherwood Forest.

This is a clearing in the forest. There is a small stream at the back with a wooden bridge. It is a scene of bustling activity. ONE OUTLAW is basting an ox which hangs on a spit turned by ANOTHER OUTLAW - the spit is slung on a portable wooden framework over a fire. FRIAR TUCK, a casque on his head, is sitting on the bridge fishing in the stream. LITTLE JOHN and ANOTHER OUTLAW are having a friendly quarterstaff bout. WILL SCARLET is playing the lute. OTHER OUTLAWS are testing their bowstrings, trying their bows, trimming their arrows.

The opening chorus involves each of the outlaws telling us how they first met Robin Hood, helpfully bringing the story up to date.

When I met Robin Hood
He said, said he, come live with me,

Under the wonderful greenwood tree,
Where the grass grows green and a man is free.
And then I understood:
From the marvellous tale he did unfold
That this young chap was an outlaw bold
Who just wouldn't do what he was told:
For this was Robin Hood.

We soon meet the Sheriff, the Nurse and the Babes who enter on hobbyhorses, together with Marian, the Sheriff's wards. Later, Willie Whiskers arrives, an old friend of the Nurse and a character unique to Henry's version of the story, who introduces his dog. When we meet Dave and Ollie the robbers (their names would change to match the actors in most later versions), they introduce themselves in song.

Robin Hood and the Babes in the Wood 1962: David Daker and Oliver Gordon as Dave and Ollie, the Robbers

Look out, look out, don't turn about
For we are just behind you.
One dirty night, you'll get a fright,
Your friends will never find you.
For we're the blackest villains,
And we're famed both far and near.
What's our favourite recreation?
Cutting throats from 'ere to 'ere.

Later we see the traditional schoolroom scene with Willie in the Dunce's cap, with the Nurse making liberal use of what Oliver Gordon always called a nap-stick – a version of the traditional slapstick with two pieces of wood that case a loud bang when slapped, without causing too much actual harm. The first act ends with a transformation scene turning the Nursery into the view of a golden fairy-tale castle, and a toy ballet introducing Father Christmas. After ice-cream has been eaten and toilets visited by the audience, the second act starts with a chorus song at Nottingham Goose Fair.

We're at Nottingham Fair,
Where you may be aware,
There is fun to be had for a pittance.
Please come in for a lark,
Now it's getting so dark,
And they only charge sixpence admittance.
There is going to be revelry,
Women and laughter,
And oh to the devil with
What may come after.
Nottingham is a city of gaiety,
Happiness for both clergy and laity;
There's no place 'neath the sun,
Where there is so much fun,
As at the Nottingham Goose Fair.

After the archery contest, won by Robin of course, Little John (a part usually given to a strong singer) sings a song to inspire the outlaws.

Bowmen of England,
Come from your woodland.

Bring us your bows
Of good old English yew.
Bring us your songs
That tell us of England.
Bring us your hearts
There's a man's work to do.
Let your horn sound
Through the hills and the valleys;
Piercing and clear
Through the hot summer's day.
Only that call
Can awaken old England,
Sleeping and silent
And not hard to betray.

There is much mileage from the other activities at the Fair, including a Ghost Train and Crazy House which had more in common with 1960s funfairs than medieval Nottingham, and the audience would have recent memories of the Salisbury Charter Fair, held in October every year. The Crazy House is an opportunity for some magic effects with UV light but the Ghost Train would become more elaborate in later versions of the script. The plot develops rapidly as the Fairy introduces the Bird Ballet, the Robbers fight (described in eight movements and great detail in the script) and the wandering Pilgrim is revealed to be the returning Richard the Lionheart. The final battle at Nottingham Castle, with boiling oil, catapults and crossbows is described with great care through more than a page of stage directions. This was the show – evolving but not materially changed – which would recur throughout the Henry Marshall years until its last performances in January 1986.

The 1962 version of the story was hailed as a great success by the *Salisbury Times*,[70] claiming that it had all the necessary components:

'a good story, colourful settings, plenty of action, sweet music and singing, lots and lots of humour and some dainty dancing.' The review also noted approvingly that the story was a traditional one, and that right prevails at the end, as it always should in pantomime.

> It's good material and Oliver Gordon, who produces, gives it all the full treatment. He and David Daker are the two 'wicked men,' and how the children hiss them as they go about their shady business! Hissing back is the Sheriff, well characterised by Jolyon Booth. Jill Graham makes a dashing Robin Hood… The dame is really a woman in this pantomime. June Watson is terrific as Nurse Enos, and is particularly funny in the schoolroom scene, where she is most ably assisted by Hugh Walters as Willie Whiskers…

The following year Frank Barrie appeared as Abanazer in his only Salisbury pantomime, the 1963 *Aladdin* – but, almost fifty years later, he still remembers his opening number, beginning:

> We come to you from Africa, a thousand miles away,
> We live on dates and paprika and say our prayers each day.
> I am a great magician, I do things you can't believe-
> I practise nuclear fission and there's nothing up my sleeve.

Perhaps not surprisingly, he may not recall the second verse, which continued, in a reminder of how much times and tastes have changed:

> Behold my slave Abdulla, yes Abdulla is his name,
> His father was a Mullah till the day Abdulla came.
> When I first bought Abdulla he seemed quite a man of grit,
> Now tho' I'm his lord and ruler, he is just an Arab nit.

The local paper was impressed with his performance and noted that he was 'a finely melodramatic wicked uncle.'[71] He also remembers how happy an experience being involved in the panto was for him, his wife and their young daughter – a golden memory as he describes it now.

> It was a very happy show – Henry was in attendance at rehearsals, bright and helpful and Oliver Gordon directed with his usual hearty good humour. Oliver also consented to play my slave Abdulla, in charge of a comedy camel and delighting the audiences with his lugubrious facial expressions and masterly timing. The cast was superb... and I'm happy to report that most of them have remained friends over the years. The audiences of the time were extraordinarily generous. They gave great strength to the repertory movement – young actors could learn their trade in front of sympathetic, family audiences who were proud that their city could field a hard working theatre company of undoubted talent and impressive versatility. Reggie Salberg had hand picked us all – he'd seen us working in front of audiences in other companies and recruited us to join his 'family.'[72]

Henry Marshall made sure in his script that the setting was as detailed as could be provided within the limitations of the Salisbury Playhouse, with a careful description of not only what should be portrayed, but which parts should be practical. Interesting to note, too, that the requirement was for a serious setting rather than the jokey one that was becoming popular at the time. It is noteworthy that it is not a laundry but the Public Baths that is the main setting, which Clinton-Baddeley suggested (writing at around the same time) 'is rarely seen today now that the laundry is a sure fixture...the laundry works its way in by slow degrees.'[73] Henry's stage direction requires both: Public Baths and laundry.

An impressive building UC is the Baths which has an ornate door. UL is the entrance to Twankey's laundry. UR a water wheel with buckets and cups which slowly begins to turn as the scene comes to life. There are no comedy slogans anywhere - this is a genuine-looking scene from Ancient Pekin.

A prologue precedes this opening scene in which Aladdin reads the beginning of his own story from a large copy of the Arabian Nights. A note on the script indicates that the first draft was finished on 25th June 1963 (which copy is handwritten and almost illegible), and it was then revised several times in July before being typed up. Donald Pelmear played Widow Twankey, a 'dainty' Dame by his own description, and the only one he played throughout his career. He remembers in particular one effect which involved some rapid street running.

Aladdin 1963: Widow Twankey (Donald Pelmear) dances a tango with Abanazer (Frank Barrie)

My main memory is of doing a tango with Frank Barrie as Abanazar. Oliver Gordon wanted Twankey to hide in a barrel, unfortunately of gunpowder, so that I was supposedly shot from the stage to the back of the auditorium. This involved disappearing via an escape hatch from the barrel, dashing round the back of the set, out of the stage door and on to Fisherton Street, a main thoroughfare, in order to get into the stalls by the main front entrance. Perhaps it startled passers-by to see a gaudily attired transvestite running into the theatre from the public highway. The 'explosion' ended, of course with a run down the length of the stalls and back on to the stage. You had to be fit for pantomime . . . ..often twice daily![74]

Throughout the pantomime the role of Abanazer is taken very seriously, and instructions are given for him to perform magic and reveal the future using a Geomantic Table – a tray of sand which glows as does his turban and gloves when under UV light. There cannot be many panto scripts of Aladdin that call for a Geomantic Table, but Abanazer's curse on Aladdin the cave has a familiar ring, although with a more effective transition to rhyme than many a lesser effort.

In the name of Allah, the all-powerful, who created the firmament,
I place this curse upon you:
May you rot here for the rest of your miserable life,
May you die of hunger surrounded by the riches you can never use.
And may you go mad before you die,
Mad with starvation and terror and fright,
Away from the air and the stars and the light.
May only the earth hear your screams and your groans,
Till the day that the rats make a meal of your bones.

After the transformation scene in the cave, and the Jewel Ballet, Aladdin re-enters in a fur-trimmed robe and Act 1 ends with a traditional tableau.

Geni: Open Sesame!
Thunder. The back of the cave is cleft in two and the night sky with

twinkling stars is revealed. Aladdin climbs on rock at back and stands, framed against the sky, holding up the lamp.

Detailed instructions as ever from the author, but in this case there are certain phrases that prove exceptionally telling; the requirement that the cave be 'cleft in two' not only gives instruction for how the scenery should be made, it seems to give a clear suggestion of how it should be moved; a sure sign of a script from a man steeped in theatrecraft. Unusually, in this version, it is the Vizier who would like to marry the Princess, but needless to say he is thwarted in this aim. The usual swapping of new lamps for old takes place, the action moves briefly to Africa, and the Geni is asked to build a pagoda for Aladdin, an opportunity to include a ballet telling the story of the Willow Pattern Plate. The ballet, we are told, should be performed to Delibes La Source: Section 14. After the obligatory songsheet (*Tiddley Winkey, Tiddley Winkey, Tiddley Winkey Woo; I love you...*), the panto ends with a walkdown to a reprise of the song celebrating

the Royal Baths, making it perhaps the only version of Aladdin to send the audience out singing *Have a Bath*. This might seem a strange choice, but it is another example of Marshall knowing his trade. I saw this production, almost fifty years ago, and I still remember the song.

When you're in the mood for slaughter,
So annoyed that you feel quite daft.
Just get in the groove with water,
Have a bath, have a bath, have a bath.
Don't mope like a dope,

Aladdin 1963 Three backstage photos of Donald Pelmear as Widow Twankey

Where there's soap there's still hope,
Have a bath, have a bath, have a bath.

Chris Dunham and June Watson were back again, this time playing the Chinese policemen. The Musical Director was Jimmy Berry, and June remembers that he sometimes enjoyed watching the show so much that he had to be reminded of where to come in.

He used to get so carried away even after so many performances and forget to play. He had never done panto before and had no idea of cues. Henry Marshall had to sit in the pit for the first week and give him the cues. That was the first time we had an organ rather than a piano.[75]

Perhaps the *Salisbury Times* should have almost the last word on this production, for once again its review[76] gives a sense of what it was to be in the audience.

Unlike some of the bigger and more sophisticated shows, which are little more than a succession of disconnected acts, our pantomime faithfully tells the story of the Peking lad lured to, and left in a cave, but who escapes and marries the princess. The story is unfolded in 13 scenes, ranging from the market place in Peking to the African desert, and from Mrs Twankey's kitchen to the enchanted cave, which is suddenly transformed from a gloomy sealed vault, full of eerie noises, to a brilliantly-lighted chamber full of dainty ballet dancers… Brigit Forsyth, who recently joined the company, makes a dashing and likeable Principal Boy, and is partnered by Gillian Royale as the Princess. They are both in good voice, with *'Go, stranger go'* an appealing number… A good pairing is Christopher Dunham and June Watson as the Chinese constables and their *'Me and My Shadow'* is one of the best of the show's many good numbers… Oliver Gordon is, as always, amusingly droll as Abdulla… Tuneful and satisfying is the music supplied by Jimmy Berry at the Hammond Organ assisted by David Nicoll on the drums.

The final words come from Chris Dunham, who remembers much of what is mentioned in the review but also the fact that the Principal Girl managed to sing in extremely refined tones for a pantomime.

We did Me and My Shadow at the end of the first front cloth. We also did the thing of shaking hands and then you get stuck together. Someone was heard to say after we'd done that routine one night, it's a good job those two are married because it's disgusting what they are doing… Oliver Gordon wasn't very good at dealing with people who didn't give him something to work with but he was wonderful at panto – you always came on at the right place, you knew where you were. And what was so good about Henry's scripts is that they were very story-orientated. I think he got that from the Alex in Birmingham. Panto's almost gone full circle and story is important again.[77]

Scene 4
The Transformation Scene

WITH THE MOVE from weekly to fortnightly repertory by the 1960s, the Salisbury Playhouse provided its audiences with a wide range of plays, musicals and entertainments. For the young actors and crew who began their career there, the glamour of the theatre only just survived the reality of the backstage conditions, as Christopher Biggins, appointed Student ASM straight from school, writes in his autobiography.

> Salisbury Rep was falling apart. There was a tiny set of different stairs and rooms and corridors but there was nowhere to pick up a cat let along swing one. And yes, there was the high, intoxicating rich scent of make-up and hair-spray. But there was also the smell of mould, mildew and damp. The roof leaked all over and most of the buckets were used to protect the seats in the auditorium. Backstage, water just drained away wherever it could. Water soaked into almost everything, and however much heat our big old radiators banged out, it was never enough to dry it all out.[78]

For Reggie Salberg, of course, there was still the audience to contend with – or some of them anyway. His brother Derek told the story of the county gentleman who tried to bring a very large dog to one of the pantomime performances. On being told that animals were not permitted, the stern gentleman protested that this was not mentioned on the advertisements. 'No,' said Reggie, 'it doesn't say that elephants, tigers and lions are excluded either.'

What repertory theatre did have, and Salisbury had it in abundance, is an attitude on the part of young actors that pantomime roles were as important as any other, and needed to be approached in the same way; although Knight Mantell remembers that some actors found panto difficult, as he did himself when first asked to play Dame. He was much happier however as the villain.

> I think pantomime really requires enormous skill of a particular type, and what you've got now are reality stars and personalities and they can't do it. Queen Rat is a burlesque version of Lady Macbeth. Dames have become drag acts with too much make-up and that's not what being a Dame's about. My interest is nineteenth century theatre and I've played Abanazer nine times. You sort of think, well, I'm going to give my Henry Irving. You have to believe in it as much as if you were playing King Lear or something, however preposterous the lines are. Even in bad pantomimes, the cave scene in Aladdin is written like it's Marlowe.[79]

Sets were becoming more lavish in the 1960s, with Stanley Rixon expecting more from his crew each year. Working on that 1963 *Aladdin*, Stage Director Marcia Wheeler remembers being swamped with scenery, with there being so much that half of it had to be kept at the stables that served as a scenery store behind the theatre, and swapped over during the interval. Despite this, Marcia also remembers the production as great fun, particularly making all the bird cages and other props that were needed. First arriving at Salisbury as Technical ASM, Marcia was then made Stage Director, responsible for Stage Management, discipline backstage and logging the show. The cast were not allowed to go more than 12 miles away from Salisbury during the run, although a visit to Southampton was possible with

Marcia Wheeler on sound in the wings, and using newly-purchased equipment. This was taken during a play; conditions were quite different during the pantomime.

special permission.

Marcia also operated the sound, with others looking after props and on the book. There was a little more room in the wings during the panto as not all the sound equipment was needed. There were also volunteers – like local schoolboy Christopher Biggins – and Marcia checked how serious they were by asking them to do a Saturday overnight get-in. She also remembers a dentist scene in *Aladdin* that never went right; at one performance David Daker as the Emperor added a gag by spitting out Mint Imperials as his teeth, but they couldn't be cleared up in time and the dancers on point all fell over. It was in this production that one actor – who should perhaps remain nameless – felt he deserved a bigger part and was not popular with the rest of the company. Marcia told her crew to ignore his protests and they adopted a policy of smothering him with kindness, which seems to have worked as he later bought sandwiches for them all.[80] The actors inside the camel were perhaps not best suited to the part, with the front half once appearing as a villager with his camel feet still on. The rear half was played by a member of the crew who later went into opera. He spoke only in beautifully modulated Received Pronunciation, and actors playing parts in dialect plays were known to deliberately dry when he was on the book just to hear

Marcia Wheeler and Stanley Rixon backstage with actor Christian Rodskjaer (later Rodska)

his version of the line.

By this time, many of the backstage characters at the Playhouse were well established. Stan Astin was still on the lighting grid, as he would be for many years to come, with his wife firmly ensconced in the Box Office from which she would peer rather imperiously at anyone who wanted to buy tickets. Mike Starke describes them both.

Lord of The Ring Mains and master of the lighting gantry was Stan Astin. A big, taciturn man, Stan cultivated a dour demeanour in a jealously-guarded rule over his dimmer-switch domain. Meanwhile, Stan's wife Pauline ruled the Box Office with a similar indomitable pride. Neither suffered fools gladly. I had a sneaking suspicion they both thought that, by coming to Salisbury, I had deprived my home village of its most accomplished idiot, and that my best course of action would be to return to my rural roots and rectify the loss.[81]

Mike Starke had joined the company as trainee Front of House Manager. He grew up in Canterbury, where he became a regular at the Marlowe Theatre, and came to Salisbury as part of an Arts Council scheme which involved placements at a series of theatres, during which he received a weekly wage of around £12, which was, he reminds us, 'a little above the pittance earned by farm labourers at the time.' He also recognises now that he could not have had a better mentor than Reggie, and it was certainly not his fault that theatre turned out not to be suited to Mike, who now says 'I did the repertory movement the most generous favour that I could by leaving it to follow another career.' Mike also remembers the stage carpenter, who often said that he joined the theatre after one very boring day in which he was asked to hang twenty doors.

Someone who always had a ready smile was stage carpenter John Scutt. Visiting his workshop down the lane from the main theatre complex one day, I found him peering into the stream that ran alongside. Poised in his hand was a home-made trident, fashioned from a stick to which three pieces of sharpened wire were attached. His quarry was one of the rainbow trout that teemed in the waterways that flowed through the city. He cheerily blamed my interruption for him losing his quarry on that occasion. John once told me of his bizarre experiences as a teenage National Serviceman. It was a salutary example of the military maxim never to volunteer for anything. After a few weeks of basic army training, John and his reluctant fellow recruits were paraded to be told they had a choice. They could either go to some grim garrison like Aldershot or Colchester, or volunteer for an exotic posting, at Her Majesty's expense, in the sun drenched South Pacific. Private Scutt was not backward in coming forward, content to remain in blissful ignorance as to why this seemingly idyllic holiday with pay was on offer. Too late he discovered he was to be one of the 'guinea pigs' exposed to test explosions of nuclear weapons.

There were other memories too for Mike Starke.

Sometime during my year at Salisbury, the film Mary Poppins came out. During its week in Salisbury, as cinema tickets were free to Playhouse staff, I joined a band of fans who went *every* day. As I recall, Mike Stroud led the way, closely followed by Christopher Biggins and Chris Harris, with me bringing up the rear. The daily cry, at the top of our voices, was: 'Mary Poppeeeens!' We must have been unbearable to anyone in earshot.

Mike also had a part in the arrival at Salisbury of the Front of House Manager who was to remain there until his retirement: Alan Corkill. Mike went from Salisbury to a placement at Her Majesty's Theatre, Barrow-in-Furness, and the barman there was Alan Corkill, who applied for the job at Salisbury, was appointed with excellent references, and was still in post many years after the new theatre opened, retiring only recently.

Mike's wife Sue worked on costumes under Wardrobe Mistress Barbara Wilson, who dressed all the shows from 1963 onwards at both theatres. Madame Barbara – as she was named by Oliver Gordon – had been at Drama School with Roger Clissold. Sue Starke had no experience of theatre when, like so many others, she was given her chance by Reggie Salberg.

I was newly-married and without a job; Reggie Salberg kindly made me assistant to the wardrobe mistress, Barbara Wilson. At the back of the Playhouse was a warren of dressing rooms and the wardrobe was two rooms at the far end of a corridor and up a rickety wooden staircase. It seemed to me that this was an area of ordered chaos. The main clothes for the pantomime, *Dick Whittington*, were gradually assembled on clothes rails in one room whilst repairs, alterations and fittings went on in the other small room. My job was to repair, clean and iron where necessary. I soon learnt to sew on buttons with double thread for strength and not worry too much about matching colours because the lights covered a multitude of sins. No zips were allowed and Velcro had not come in to general use so it was buttons and strips of hooks and eyes for fastenings. One chest of drawers held overflowing piles of cotton tights of many colours. One of my jobs was to insert extra gussets into these garments to fit the larger actors. Barbara was a slight, bird-like figure. Despite her furrowed brow, Barbara had an infectious laugh and sardonic sense of humour. Her almost permanent worried look belied the fact that she was an expert and accomplished designer whose work was universally admired by directors and actors alike. As this sorcerer-seamstress's apprentice, I had my own reasons for wearing a worried look when working with her, for Barbara was practically a chain smoker and would absentmindedly leave burning cigarettes on highly inflammable work surfaces while preoccupied with her next costume task. At times she would light up again, reinforcing her potential as a pyromaniac. However, we both survived to tell the tale.[82]

Reggie Salberg always remembered the 1964 *Cinderella* as his favourite pantomime 'with Marilyn Taylersen enchanting in the title role… the best we have ever produced.' A local girl whose father was a butcher, Marilyn was a student at RADA when she got the part. She later took a degree in Anthropology, surely a unique achievement among Salisbury company members. The *Salisbury Times* was most impressed with the production as well, and noted rather eruditely that it was 'tradition, judiciously blended with modernism' that characterised the show. The paper's review[83] gives a sense of the joy of the production in performance.

The whole is a pantomime to remember. For one thing, it is slanted almost violently towards the children who are given a whale of a

Cinderella 1964: Dandini (Stephanie Cole) meets the huntsmen when standing in for the Prince

time with schoolboy humour, chances to participate with responses, and to sing their heads off. There is even the thrill of catching well hurled packets of chocolate buttons... on the night I viewed this pleasing spectacle one happy boy fell completely into the next row catching his packet of sweets... Prince Charming and Dandini are given dazzling manhood by Brigit Forsyth and Stephanie Cole in the best tradition of pantomime. Even more has been made of the Ugly Sisters by the irrepressible Oliver Gordon and David Daker... the two have many excellent scenes together: they fool their way through a haunted bedroom scene; release a lot of inhibitions by some most satisfying crock crashing; dash about on a rooftop and generally see to it that no scene ever lingers on its way. They are heartily backed by the hire purchase brokers Michael Poole and David Ryall who manage to infuse schoolboy humour of the type that rocks us at ten and has deserted us by twenty... In the Royal Ballroom the golden clock has hands which, to add to the touch of versimilitrude all children insist upon, has hands which carefully move – even if a little spasmodically… perhaps the most genuinely pleasing comment the cast could receive was given in one word by a ten-year-old lad after Monday's performance- 'Smashing.'

It was this production that saw Oliver Gordon play Dame for the first time, surprising some who seem to remember him being a fixture in the part. Chris Dunham remembers that he was quite nervous about the move, but it turned out to be a great success. 'Oliver played the high class one and David Daker was the common one. The plate smashing scene at the end was very good, very deadpan. They got on very well together and Daker was quite sort of strapping and Oliver was thinnish. He was a lovely, lovely man and they worked well together.' [84]

By this time, Chris Dunham's wife June Watson had moved on, having come to the end of her time as character female in the company. 'Steph and I overlapped by a couple of plays and then I left. I took over from the great Maggie Jones. Then Steph took over from me. You were in a slot. Once a year I got to play a leading lady, and I think it was Spider's Web that was my turn. Charmian May took over from Steph. I've never done a panto since because I can't sing…' [85]

Cinderella 1964: "What is that?" "Your finger" The Sisters (David Daker & Oliver Gordon) with John Peel (Desmond Gill)

The script for *Cinderella* can still be found in the Lord Chamberlain's collection, and begins with some characteristically brisk stage directions for the opening scene of the Royal Hunt.

> There should be plenty of trees and bushes for the fox and Prince to hide behind, and one prominent tree stump. It is just after dawn. In the dim reddish light we see a Fox (Principal Dancer) crouching UL almost invisible in the dimness, but seen more clearly as the light grows stronger. Distant hunting horns in music. Fox raises its head, looks round, listens. Horns, nearer. Fox scuttles across R and listens again. Then goes across L again. Yelping of hounds over loudspeaker. Fox dashes off R. Yelping comes nearer. John Peel enters, a hearty yeoman type, in the correct costume . . .

It is that insistence on the correct costume for John Peel – hardly a major character – that is another sign of Henry Marshall's attention to detail. The Prince soon enters, and sings one of Henry's lyrics.

> Show me a shady nook
> A country scene
> I'll read my favourite book
> And feel serene.
> Far from the bustling throng
> With just the blackbird's song
> Happy the whole day long
> I'll be...

In a later scene, Buttons (Christopher Dunham) sings the Tiddler song, which was a regular feature in Henry's pantomimes, and usually sung with the actor sitting on the edge of the stage with his fishing line dangling in the orchestra pit.

Cinderella 1964: Mimi (David Daker) and Fifi (Oliver Gordon) in hunting outfits

Oh, I like catching tiddlers,
'Cos I like them for my tea.
And when I catch a tiddler
I am always full of glee
I sit and wish for my little fish
All piled up high upon my dish
A tiddler dish is so delish-
I hope you all agree,
For that's the fish for me

In this wholly traditional version of *Cinderella*, none of the key scenes is forgotten, and even on that small and cramped stage, a haunted bedroom set featured appearances and disappearances through trap-doors that were in direct descent from the antics of

Harlequin and his companions; as writer and director, at least, knew full well. The script gives detailed instructions for the scene with the Sisters and the Brokers Men.

> He pursues the monkey into cupboard. In Fifi's room, Mimi is looking in cupboard. Bed returns. Mimi turns back covers. Purchase sits up and raises hat to her. Mimi goes into cupboard in fright, comes out again pursued by ghost which exits. Bed with Purchase disappears. In Mimi's room Fifi finds and loads a pistol. Mimi runs into room. Fifi shows her pistol. A double ghost enters. Fifi fires at it. Its head comes off. Mimi catches it, throws it to Fifi, who throws it back. Headless ghost exits. As Fifi and Mimi play football with ghost's head, monkey comes out of cupboard, stands in between them, catches head as it goes to and fro and goes into cupboard with it. Mimi and Fifi try to get into bed in Mimi's room. Hire and Purchase sit up in bed holding HP document. Mimi and Fifi scream, rush into Fifi's room. Fifi takes Indian club from bedside table, indicating they will defend themselves with

Cinderella 1964: Dandini (Stephanie Cole) and Prince Charming (Brigit Forsyth)

it, put it on table, get into bed, kiss goodnight. Hand of portrait picks up club hits them both on head. They pass out. Bed disappears into wall. Blackout.

The Prince was named Florazel, and always wore the star of Florazel, making it easier to see who is taking the part of the Prince when he changed roles with Dandini: a nice practical touch to ensure that children can follow the story. His song in the second act was a rousing one.

> The small sword of Florazel
> Will keep my honour bright
> I know how to use it well
> I'm ready for a fight.
> If some affray should come my way
> I will not turn aside.
> I will defend until the end
> My honour and pride.

His loyal manservant Dandini, played by Stephanie Cole, confirmed her duties in song after being given the task of finding Cinderella.

> I promise you it shall be done
> We will search your kingdom through,
> Looking high and low, until we know
> The girl who wore that shoe.

All this, and a running buffet (a table with human legs) at the ball, a chase across snowy rooftops with Father Christmas, and lots of broken plates: all rounded off with a song sheet which consisted of *Lily of Laguna* and the Beatles' *She Loves You Yeah Yeah Yeah* – sung

Cinderella 1964: Hire (Michael Poole), Fifi (Oliver Gordon), Mimi (David Daker) &
Purchase (David Ryall)

at the same time… No wonder it is a production that has stayed in the memories of all involved. Marcia Wheeler was once again Stage Director and remembers preparing the set.

> We shut for several days to nail sliders down on the floor and get the trucks in. The trees were on a tug truck and you could just pull them across, and all the little side bits went on sliders. There was a bedroom scene with trick doors and openings. With no flies we had to use tumblecloths.[86]

The Fire Brigade had to come and pump out rain water backstage, and one actor made a rapid exit, ran down the corridor and fell straight into the coal hole. Sometimes pieces of masonry fell off a backstage door, prompting Reggie to remark wryly 'It hasn't been the same since the elephant went through it.' Whether this was Nellie in *Robinson Crusoe* or a real elephant, no-one seems quite sure.

Stephanie Cole had left the Bristol Old Vic Theatre School in 1960 and then joined the Bristol Old Vic itself. She joined the Salisbury Playhouse company in 1964, and *Cinderella* was her fourth panto after previous appearances at Bristol, Lincoln and Canterbury. The rehearsal period was as short as those of all the other plays in the season, but, as she now remembers, 'we were young and learning was quick.'[87] Stephanie sang *'Oh wouldn't it be wonderful'* to Brigit Forsyth as Prince Charming. Many of the memories of that time relate to the problems of the aging theatre, with Stephanie recalling a production of *Romeo and Juliet* in which her Nurse cowered under an umbrella in the wings with Vivien Heilbron's Juliet, both wearing Wellington boots and hoping they would remember to remove them before going on stage. She also remembers acting on stage and glancing into the wings only to see sparks flying from the lighting grid.

The production of *Cinderella* had real ponies for the transformation scene, and unlike modern practice, the animals lodged at the theatre rather than just arriving each night in time for their cue. They were also taken to the Boxing Day Hunt Meet in the Market Square in the hope of gaining some extra publicity. As luck would have it, the scenery workshop at the back of the theatre was originally a stable and still had a cobbled floor with drainage channels, and a manger in place on one wall. The ponies lived there with the woman who looked after them, and had to make their way to the stage by walking along the Dressing Room corridor. They are not remembered too fondly however; they bit the stage Carpenter and made a mess on the stage at the Dress Rehearsal – though not after that so it was probably first night nerves.

Jessica Benton was one of the dancers in the production, using ballet shoes that had been broken in and worn by Principal Dancer Susan Saloman, herself remembered as an excellent dancer who often

Cinderella 1964: Cinderella (Marilyn Taylerson) in her coach

walked around backstage *en pointe* just for the practice. Principal Boy for the second year running was Brigit Forsyth and she has very happy memories of both productions, especially her first entrance coming out of the dragon in *Aladdin* and the small sword fight with Stephanie Cole in *Cinderella*. Brigit Forsyth grew up in Scotland watching Stanley Baxter and Rikki Fulton (with whom she later worked) at the King's Edinburgh, so traditional pantomime was very familiar to her before she same to Salisbury.

> I had the most marvellous time. Oliver Gordon was mercilous – his big aim was to corpse you – and he was just so funny. And I remember his direction being mainly 'Piss off down left, cock.' If asked about motivation, he would say the motivation is your pay-packet... Henry

Marshall was around for rehearsals and would help out with gags, showing us how to time it if it wasn't quite working. Barbara Wilson was so clever with what she did with the costumes and Reggie was always so sweet. When I was in a play somewhere else he very kindly said 'Don't read the notices' but of course I did...[88]

Brigit Forsyth also organised a Burns Night event one Sunday to which Reggie came, causing his wife Noreen to say that it was the only time she had seen him out of his pyjamas on a Sunday. The production of *Cinderella* did not run totally smoothly however, as Reggie Salberg complained again in an interview with *The Stage* about the people who book tickets by telephone and then don't turn up. He complained that this happened with almost 300 seats over the run, and caused the company to lose £60. Those seats could have been sold many times over of course, for the theatre had turned down more than five thousand bookings.

Marcia Wheeler still remembers with horror the performance when the trumpeters raised their instruments only for the sounds of *Hark the Herald Angels Sing* to be heard, causing much on-stage mirth. Marcia also used dry ice for the transformation scene, the first time it had been used at Salisbury. She got it from Southampton and kept it in a box full of straw, with an actor and an ASM in each wing with a kettle at the appropriate moment. The production also marked a milestone in that Oliver Gordon played Dame – or Ugly Sister in this case – alongside David Daker. They had worked well together as the robbers in *Babes in the Wood* the previous year. At one point, Oliver Gordon's Fifi wore a bread roll necklace and muff made of a hollowed out loaf called a rifle roll. After a few performances it got very dry and he would choose a suitable moment to crack it over the head of his sister Mimi; Marcia and her colleagues took this as their signal to make another one.

David Ryall and Michael Poole played the Broker's Men, and it was David Ryall's first – and indeed only – pantomime. Like so many actors he had been introduced to theatre through pantomime and particularly remembered the throwing of sweets – so much so that he was planning to include that in his performance.

I was determined on this, despite Mr Salberg's reluctance. 'Well, if you want to do that you'd better buy them yourself.' So I did, at the shop next to the theatre. Imagine my dismay when, upon joyfully tossing the fruit gums etc to the audience mid-song, I felt a sharp pain on the side of my face and realised to my horror and disgust that they were throwing them back! Times had certainly changed, I thought ruefully.[89]

Cinderella 1964: Fifi (Oliver Gordon) with her muff made of a loaf of bread

It was just after the run of *Cinderella* that David Ryall auditioned – successfully – in front of Laurence Olivier at the Old Vic and was offered a place with the National Theatre; and then got back on the train to do the evening performance at Salisbury. Fifty pieces of crockery were needed for every performance, and Marcia Wheeler got most of these from house clearances together with cracked plates from hotels. The plate smashing didn't meet with universal approval however. In one of Reggie's acerbic programme notes some years later he remembered:

The oddest complaint was from a mother who said that her little Oswald had been frightened by a comedy scene involving the breaking of plates: I was sympathetic until I learned that little Oswald was fourteen years old.

On the whole, then, the show was a great success and is fondly remembered; the get-out less so, since the stage Carpenter fell off a ladder and was off work for a week, and the Scenic Designer ended up in hospital having stitches put in a badly-cut hand.

By the time that Oliver Gordon took over as Dame from this production onwards, there had been a wide range of performers playing the role at Salisbury. Ronald Magill was one of the first Salisbury Dames. He appeared with *Stars in Battledress* during the war and then went into repertory when he was demobbed and had a long career in theatre before finding fame as Amos Brearly in *Emmerdale Farm*.

Cinderella 1964: The Sisters (David Daker & Oliver Gordon) ready for the Ball

In addition to Donald Pelmear and June Watson, other Dames in the early years included John Graham, Brian Kent, Tony Steedman and Christopher Benjamin.

Tony Steedman is remembered by Reggie as being particularly good as Dame but, he later remembered, 'we didn't love him on the last night of the run; he had a five minute spot to himself in the second half but at that final performance decided to have a last fling and stayed on stage for nearly

Dick Whittington and his Cat 1965:
Oliver Gordon as Lady Fitzwarren in
the dressing room

half an hour during which he told some jokes which were not in the spirit of our pantomimes!' Reggie also remembers having to placate a clergyman who had brought a large party of children to that performance from another city – after giving up on the theatre there because of blue jokes. Unusually, a stand-in also had to take over for part of the run when Tony Steedman was ill, with Tim Preece upgraded from one half of the elephant, and Reggie had to get Board approval to take on an extra person to help with the stage management as a result. [90]

By this time Roger Clissold had arrived at Salisbury. He also appeared in several of the pantos at this time, and developed his understanding of, and sympathy for, the Henry Marshall scripts, which would stand him in good stead when he later became Artistic Director of the theatre. In the early days, however, he was himself directed by Oliver Gordon, by now well established in the role of Dame, as Sonia Woolley found when she was asked to help him get ready.

> I used to do his make-up. He was very fussy about how he looked and he said 'I can't make up myself, you can do it for me.' I had to go down every lunch-time before the matinee, go into his dressing room, because I wasn't in the first couple of pantomimes, and put on this make-up in exactly the way he wanted it. I had to order it, make sure that we got all the right things, and it was a HUGE make-up. They don't wear nearly as much today. Although I suspect Dames

probably do. But I mean great big eyebrows, whiting out his proper eyebrows with soap, putting on the base and he had quite a strongly coloured base, a very pinky colour, I don't remember which Max Factor it was but it was a specific one he liked. And then the eyebrows and then huge amounts of violet blue eye-shadow… And then there were eyelines and then huge false eyelashes which had to be put on with glue and they were enormous and very difficult to fix. By then Oliver was well into his sixties if not more, and it was very difficult to fix those on a rather lovely, mobile but very wrinkled face. And men's faces are not so used to taking that sort of make-up, so that was a bit of a challenge. They had to be firmly stuck on, and then obviously he had his wig and things on top of that. [91]

Stephanie Cole played one of Salisbury's series of female Dames when she was Margery the Cook (and the Empress of Morocco) in the 1965 *Dick Whittington*, although she remembers the role as more of a mother than a Dame, with Oliver Gordon's Lady Fitzwarren playing the Queen dame opposite the more knockabout comedy she was given. This production, with a young Christopher Biggins in his first pantomime, included many dances choreographed by Felicity Gray: Ballet of the Shoes, Ballet of the Golden City, Adagio Dance (Lady Fitzwarren, Blackbeard and Mate, with eggs being carried inside a dress) and – perhaps rather perplexingly, a Can-Can as the finale.

This was the first of two pantomimes at Salisbury for Christopher Biggins, then a very young student ASM. He is now a leading pantomime Dame himself, but it is Oliver Gordon's Dame that, he now says, taught him so much about pantomime.

He was a big influence on me; a good, old-fashioned director. A lot more directors could learn from him. I learnt slapstick was very important he was wonderful at that. He was the kind of Dame that would throw himself through trapdoors. I think that came from the cricket, which was very important to him and Henry. It was very physical comedy which reminds me now of a Dame like Berwick Kaler at York . They both have the same physicality. It was a very happy period, Henry wrote very good pantomimes and then his

Dick Whittington and his Cat 1965: The Can-Can dancers in the finale.

brother took over to produce them. As with all repertory, the audience loved the familiarity of seeing the actors they knew playing Macbeth one week and pantomime the next. They were amazing times for repertory companies; nobody got big money but those pantomimes earned money to keep the company running. Reggie Salberg was very keen on the panto and I am thrilled to have started my career under Reggie; he was responsible for play after play of a high standard. And there's nothing quite like a repertory pantomime.[91a]

The cast also included a future choreographer, Olivia Breeze, as Alice Fitzwarren. She remembers her involvement in the pantomimes with great fondness. 'Henry's pantos were wonderful, and I loved it in Salisbury.' She did, however, have to work hard to persuade Henry to change one of the songs he gave her. Instead of Henry's 'Temple Bells', Olivia wanted to sing a Johnny Mathis number of the day called 'A certain smile.'

> 'I thought it was a wonderful song. I said, can I sing it Stage Right with a number 36 light on me. He puffed on his pipe and asked me to sing a few bars to him, before he said, yes, I suppose it is a little bit better. And he let me sing it. Henry was always terribly eccentric; I'd ring to speak to Steph and he would say she was in Holloway...'[92]

The script for *Dick Whittington* begins with one of the most detailed of Henry Marshall's set descriptions, which at times almost rival George Bernard Shaw in their prescriptive detail.

> Along the back of the set are the shops of various tradesmen, each with the arms of their guild displayed. These are on a shield which is hung on a pole projecting from the building over the door. The line of shops is broken UC by another street which stretches away into the distance. Just DS of this intersection UC is the Cross of Chepe. UL of this, the shop next but one to the street corner is Sir John Fitzwarren's shop with arms of the Mercer's Guild on the hanging shield. These are gules, demi-virgin with hair dishevelled and crowned, and issuing out and within an orle of clouds all proper. DR of the Cross is a Pillory. It is morning. The clock of St Thomas' Church nearby strikes six. The Constable enters, carrying an iron cresset in which is a lighted candle.

The cast is larger than later versions of the story and the plot that much more convoluted, with Jack Stevens a rather more dubious character than when he is played as Idle Jack. In this production he is in league with Blackbeard to steal the money from the Alderman's safe, so there is no need for the magical wiles of King Rat to be used to make him do so. King Rat, in fact, is non-speaking and appears only once in Act 2; and the main villains are Blackbeard and, in his Locker under the sea, Davy Jones. The cat, who alternates between being called Tiddles or Tomasina in the Marshall pantos, is here the focus for Jack's resolution as he sets out on the road having lost his job at the Fitzwarrens.

> Oh Thomasina I must try
> To be a man and not to cry.
> Sustained by you, my only friend,
> I know this stony road will end;
> Although ill luck has come my way,
> I'll be apprentice, come what may.
> Come friend, the day's but half begun
> I bear the name of Whittington

As is traditional with this panto, there is a lengthy and messy cooking scene, this time the version where the characters follow instructions from Womens Hour on the wireless. Jack and Lady Fitzwarren also do the mirror routine, and the front-cloth scene *The back door of the warehouse* gives an opportunity for an acrobatic piece which goes right back to the Victorian harlequinade, as the stage directions make clear. The details of what should happen in this scene are explained in great detail, with the use of a double for Lady Fitzwarren, and over more than a page of the script, but the details of the trick cloth used will explain the potential.

> From L to R. Flap doors opening in the middle. Window with flap. Swivel door in centre. Then another window with flap. Finally another

flap door opening in the middle. Between flap window and flap door
L there is a slate on the wall.

That was not the only connection with theatrical heritage
to be seen however; in a first for a Salisbury panto (apart from
Cinderella's horses), and with echoes of the Victorian productions of
Henry Beerbohm Tree, live animals were involved. Rabbits, owned
by Costume Designer Barbara Wilson, appeared through a trapdoor
on a grassy mound, and then lived in the costume store for long
afterwards. After Act 1 ends with the traditional evocation to Turn
Again Whittington, together with a chorus of the Cries of London,
the second act opens with a rousing seafaring chorus led by Michael
Poole's Blackbeard.

I sailed away on a ship one day
Away to a foreign shore.
When I got there, the land was fair,
The wine was strong and the girls were bare,
I'll never come home no more, no more
I'll never come home no more.
Heigh ho, heave ho
Shiver me timbers, how she blows,
Heigh ho, heave ho
Yo-ho for the shining main, my boys,
Yo-ho for the shining main.

After the rats have been caught, the songsheet (*Rinkety-Tink*
with a whistling refrain) sung and the Can-Can danced, the walk-
down is to a reprise of *'Come along Tomasina.'* Mike Starke explains
how Reggie acted as script editor, always alert to the limitations of his
audience.

Reggie took it upon himself to scan Henry's Dick Whittington script for any possibly risqué innuendo. A line sprang up from the page at him: 'No, no, Henwy, we weally can't have this.' (Reggie had trouble with the letter 'r')

'What?'

(Reggie; reading): 'Alice Fitzwawen is distwaught at Whittington leaving London and says: 'Oh Dick, oh Dick; I do miss my Dick."

(Henry, in baffled innocence): 'So?'

'Believe me, Henwy. You can't have it.'[93]

The *Salisbury Times* began its review[94] by mentioning Oliver Gordon's tango with Michael Poole's Blackbeard and Ralph Watson as Mate. Despite Reggie's misgivings, the reviewer was most impressed that 'it is all good clean fun with no suggestive lines anywhere.' Carolyn Moody's Dick Whittington has 'a most pleasing voice which blends well with that of the heroine, Alice Fitzwarren, played sweetly by Olivia Breeze.' Jane Quy as Thomasina was 'a lovable feline,' Chris Harris 'a bubble of fun as Idle Jack' and the fights were, as usual a strong feature. Particular mention

Dick Whittington and his Cat 1965: Lady Fitzwarren (Oliver Gordon) backstage

was reserved for 'those in which Dick out-fights Blackbeard and again when he outswords the ambitious Vizier played by Michael Stroud.'

When Chris Harris, now a well-known pantomime Dame and director, arrived at Salisbury in 1965 for that production, it was to take part in his first panto. Spotted by Reggie Salberg playing Huckleberry Finn at Lincoln, he arrived to find props for *Dick Whittington* already being made. As he remembers rather ruefully, 'You could ask for proper props for panto then, a massive foam hammer painted yellow or whatever you wanted.'[95] Rehearsals were held with each actor having pen, script and cigarette in hand. Salisbury resident Jenny Crews was in the cast and her mother, a local dancing teacher, taught Chris to tap dance – a skill he was to use later in one of his one-man shows. Above all though, he learnt from Oliver Gordon the importance of the storyline and the need to keep it moving. Oliver had a repository of ideas in his head. 'If you don't know how to finish a scene,' he remembers Oliver saying, 'get the gorilla suit on down left and chase it with a red hot poker to down stage right exit.' Only he might not have used exactly those words...

Chris found that he shared a sense of humour with Oliver Gordon, which led to him becoming Salisbury's first Principal Boy in the following year's *Jack and the Beanstalk*, an athletic performance which involved a climb almost to the flies (not that there were any) during a chase in the Giant's castle. Chris remembers the production in particular for the performance when John Swindells as the Giant fell on him, leaving him pinned to the stage and in danger of changing the ending of the story. To the sounds of muttered 'I've got to win' and 'I can't move' the curtain had to be brought in and the giant hauled to his feet. By now, Oliver Gordon was well-established as Dame, and very much in the Dan Leno music hall tradition. Many will remember him standing with his arms raised, and those massive hands. The stance is one that Chris Harris attributes to Oliver having played Diggory in *The School for Scandal*. It had apparently been traditional for Diggory to be played in this way to indicate that he was suffering from arthritis.

Choosing to have a male Principal Boy was a big step for a series of pantomimes as traditional as those at Salisbury, although the 1950s and 1960s saw developments in this direction with Norman Wisdom and Cliff Richard leading the way, despite the protests from

Oliver Gordon in Chapel Place, alongside the theatre, in 1965

the traditionalists that it 'never really works.'

The male impersonator is indigenous in the English theatre, essential to burletta, extravaganza and burlesque, and consequentially essential to the late Victorian pantomime. The rhymed couplets which any decently bred Principal Boy will still produce in moments of drama or sentiment are the relics of those rhymed entertainments in which her kind were nurtured. A great tradition remains embalmed in what we are pleased to call the pantomime.[96]

Those rhyming couplets are still found, of course, in the closing stages of many pantomimes today, although not all companies follow the superstition of not speaking those final lines till the opening night. Some researchers suggest that the tradition of these lines being in verse arose because this would ensure these important lines are not forgotten.

Michael Stroud was in *Jack and the Beanstalk* too, and remembers Chris hanging like a sloth among the black drops hiding the lights, with his feet round the rope, as the cast all sang *Farewell Jack*. They soon became friends and Michael says now that he is the first friend (that he made in the business) who is still a friend. The first play Michael had done with Chris Harris was *Murder at the Vicarage*, 'with Steph Cole giving her Miss Marple.' *Jack and the Beanstalk* was set in the village of Crumplehorn in Cornwall, and the pantomime opens with the scene of a fairy-tale village, castle in the distance and a stream and willow tree nearby. The Chorus all have specific characters as is clear in the following directions for the opening scene, and unusually Dame Durden – not in fact the Dame but a whimsical village lady played in a local accent by Stephanie Cole – is already to be seen as the curtains open, for in this panto it is Queen Iodine of Cornwall who is the traditional Dame character. She will arrive mid-scene with blunderbus, exclaiming that she is off shooting peasants, but first of all we need to meet the villagers.

> When the curtain rises, Jenny Wren, the May Queen, is standing C in front of the maypole, which is striped like a barber's pole and has a garland of flowers at the top. She is surrounded by Morris dancers (girls) with bells on their legs. DL on a stool sits Dame Durden, surrounded by the Chamberlain, an old man with a long beard and

Jack and the Beanstalk 1966: The opening scene with Dame Durden (Stephanie Cole), the Chamberlain (Michael Stroud) and PC Boggins (Christopher Biggins) among others

a stick, a man with a fiddle, a man with a hobby horse, and Jonathan, who is dressed as the clown of the Morris dancers and has a bladder on a stick.

Many classic Henry Marshall/Oliver Gordon routines are included, with much use of revolving doors and hidden traps, and the Queen and Inspector Migraine perform the tree of truth routine, with the fruit of falsehood falling on them when they tell lies. The traditional pathos of the farewell to the cow as she is taken to market is not forgotten, with a song including the unforgettable rhyming of cows with mouse.

> So farewell Tallulah, a jeweller could see
> No diamond on earth could be worth more than thee.
> As fish to a pussycat,
> As cheese to a mouse,
> You're quite indispensable,
> Cow of all cows.
> You're quite indispensable,
> Cow of all cows.

Jack makes much of his Cornish background throughout, as befits a tale strongly based on the original Jack the Giant-Killer legend from Cornwall. Before he climbs the beanstalk to end the first act, Jack sings of his heritage and determination.

> Give me a song to take along,
> Speed me on my way.
> This is the time for me to climb
> Up there, far away.
> Out in the blue there's a deed to do,
> I'll go through storm and stress.

I'll fight for the right with honour bright
To rescue my Princess.
Hand me a lantern,
And give me a rope,
And I'll do the best I can,
I will try till I die or my feet touch that sky,
For I was born a Cornishman,
I was born a Cornishman.

The second act opens with a Cloud Ballet at the top of the beanstalk, followed by many adventures in the Giant's Lair and involving chases, much breaking of crockery and the catching (or not) of eggs on plates. The Queen, the Chamberlain (Michael Stroud), Dame Durden and Inspector Migraine (Raymond Bowers) sing the popular panto song 'We must be ever so, ever so quiet – Shh, shh, shh' when creeping up on the Giant, with the traditional loud noise at the end of the chorus. With his usual attention to detail, Henry Marshall states that this should be the Bach D Minor. In place of a songsheet, the main comic characters form a band and play a version of the Poet and Peasant overture, and the walk-down is to a reprise of *I'm Dancing*.

It was during this production that Brian Protheroe, playing in the pit, taught Chris guitar skills. This was also the first year in which Marie Phillips, by now with a four piece band, was amplified, so the actors had to learn to sing louder. Brian had joined the company early in the year, straight from the local amateur dramatic society Studio Theatre. Noreen Craven, Reggie's wife, directed and appeared in *Lysistrata* for Studio Theatre and spotted him in the cast. His first part was as Paris in *Romeo and Juliet* and he stayed for most of the next year. Michael Stroud remembers that Reggie – 'who was a wise old bird' – told Brian it was time to move on before he got too comfy, 'and it's not a comfy profession.' For the pantomime, however, Brian was in the pit on guitar, under the direction of Marie Phillips, who was, he says 'a sweet old thing; quite refined and proper.' Watching the show every night from the pit, he has some clear memories of routines.

> Oliver Gordon and Raymond Bowers (playing Queen Iodine of Cornwall and Inspector Migraine) did this frontcloth routine about guessing the town. Raymond took off his hat and punched the middle. What's that? Prestatyn. Took a bite of an apple. What's that? Eton. Took out another apple. What's that? Nuneaton. Ollie loved doing the Dame and relished the double act opportunities. [98]

Two of Brian Protheroe's other memories of that production are not quite so happy however. At the Technical Rehearsal he watched in horror as Ollie fell into the pit when crossing the temporary bridge to the stalls – something he had to do regularly as he was producing as well as appearing in the cast. He seemed none the worse however, and could also be terrifying, as Brian – a local boy – found when he was late back for a rehearsal at Bemerton Church Hall after running all the way home to Bemerton Heath for lunch. He was never late again and, although he did not appear in a Salisbury panto, Brian did go on to write five or six pantomimes of his own with David Cregan, for which the brief was to go back to the original story: a task for which Salisbury must have been a good preparation. Oliver Gordon obviously had the knack of ensuring latecomers never repeated the experience, as Michael Stroud remembers: 'I was late for rehearsals one morning, came rushing in, I think it was an alarm clock thing. Ollie said it doesn't matter what it is, you're late. Coffee break now and when they all come back they'll be called on stage and you have to apologise. I was never late again…' [99]

By the 1966 *Jack and the Beanstalk*, Christopher Biggins had progressed from chorus member to a small part, as PC Boggins: the part, created for him, would recur in later productions of the same pantomime long after he had left the company. It was in this production that Vivien Heilbron played Fairy, leading Reggie to remember her later as one of those most memorable in the role. That is not, however, how she remembers it.

Having just played (almost back to back) the eponymous heroines in *Romeo and Juliet* and *Portrait of a Queen* (Victoria), I was exhausted. I fear I could not put my heart and soul into the pantomime, which I, being a total admirer of Oliver Gordon's style as Dame, would have happily watched night after night. Being in the pantomime night after night was rather a different matter. I hope I performed as Fairy with something approaching the required charm but I cannot honestly say the enterprise had my undivided attention. I had several entrances which were rather like one another, and the doggerel-like Fairy verse carried unvarying messages of hope and encouragement to Jack and other assorted goodies in the cast. I think I got them mixed up on at least two occasions. Unfortunately, one of the those lyric verses was the cue for the pianist and the little dancers, and thus they performed the Bean Ballet while dressed as Mice (or vice versa, I simply don't remember). I do recall (choreographer) Felicity Gray's reproachful face and I wish I could have reassured her with more sincerity and fervour that this accident would not happen again. I was brought up in Scotland and saw all the great Scottish comics play Dame (Rikki Fulton, Jimmy Logan) and Oliver was as funny as they were, with a genteel demeanour and an air of benign condescension which was most disarming. During the pantomime, he took the company out before the Saturday matinee and brought us all a schooner of sherry – you wouldn't do that now. I can't smell dry sherry without thinking of Oliver Gordon. He was a great director of comedy and his advice stayed with me and stood me in good stead in other companies. [100]

Productions got bigger and more ambitious, although the 1967 *Robinson Crusoe* – with an astonishing cast of 28 – is remembered by Sonia Woolley for the embarrassment of having to black up at a time when this was already beginning to seem unacceptable.

> We had to be cannibals... it was awful because Oliver decided we should all black up. In those days that was considered OK, but a lot of us were uncomfortable about it: it didn't feel right. We did it at the Dress Rehearsal and it was so awful, we couldn't get the make-up off in time. It was absolute chaos. In the end we wore brown tights and sort of body stocking things and then had to do make-up to match them and then prance about waving drumsticks. I didn't enjoy it...[101]

Paul Haley suffered from some of the same doubling problems as Kim Grant did in 1955, making the whole experience an unforgettable one. 'It was some of the hardest work I've ever done, particularly when you think of it twice daily. I remember it as being very busy and truly bizarre in my case. As I (roughly) remember it ......In the opening we all sang a typical Henry song about the Port of Hull as the ship sailed. We were all either townspeople or sailors. Once at sea I sang *'Shenandoah'* with backing from the assorted (very) sailors. That was when Knight (Chris Mantell as he was in those days) walked around with the ship's wheel after it detached in his hands. I had my back to him to and couldn't understand why a fairly forgettable song and performance was getting so many laughs.' The ship's wheel incident has achieved legendary status, and we will hear more about it from other cast members in a moment; but first Paul completes his summary of the plot and what it involved for the cast.

> Once at the island a quick change from sailor into the King Kong gorilla skin for a fight with Crusoe (Norman Comer). He used to whack me over the head mask with his sword and tells me he has a

photo somewhere showing him doing exactly that. After that back into sailor costume for more larks then it was the interval. Act II opened with the attack by the cannibals on the stockade. Being a big bloke, I was logical casting for the Cannibal Chief. This entailed us cannibals spending the whole interval browning up all over except for our grass skirt area. No relaxing interval cup of tea for us. After the stockade fight scene was over it was into Captain Woodes Rogers' costume for me, in time for another fight rescuing Robinson. On the voyage back to England, as the Captain, I visited the galley to see what the commotion was, just in time to cop all the slosh remaining in the buckets as the climax of the slosh act. Captain's finery ruined, I retired to the dressing room to put on another set of Barbara Wilson's best for the walk down. My skin was red raw for weeks. We seemed to do nothing but wash off make up, body paint and slosh and then start all over again.

By this time, the script (licensed for performance by the Lord Chamberlain on 19th October) was using some imported songs alongside the original ones, including *Pretty Little Polly Perkins of Paddington Green*. Although much of the music was written by Henry Marshall, there were always familiar songs included too, although not often current ones. As has been noted by others, 'the borrowing of music is a peculiarity the pantomime has never lost.'[102] The stage directions are less detailed although the plot is still quite complex and involves many named pirates. Routines include Pancake Day, the mop drill, and the delivery of the fragile parcel. After the shipwreck, a UV scene with fluorescent fish leads us to King Neptune's Kingdom, where the following interchange occurs between Michael Stroud and Oliver Gordon.

Neptune
Enough of impudence! Why are you here,

Where only fish and seaweed should appear?

Mrs Crusoe
Look here, you chlorophyll King Lear
I was sitting in my cabin, drinking beer.
I read the Times and had a little chortle
When all at once the sea came through my porthole;
I ran on deck, and feeling rather dotty,
Jumped overboard and landed on my botty.

Neptune
Unhand me, woman, and begone,
Before I use my powers to do you wrong.

Mrs Crusoe (producing fish from costume*)*
Oh look, a skate. And here's a little scallop;
I've had my chips. I'll swim to Nether Wallop.

The mention of local village Nether Wallop (or sometimes Middle Wallop) was always considered worthy of a laugh in a Henry Marshall script. Act 1 ends with an animal ballet and Act 2 begins with the cannibal dance number remembered with some embarrassment by some of those involved. Demands were high, however, for we note in the script the requirement that the (female) Witch Doctor 'dances a dance of primitive exultation.' The songsheet was, of course, Nellie the Elephant, and the whole production was a great success according to the review in the *Salisbury Times*[103].

Robinson Crusoe was a success before it started because of the heavy bookings, but now that the curtains have gone up and down on the first performances one may wonder if its five weeks run will be long enough. Lucky are those young folk for whom this will be their first visit to a theatre because this production is the most traditional of traditional pantos. It has far more to it than the usual magical ingredients; more even than a good story kept running without undue interruption: there is plenty of music, a blazing kaleidoscope of colour; lots of fun and (of course) that special magic, audience participation. Yes, no matter who, Billy Crusoe (Lionel Guyett) will get them to sing, to clap, to answer back, so that old and young, critic or child, man or woman, finds great joy in roaring out the story of Nellie the Elephant.... Three ballet scenes of charm and merit add interest and colour for the older patron and the whole makes one of the best balanced pantomimes in the lengthening list now standing to the credit of the Playhouse.

This was also the production in which Roger Clissold played Miles the Crocodile, sliding around the stage on a padded ironing board – effective for the audience but tricky to cope with backstage. For Frank Ellis, this was the first of five Henry Marshall pantomimes at Salisbury. He looks back on them, and all his time at Salisbury, with great fondness.

It was a wonderful place to work, thanks in great part to Reggie Salberg, who was like a father to us all. Being in the company was truly like being a member of a family, and we all really enjoyed taking part. One of the great joys was that many of the people in the building, not just the actors, took part. I remember, for instance, that Paul Taylor, John Scutt's assistant in the workshop, was in a couple of them, as was Philippa 'Legs' Eden, the Assistant Designer. Looking back, doing two shows a day didn't seem like the hard work it does now. But then, of course, we were all much younger and fitter. I was also extremely lucky to have worked with the wonderful Oliver Gordon, who directed and played Dame in the first three I did at Salisbury. He was a lovely, lovely man and a joy to work with. [104]

Robinson Crusoe 1967: The pirates and most of the cast sing about Pancake Day

Frank also remembers – as do most of the other people on stage – the moment when the ship's wheel, apparently being steered by Knight Mantell as Elisha Morgan, came off in his hands. This caused great and not always suppressed hilarity among the pirate crew, and Knight remembers it too.

> We were singing Shenandoah with Paul Haley leading. Because, I couldn't sing, I was placed at the back of the stage but one night the ship's wheel came off in my hands – I think I might have engineered that – and I walked off with it sideways. That was another event that got me into Reggie's office.[105]

Lionel Guyett remembers the incident too.

> Paul Haley began to go and this infected the entire cast – we were all giggling – eventually we turned round and Knight had wrenched the wheel off its stand. We had to leave the stage and Oliver Gordon dressed us down and told us it must never happen again as we insulted the audience and the material.[106]

It was during this production that Roger Forbes got offered a job at the National Theatre, where Lionel Guyett soon followed him, and Knight Mantell had to take over as one half of Nellie the Elephant with David Gooderson. According to Michael Stroud, also in the cast as King Neptune, this was not a popular role to play.

A terrible thick heavy disgusting rubber elephant arrived. David said 'I am not going in the front.' This came in usually out of step and all you could hear was 'What the ****…' One time Knight went into the prop room and disappeared for quite a while and everyone thought what's he doing. He had made a papier mache elephant turd with a little curl on the top. He somehow got it into the elephant's costume, so when Nellie got up to make her exit, this terrible thing like a Dundee cake was left there.[107]

Lionel remembers that the cast made the best of the limited backstage facilities: 'We bought sandwiches and played poker. The dressing rooms were awful. There were cold taps and one hot water heater with a small tap – no showers.' Paul Haley has backstage memories that include the playing of poker too.

I must say a strong memory of that show was the poker school started by Roger Forbes. There was a room off the dressing room corridor right at the back, almost outside, that had at some time been a kitchen. It was used for props and as a general junk room and prop workshop. There was an old gas oven in there and we used to heat the room during the card school by having the oven door open. There was a permanent smell of the theatrical size that had for years been boiled on the cooker; a smell today's actors would never have known. The card school started at the half before the matinee and ran more or less right through both performances and between shows. Not a lot of money was at stake but it was huge fun as I remember. People dropped in and out for a few hands depending on the gaps between cues. There we would sit in dressing gowns, cannibal outfits, half an animal skin whatever, hoping for a good hand before the next cue.

1968 saw a return of *Babes in the Wood*, but with a few changes now that Oliver Gordon was playing Dame, and with the robbers renamed Jim and Pete (James Tomlinson and Peter Robert Scott). The prologue was still there to set the scene, but it had become shorter; Robin, however, was still ready to sing of the joys of life in Sherwood Forest.

Babes in the Wood 1968: The Company at Nottingham Fair

Listen to the murmur of the forest
Don't you sense the peace it brings?
Can't you feel the breeze
That gently stirs the trees?
Can't you see the sun,
His journey just begun?
Listen to the ripple of the trout stream
That's the song that Sherwood sings.

By this stage, there was also some use of popular songs of the day, with Ben Aris as Robin singing *Born Free* at one point, though his Merry Men were still happy to join in their traditional Marshall lyric.

Merry men so brave and trusty
Don't find life so dull or dusty
For our swords will not grow rusty
While we wear the green. Oh . . .

One of those Merry Men was David Beames, appointed as Student ASM by Reggie Salberg earlier that year, on a salary of £2 a week, though he later pleaded poverty and managed to get it raised to £5. He remembers that his first job was to push Oliver Gordon's Daisy Dimple over the little bridge in the opening scene. 'There was no call system and I did the knocking on doors and I was quite often on the book.'[108] David grew up in nearby Winchester and later went to the Bristol Old Vic Theatre School, as did so many of the Salisbury company through the years.

Frank Ellis was teamed up with Knight Mantell again in *Babes in the Wood*, and this time it was Frank who had to change into his schoolboy outfit for the big classroom scene but forgot on one occasion that he first had a frontcloth piece with Knight as Sheriff of Nottingham. On that occasion, the Sheriff had to complete the

Babes in the Wood 1968: Willie Whiskers (Frank Ellis) with the Sheriff of Nottingham (Knight Mantell)

scene without Willie Whiskers, in this version his elderly and very stupid henchman. Frank still remembers hearing the Sheriff over the tannoy, shouting 'Willie, Willie, where is that idiot...' By this stage, the schoolroom scene had developed as a routine and included plenty of number-based gags on the blackboard as well as the traditional by-play with nap-stick and tipping bench, but other traditional routines were included as well.

One of the most amusing scenes is that representing the Gallows Oak in the Forest of Sherwood when the two robbers physically take possession of two trees with startling results... Two of the prettiest and daintiest babes imaginable are Anne Preus and Jane Quy. They captivate all hearts and take part in the night nursery scene wherein they are saved from the robbers by the Fairy (Sonia Woolley) who then produces a veritable fairy toyland with toy soldiers, dancing dolls, a prancing golliwog and a clawing cat with a background of enormous playing cards. Spectacular is the transformation scene when the birds arrive to cover the sleeping babes with leaves, and exciting is the siege of Nottingham Castle.[109]

The nursery still transformed, but to a Magic Toy Cupboard for the ballet, which was perhaps less challenging that the previous golden castle. The second act opening at the fair, however, had gained a Ghost Train as well as the Goose Fair and Crazy House. Also added to this production was the balloon dance routine, performed by the Dame with two male members of the chorus. There was also a Dancing Bear, so it seems likely that the chorus members were kept very busy with costume changes. After the meeting with the Pilgrim, the fight between the Robbers and the Archery contest, Robin (a male Principal Boy, Ben Aris) was ready to sing again.

Babes in the Wood 1968: The Babes (Jane Quy & Anne Preus) and the Fairy (Sonia Woolley, upstage) are transported to Toyland

I came to Sherwood Forest
With a feather in my cap
A fighter never looking for a fight
My bow is always ready, and I keep my arrows sharp
I use them for fighting for what is right.

After the audience song (one half singing, the other half providing an accompaniment of 'plip, plop') the walk-down began with 'a stately pavane' and then finished with a reprise of a number from the first act.

Money, money, money,
Money to spend.
Isn't it funny, funny, funny,
What you can lend.
If only you have got the cash
To carve a niche or cut a dash,
When you get rich you'll make a splash
On that you can depend.
On that you can depend,
And this is now the end!

End of production parties were always memorable, and sometimes for the most surprising reasons, as Mike Starke explains.

I think it was at the end-of-production party on stage that Reggie joined the cast to celebrate the triumph these packed-house productions invariably were. Oliver Gordon and Reggie somehow got into an animated debate on the relative strengths of each other's stomach muscles. Reggie, who sported a comfortable midriff rotundity, in contrast to wiry Oliver's racing snake physique, vehemently denied his tormentor's cajoling that this spoke of flabbiness. He lay down on the stage and insisted Oliver stand on his tummy to prove his point. The surreal scene collapsed in laughter all round, and the mists of time and wine cloud recollection of the case being proved or disproved. [110]

Mike Starke had many tasks to fulfil, but he played a particular role for Oliver Gordon, however, which was not related to theatre or cricket.

Oliver was tall and slender, with a slight stoop. His voice boomed like pebbles rattling in a drum and always at top volume, perhaps because he was partially deaf. It was this affliction that led to me being cast as his stooge in his role as spectator at live performances in the City Hall close to the Playhouse. Oliver had a passion for watching the professional wrestling bouts staged there on Saturday nights. An integral part of the enjoyment for Oliver was the dramatic dialogue between the protagonists, often drowned by the roars of approval or opprobrium from the crowd. It was my job to act as Oliver's ears. If he missed a particularly juicy bit of badinage, he would jab me in the ribs with a bony elbow, honed by years indulging in his other love, cricket, and shout: 'What did they say, cock?' Oliver called everyone 'cock'. It was formal address for him; by no means a disparaging term. Oliver didn't do disparaging. He was a gent. A quirky gent, but a gent.[111]

Peter Robert Scott met his wife, Christine Edmonds, when they were both in the company at Salisbury in the 1960s, and they were directed by Oliver Gordon many times. He was, they say 'a dear man, and a gentleman of the old school' but on occasions he reduced the entire company to fits of laughter without realising what he had done. 'In the schoolroom scene in Babes in the Wood, he broke his slap stick and not knowing what it was called, said 'oh bother, I've broken my wanker' and proceeded to call it that throughout the scene not realising what he was saying.'[112] This was also the production in which the Babes Jane Quy and Anne Preus, teased throughout by Robin Hood (Ben Aris) got their own back on the last night by covering the mouthpiece of the horn with sellotape; leaving it completely useless, much to his fury.

Babes in the Wood 1968: The Sheriff (Knight Mantell), Tina (Anne Preus), Judy (Jane Quy), Maid Marian (Christine Edmonds) and Willie Whiskers (Frank Ellis) arrive on their hobbyhorses

For young actors, Ollie was a link with a previous age. Knight Mantell remembers the way he held his hand with finger and thumb extended. After taking over the role, Oliver played Dame every year until he died in 1970, but Knight also remembers his work as a Director.

With him directing you always knew you were in the right place to play the part; now, you are invariably in the wrong place. There are people who are important in a scene, and people who are not, and he understood that perfectly. He was a weekly rep Director, and when he went to Salisbury it was fortnightly rep: he didn't know what to do with the extra time and would send the cast off to the cinema. He was a lovely, lovely guy but more interested in cricket really. He used to say 'You piss off right cock' or 'You piss off left cock' and that was about it. Everybody remembers Oliver with affection, he was really nice. [113]

Oliver Gordon's last pantomime – as producer and Dame – was Aladdin in 1969. His previous part of Abanazer's slave was changed to a female character, Fatima, and Wishee-Washee joined the cast, and sang *There's a hole in my bucket* with Widow Twankey, as is only to be expected. The cave scene was enlivened this time by a shrieking cockatoo, and the Royal Baths was the venue for a scene in which giant props were used to bathe Esmeralda the camel. The usual laundry jokes also appear, and pencilled corrections in the surviving scripts indicate the passing of time: holding up a pair of bloomers and asking who they belonged to had originally received the answer 'Bessie Braddock' but this was now replaced with 'Twiggy.'

Chris Dunham was back, playing Vizier and responsible for the choreography. He remembers Oliver Gordon being determined to complete the run although he was so ill, and he wouldn't cut anything. 'He insisted on going through the mangle in the laundry scene; he was

Aladdin 1969: The citizens of Peking with, among others, Wishee Washee (Peter Robert Scott), Widow Twankey (Oliver Gordon), and the Chinese policemen, Hi-Tee (Robert Whelan) and Lo-Pong (Frank Ellis)

bent over in the wings and then straightened up when he had to go on. I assisted Oliver on this and then stayed on and started directing plays.' [114]

Oliver Gordon is fondly remembered still and his great contribution to pantomime – and theatre – is perhaps best summed up by Reggie Salberg's programme announcement of his death.

It is with great sadness that we report the death in Guy's Hospital of Oliver Gordon. Until recently he had seemed ageless but those of us close to him knew that he had suffered considerably during the past two years. His last appearance here was in *Aladdin* and he often played in an agony which seldom showed in his performance. He was a wonderful man and hadn't an enemy in the world. We will all miss him, but can console ourselves with the thought that few people can have enjoyed their lives so much. The theatre filled his life in the winter and before he turned to producing I think he played as an actor in every London theatre. In the summer he turned to his even greater love, cricket, at which he excelled and he still struck terror in the hearts of opposing batsmen even when in his sixties. A great character and a truly kind man.

Aladdin 1969: Oliver Gordon as Widow Twankey, his last appearance as Dame

The first pantomime after Oliver Gordon died, *Cinderella*, was directed by Christopher Dunham. All but two of the 58 performances were sold out before the show opened on 19th December. Reggie remembered the production as being very successful but also recalls the escape of the pantomime ponies, an episode which has passed into theatrical mythology and exists in several different versions:

> My abiding memory… is of a wintery night in 1971, when down the lane by the old Theatre I glimpsed Cinderella's ponies, who had escaped from their makeshift stabling, disappearing towards the snowy car park. By the time the stage Manager… and I caught them they were heading up Castle Street where bewildered motorists… had stopped their cars to view the spectacle. We got them back just in time for their entrance but never before or since has Cinderella's coach been drawn by such mud-besmattered ponies.

Michael Stroud, playing Ugly Sister opposite Roger Hume, remembers the incident too, and the effect it had on Christine Edmonds as Fairy Godmother who was patiently waiting for them on stage.

> It was snowing and they were snowy white Shetlands – bad-tempered but pretty. Ponies got taken back in haste, and they put them in the traces the wrong way round – there was a frontcloth going on with Christine as Fairy Godmother and all you could see was the frontcloth wobbling. Then there was a lot of whinnying going on and she was standing there saying 'I am your Fairy Godmother' and a gallon of steaming yellow horse piss came out under the frontcloth. [115]

At least the incident wasn't as serious as it was when Michael Stroud played the same role in Dundee and one of the horses collapsed and died in the wings, catapulting Cinderella out of her coach. He had been planning to play Ugly Sister at Salisbury opposite Oliver Gordon, who kept ringing him up with new routines, but Ollie's early death meant that those plans were never realised. When Oliver Gordon died, the many contributions from patrons and friends enabled the setting up of a fund to pay for under-privileged children to visit the pantomimes for many years. The local press were relieved to find that the tradition of pantomimes was safe in the hands of his successors, and with his brother Henry still providing the script.

> ...the production is outstanding for another reason – its lavishness. No effort has been spared to dress principals and supporting cast most lavishly... And there are many other things that are beautifully done... the flight over the rooftops, the haunted bedroom and the pantry, wherein the two ugly sisters, Fifi and Mimi (Michael Stroud and Roger Hume), go in for a wholesale smash up of the family china... Cinderella, daintily played by Heather Bell... Peter Robert Scott is extremely good as Buttons. Both Tim Meats and Elwyn Johnson as Prince Charming and Dandini act their parts well. Christine Edmonds looks convincing both as an old woman and as the Fairy Godmother... The singing, generally, is good, and there are some very graceful dance numbers, all accompanied by Marie Phillips at the organ, Jonathan King, piano and Stephen Banning on the drums.[116]

Dandini was a prelude to two later male Principal Boy parts for Elwyn Johnson. He remembers Henry Marshall as being present during rehearsals and performances, and always ready with a twinkle in his eye and a joke to pass on. He was, says Elwyn, 'an encyclopaedia of traditional, tried and tested jokes and routines, which made his work a safe, secure and deeply enjoyable experience. He looked like Shakespeare, and for the thousands of children who came to his pantomimes, he performed the same introduction to the joy of story-telling and the magic of theatre as the Bard, but his jokes were a bit less obscure... I would hope, as the kids got older, they returned to

Cinderella 1970: Fifi (Michael Stroud), Buttons (Peter Robert Scott) & Mimi (Roger Hume)

the Playhouse to experience the irreplaceable wonder of live theatre for the rest of their lives.' [117]

There were fourteen scenes; as Chris Dunham says now, 'what we used to do on that tiny stage...' [118] After Oliver Gordon's death, Reggie remembers the concerns that the spirit of the Salisbury pantomimes might be lost, but with first Christopher Dunham and then for many years Roger Clissold as Director, the productions were in very safe hands: 'both had been in pantomime with Oliver and have carried on his traditions in a way which would have made him happy.' Of course, changes were made over the years, but the productions always stayed firmly within the style of production that Salisbury audiences had come to love. One change was the disappearance of the group of dancers who were usually enlisted by the choreographer from local dancing schools. 'They sang a bit,' remembers Sonia Woolley, 'but mainly danced and stood around looking pretty.' [119] In their place, Roger started doubling parts for the cast and the enlisted group of dancers was no more. This reduced the opportunities for female members of the company, since there are far fewer female than male parts in most pantomimes.

Jane Quy was another local girl, and had been a regular in Salisbury pantomimes since 1962 and was still appearing at the end of the Henry Marshall years. Sonia Woolley and Jane Quy both found they were pregnant during the 1968 *Babes in the Wood*, leading to much discussion about a pantomime having a pregnant Fairy and a pregnant Babe. Jane got her first job at Salisbury at the age of 17 and was paid £1 a week. Having grown up in Guildford, she was supposed to be going to Bristol University, but she just wanted to go on the stage.

> My first job there was on the book for *A Christmas Carol*. I stayed with Marilyn Taylersen, who was also in the company. Her mother took me in; they lived in the bicycle shop next door. I gave them the £1 and they looked after me. Because it was next door we used to get changed there and rush across the road. I played the cat in *Dick Whittington* but nearly suffocated inside the costume. [120]

Jane appeared in ten of the Henry Marshall pantomimes at Salisbury; more than anyone else except Oliver Gordon. She particularly enjoyed playing Babe in *Babes in the Wood*, which she did three times. On the last occasion a young friend came backstage and said to her, 'Oh, you've grown up again...'

In the early days, there were always imported dancers from local dancing schools or from drama schools like Arts Educational. Some were local, like Jenny Crews. One of those dancers was Jessica

Benton, who met her future husband, Charlie Waite, at the theatre where he was a Student ASM. They still live near Salisbury, and Charlie is now a well-known landscape photographer, but they met in the cast of *Jack and the Beanstalk* in 1966, as Jessica remembers.

> We ignored each other for the first few rehearsals because I thought he was gay and he thought I was stuck up. We were both 16, and at the ripe old age of 61 we are still together; a neat reversal of the numbers. The choreographer, Felicity Gray, reprimanded me once for being late to a rehearsal. Charlie had asked me to go to the cinema with him and as it was the first time a boy had asked me out... I went! On another occasion, I washed Charlie's costume between the matinee and the evening performance (I was showing off I suppose). Of course, not only was it still wet come the evening, but it had shrunk considerably and all the colours had run. Barbara Wilson was furious.[121]

Jessica also paints a vivid picture of the backstage conditions, as they are remembered by so many of those who appeared at Salisbury, with the unforgettable figure of Ollie Gordon at the centre of the pandemonium.

> At the old Playhouse, to exit SL and reappear SR moments later as if by magic, the actors had to charge around the back in the dark, through a sort of very narrow tunnel with damp walls, and for some reason there was always a puddle of water in the middle. Dancers in ballet shoes usually re-emerged with wet feet. It became quite a skill negotiating that puddle; running through it one night I collided with a stage hand coming the other way and the cup of hot coffee he was holding went all over both of us. The wonderful Oliver Gordon wearing his various enormous Dame costumes along with giant false bust would charge through the tunnel sideways shouting 'Watch out, cock!' which was his pet name for everyone. Musicians, actors and

front of house were all called 'cock.' He was much loved by one and all; never to be forgotten.

Peter Robert Scott and Christine Edmonds also remember the state of the building and that this was much easier to put up with because Reggie had the knack of having actors in the company who got on together, and he offered them the chance to appear in plays that gave them new challenges and kept them involved, leading to many long-term friendship as so many other actors from that time have said. Backstage, however, was at its most challenging during the pantomime.

The conditions under which we were working in the old theatre were cramped and grubby to say the least especially at panto time when the cast was augmented with local people, wives of actors, backstage staff etc as well as the actors themselves, all cramped into tiny dressing rooms, with one washbasin per dressing room and two loos for the entire cast, no wing space, no time between shows to change and go and eat. To facilitate the change over in the auditorium, Reggie himself and whoever else was free would clear it of the detritus left by the matinee audience. Alan Corkill, the House Manager, used to provide sandwiches and soft drinks for everyone in the bar. Later on a wonderful woman called Tricia Martin came as Stage Manager and organised everything and provided hot food backstage for everyone as well as all her other duties.[122]

Pantomime Musical Directors at Salisbury have mostly stayed for several years, and each brought their own style of performance to the productions. The first regular Musical Director was Sydney Carmen, perhaps best introduced by his ad in *The Stage* from 1942:

Released from National Service
Sydney Carmen

Pianist-Conductor (50)
Radio Composer-Arranger
Open to First Class Offers
No Touring   17 Nelson Road
Tel 5277 Bournemouth, W[123]

Obviously, the trip to Salisbury didn't count as touring. Ian Mullins remembers Sydney as the regular musical director and accompanist in the 1950s whenever the company put on a pantomime, musical or revue. 'He was,' says Ian, 'very good to work with and very understanding with non-singers.' [124]

Another musical director, Reg Baker, is remembered in particular by Chris Dunham for the flamboyant entrance he liked to make, down the central aisle of the Stalls rather than sidling into the pit without the audience noticing. Then came Marie Phillips, a local piano teacher who played for eight pantomimes and many other musicals and reviews as she got on well with Oliver Gordon. She was quite elderly and, Sonia Woolley says, very small and bird-like and very precise with people about singing properly and opening their mouths wide enough. Knight Mantell liked Marie a lot, but recognised she was part of the old regime: 'Henry and Ollie and Babs and Marie and Stan on the board – they were all Reggie's old friends and they didn't cost a lot.'[125] Pantomime rehearsals always began with the songs, round the piano with Marie.

Following Marie Phillips was Christopher Littlewood, who worked on eleven shows and was a new style of Musical Director, very much a professional theatrical musician. Richard Frost remembers him as a very good musical director and very strict, though Richard was never sure how much he liked some of Henry's music. Graham Richards remembers the methodical way in which the cast were taught the music by Christopher.

We were assembled on the first day on the stage with the chairs in a semi-circle and Chris was in the pit. And he said The number starts like this 'In - the – vill - age - of – Crum – ple - horn' and then we all had to sing it. And that's how we started. Very few people had little tape recorders or anything. We put little arrows to remember where to go up, and then of course we got to the harmonies. And that was the first day of rehearsal. After a while, performing twice daily he would get a little bit bored. There'd were certain parts of the pantomime where he played incidental music as somebody came on, so he'd play perhaps a bit of La Traviata or Gilbert & Sullivan. It never took away from the effect.[126]

Christopher Littlewood's first panto at Salisbury was the 1971 *Dick Whittington* when he played piano in the pit with Marie Phillips; over the following years he became Musical Director and later composer of music and lyrics for many of the pantomimes. He remembers interpolating tunes as Graham described: 'I used to organise a competition called Spot the Tune, and treat anyone in the company who could find the hidden melody. If they couldn't get it – and they had to put it into the script or a lyric somehow to show you had spotted what it was – it started to become more prominent by Act Two. Maybe a couple of times in the ten years I was there an audience might have spotted what was going on, but generally I think not. This kept everybody on their toes. It wasn't subversive it actually was helpful.'[127]

Christopher originally came to Salisbury because of his love of archaeology, and was looking for a job that would enable him to stay in the area. He knocked on Reggie's door and somewhat to his surprise was given the job of pianist for the panto. Although Marie Phillips was still Musical Director, there was a general impression that it was time to move on to the next phase of music for the productions. 'The problem was that she would insist on bringing her organ into the orchestra pit, which was tiny of course. So this thundering organ came in with pedals and things, and Marie was quite happy at it; she would give body to the show by having the organ. She was a lovely lady but it was sometimes difficult staying in time…'[128] Christopher soon met all the team, and remembers Henry Marshall being very welcome but a stickler for detail. He remembers him as 'a stocky man with an intellectual beard. He was very, very precise and he would stand like a fencer. He hadn't lost his hair then, he was a bit Shakespearean. I had to say to him, I've got a problem, and he said Marie! No, I said, I can't read your music. He said, I do it that way so you can change it. I got on very well with Henry, and when the blow came later when he was told I was going to write the music, I cannot tell you how gracious he was.' It was Roger Clissold's efforts as Director, however, that ensured that Christopher decided this was the place for him, 'Roger was terribly new and eager to please. I think he probably got the right spirit for this one; it made me want to be in Salisbury. It was a huge success.'

Richard Frost joined the company in 1971 too, and soon found himself playing Roger Clissold's old part in Dick Whittington: King Richard I.

Oliver had died in 1969, but they were still talking about his funeral, and immediately you were steeped in Oliver Gordon. I remember when I had my interview with Reggie in his flat in Chepstow Villas. I had worked with Noreen when she directed a play when I was at Canterbury, and she said Oh I think you'd like Salisbury and they'd like you. I wrote to Reggie and I've still got his card, he wrote tiny, tiny writing. He said my wife's talked about you, perhaps you'd like to come. It wasn't an audition, I just went to his flat in London. Before I knew it I was there playing Tim in *Salad Days*. My hair was just going grey and he just asked if it would show from the front. By that time there was a company of non-cricketers but at one time both at the Alex Rep and at Salisbury it was very important that you could play cricket as well as act.

As Roger Clissold had been in them, he wasn't going to change things. He used to have a huge chart with all the scenes you were in and what costume you were wearing. It was all tabulated, that fascinated me. He would confer with the Musical Director and say 'Didn't we used to do this?' I felt very much that the tradition was there. As I recall, Henry was there at rehearsals quite early, maybe because it was Roger's first. Reggie and Noreen always put on a New Years party and I had black hair so I had to go out and bring in the coal. And we got a Christmas bonus. Both Reggie and his brother Derek were the most wonderful managements to work for. They don't exist any more, that sort. [129]

There were some differences however, and Michael Stroud says that when Roger Clissold took over, 'he was a bit more 'what's your motivation' where Oliver wouldn't have known the word. He was a young blade, a younger school.' Once again, Henry Marshall's direction of the fights came in for special mention in the review in the *Salisbury Times*.[130]

Dick (Elwyn Johnson) becomes embroiled in some rare fights, one with knives when he is challenged by the burly braggart, Blackbeard, played very well by Tim Meats, and one when with shield and scimitar he engages the fiery Vizier (John Golder)... Derek Pollitt is very funny indeed as the Dame – Lady Fitzwarren – married to the

Roger Clissold in 1973

ageing and shortsighted Sir John characterised by Michael Stroud, who all too often mistakes others – not always human beings – for his lady. Mr Pollitt has the kind of voice and expressionable saucy face to suit the part… Richard Frost as a frightening Davy Jones who brings about the wreck of the Unicorn, and Mr Frost doubles as a very elegant King Richard… And for those who will be taking children to an evening show it is not too late – the curtain is down about 9.30.

It was in 1971 that a Salisbury pantomime story made the national press and television news, after a little girl unhappy by the banishment of *Dick Whittington and his Cat* was taken backstage by Theatre Manager Alan Corkill so that she could meet Penelope Nice's Tomasina and be reassured. It was also in this year that Daniel Pettiward, stalwart supporter of the Playhouse and contributor to pantomimes and revues, wrote an article for the Salisbury Journal giving some background to the production. He explained in the article that pre-Henry Marshall days had seen imported comics bringing routines with them and scripts passed on by other theatres. That was by now long past history, as were the local dancers, now replaced by smaller numbers of company members forming the chorus. Pettiward is pleased to note that, in his production, Roger Clissold has 'gone out of his way to uphold tradition and preserve the magic formula which has made the Playhouse pantomime.' He also noted the inclusion of the genuinely medieval Ratcatcher's song. Among other unsung heroes mentioned in the article are 'the late Mrs Deering of Broadchalke' – Deirdre Deering – who made cat masks and many other hats and head-dresses over the years. Also given a nod of appreciation is designer Neville Dewis, painting the backcloths 'in the unheatable wastes of a disused building in Churchfields.'[131]

In 1972, Christine Absalom – in her second professional pantomime – was one of the Villagers in *Jack and the Beanstalk* singing the song about Mayday (sometimes surreptitiously changed to Payday by the cast). The other big moment for Christine was the walkdown complete with 'floral garlands and beautifully choreographed by Liz Moscrop.' By this time, the cast were allowed to travel home for Christmas if it wasn't too far away and if there was a train back to Salisbury on Boxing Day – which there was in those days. Several of the cast met up at Waterloo and shared a compartment as Christine explains.

> We took over one of those old fashioned compartments that seated about 10 people all squashed together on bench seats. Out came the picnics, carefully prepared by loving parents, and best of all the hip flasks (now that wouldn't happen today). A party atmosphere prevailed throughout the journey, and we performed faultlessly for 2 shows that day. Great times. [132]

Jack and the Beanstalk 1972: Jack (Brian Honeyball), Simon (David Grout) and Dame Durden (Geoffrey Brightman) bid farewell to Tallulah the Cow (Jenny Burke & Amanda Boxer)

Another one of the villagers was Sara Coward, who only ended up in the production unexpectedly.

It was pure chance I was in the panto at all – I'd arrived in Salisbury a few weeks before, at 24 hours' notice, to take over the leading part in *There's a Girl in my Soup*, after the principal lady had had a car accident. Luckily the wonderful Reggie Salberg liked my work, and asked me to stay on to play some lovely parts in the Spring season. As a stop-gap, he suggested I stay for the panto as well and just 'tart about in the chorus' – which I did. My romantic leading man, Gilbert Wynne, transformed into the grumpy king, and lovely Geoffrey Brightman shone as Dame. One moment I do remember was between the two of them – Gilbert as King invited Geoffrey to visit his 'palARSE' and Geoffrey responded with an invitation to his 'cottARGE'. It was a very happy time! [133]

The story was still set in the Cornish village of Crumplehorn, and Henry Marshall was as particular as ever in how the opening scene should look.

In the far distance, on a hill, a fairy-tale castle. Nearer, but still some distance away, the village church. UC a footbridge, with handrail, over a stream, and nearby a willow tree. A few higgledy-piggledy houses, and a shop with a sign reading Cornish Pixies.

With this fairy-tale village revealed, the happy villagers struck up their opening number, which some of the actors involved can still sing to this day.

In the village of Crumplehorn,
Far away in the fields of corn,
We have heard of what other folk do,

When they want to be with it.
Why should we be with it?
Happy the days of long ago,
There were lots of things that we used to know,
Happy the folk of the fairy tale,
When the girls were girls and the men were male.
Ours were the happiest days, boys,
Ours were the happiest days.
Happy the days when we all could roam
Over quiet hills to a peaceful home.
Happy the evenings in Lovers Lane
With no motor car and no aeroplane.
Ours were the happiest days, boys,
Ours were the happiest days.
The happiest days
The happiest days
The happiest days!

Oliver Gordon's old part of Queen Iodine was transformed to King Cuthbert, and the script preserved in the Henry Marshall collection seems to be an earlier one with lots of amendments on pink paper sellotaped to the pages. Some things never change however, and the Fairy (choreographer Liz Moscrop) still worked her magic on the beans to produce the beanstalk which would bring Act One to a rousing finish.

Oh magic beans that lie within this well,
Grow quickly to a stalk by this my spell.
Towering on high into the distance far
To touch the sun and reach the farthest star.
Oh magic beans that in the dark now lie,
Become a magic beanstalk in the sky.

Act Two saw a plate-smashing scene with the King (Gilbert Wynne, 'played with something of a difference which is hard to define') and Dame Durden (Geoffrey Brightman, 'blessed with a nice north country accent, romps through it all, gagging, singing, dancing and showing some very nifty ability in the kitchen scene[134]'), whilst poor Princess Isabel (Rosamund Shelley) sings from the cell into which David Sadgrove's Giant Thunderclub has placed her[135].

I hear the wild bird calling,
Pity a poor princess.
The days are dark and the nights are long,
With never a soul to hear my song,

Jack and the Beanstalk 1972: King Cuthbert (Gilbert Wynne), PC Rafter (David Beames), Lord Chamberlain (Frank Ellis) and Dame Durden (Geoffrey Brightman)

Hoping in vain to live again,
Oh rescue me in distress.
I hear the wild bird calling,
Pity a poor Princess.

The Princess is rescued after a lengthy – and carefully described – chase scene involving fake doors, rollers and vamp doors, the whole thing described in more than a page of stage directions. Giving most of the cast a chance to recover – or at least to get into their walk-down costumes - the songsheet, of course, was in honour of Jenny Burke and Amanda Boxer as Tallulah, 'a very lovable beastie.[136]'

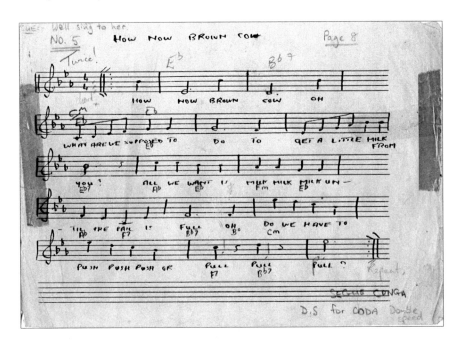

Henry Marshall's much-amended score for the Brown Cow songsheet

Why does a brown cow give white milk,
When it always eats green grass?
That's the burning question,
Burns like indigestion.
You don't know, I don't know,
Don't you feel an ass?
Why does a brown cow give white milk,
When it always eats green grass?

Gilbert Wynne has many lovely memories of his time at Salisbury, but thinks now that he was 'the unfunniest and worst panto king ever' in that production, although he feels he was more successful when he returned five years later. 'I think panto acting is an art by itself, one I did not possess. But I still enjoyed it, and was lucky to be in two pantos written by Henry Marshall.'[137] David Beames had returned to the company by this time, after training at Bristol, first as an Acting ASM and then as a full member of the company. Cast as PC Rafter ('peace hereafter'), he had progressed from his previous involvement in the chorus and found Geoffrey Brightman's Dame to be quite different from Oliver's. 'Oliver Gordon was in no way camp, frock or not. Geoffrey was a very funny High Camp Dame.'[138] Cast as Jack was the latest in the line of Salisbury's male Principal Boys, Brian Honeyball. Years later, David Beames was surprised to meet up with him again when touring in Brazil, where Brian now lives.

By now Musical Director, and with piano, bass guitar and drums in the pit, Christopher Littlewood was pleased to be working again with Geoffrey Brightman since they had appeared together previously at the Library Theatre, Manchester. He very much enjoyed Geoffrey's Dame Durden, who was very motherly in the northern comedy tradition. Henry Marshall was pleased when Christopher added *Life is What You Make It* from Victor Herbert's operetta *Sweethearts* for the Dame and Princess Isabel, who was known as

Princess Isabulge to the cast due to the unfortunate visual effect of the medieval dress. He also remembers that in those days the whole cast helped with getting in the set, and if Henry was particular, so was Neville Dewis the designer. Barbara Wilson, as ever, produced endless costumes on time. In this panto, the vocals were particularly strong, as Christopher remembers. He was always loyal, too, to Derek Brook, a drummer who was 'very quiet, very old-fashioned but very good at panto.' There was no written drum part for Derek in Marie's day, but when Christopher took over, he wrote one for him.

That show was also Graham Richards' first professional pantomime, and he was back the following year for *Robinson Crusoe*.

I can sing Henry's music to you because I've got that kind of memory. I didn't know much about Salisbury when I got my first job. Cricket was always talked about. I'm sure Henry came to *Jack and the Beanstalk* to see how we were getting on but I remember him more the following year when we did *Robinson Crusoe* because he came in and did the fights. In that first panto there was a woofenpoof, a hairy caterpillar thing. Because I hadn't grown up on pantomime and seen all these routines I was fascinated. My Dames were both Geoffrey Brightman, he was a big character man who came down from York Rep. As you know there was no room, and I was an ASM for *Jack and the Beanstalk* so I had to set the props. And I used to be based SL - wasn't that where the coal was kept? There was no room whatsoever. There was an 18 carrot necklace and all that business and there was no room to put anything. There was even a maypole in *Jack and the Beanstalk*. The designer Neville Dewis insisted there should be a bridge in the opening scene and he was outraged because the stage Manager forgot to set it. I remember that Liz Moscrop was choreographer and playing Fairy Liquid. She had been a ballet dancer and had become an actress. Just before we opened she had to put the shoes on as they wanted her on pointe. The agony, on pointe for quite a long time. She danced solo in the cloud ballet with the floaty fairies. Also for Robinson Crusoe we had a very clever DSM called Andrew Empson, who's now a Producer, and he was so good at making things when we got to the jungle scene he made these ostrich heads, two of them over the very clever little set. They would appear and the children were captivated, but we then got a note during the run as the ostriches began to appear in scenes where they shouldn't. [139]

Despite the difficulties, or perhaps because of them, strong bonds were formed between those who began their acting careers at Salisbury. Some even went on holiday together, as Knight Mantell did with Maria Heidler and Joyce Rae, and he remembers them both sitting in the Bishop's chair at Valderosa Cathedral, a famous chair because it was said that anyone who sat in it would be married before the year was over. Both women sat in it, much laughter followed, and both were married within months to people they had been in pantomime with the year before. When Maria Heidler joined the company in 1973 her first professional part was in *Mother Courage*, but this was soon followed by *Robinson Crusoe*, in which her main featured role was as Ermintrude the Monkey.

I have very little recollection of that first panto, except that I learned an invaluable lesson in Professionalism that has stood me in good stead for the rest of my life.

Towards the start of the run there must have been a Friday night party that ended up in somebody's digs out of town. Very few of us had cars in those days, and it was agreed we'd go in for the matinee the next day in the theatre van. Now, this was a cantankerous old jalopy and it decided to take Saturday off - it just refused to start! It was getting near noon and the panic was rising. No matter what the boys tried, it just wouldn't start. The AA must have been called, but by now we were trying to fathom out the Country Bus schedules.

There were two of us who had to be at the theatre by 1.25 - the 'Half'. The show went up at 2 o'clock; we were a good half hour's drive from Salisbury and that would mean gunning it and having every traffic light in our favour once we reached town. We found a bus would be coming through about 1pm but doubted if it would stop at the local stop as it was a through-bus, possibly from Swindon. Waffling about what to do for the best, and still trying to get the van to start, it was obvious that it would even be too late for someone to drive out and get us. There were no mobiles in those days and phone calls into Salisbury were long distance and put through operators. Mainly, there was a lot of shame that we'd allowed ourselves to get into this predicament - which not only let us down, but the entire cast and crew of Salisbury Playhouse - and the audience if the curtain had to be held. Eventually, feeling quite sick with panic, the two of us went out and stood at the bus-stop. Finally we saw the bus coming and my companion bravely stood in the middle of the road and waved it down. Somehow we managed to scrape together the fare in small change and sat silent as the bus drove oh--so--s-l-o-w-l-y toward Salisbury. Finally the bus pulled into the Bus Station which, of course, was in the middle of Town, and we had to run like gazelles up Fisherton Street to the Playhouse. It was now well gone the 'Half' and as we careened up the alley to the stage Door, there were Mr. Salberg and Mr. Clissold standing, waiting. A phone call had got through to say we were on our way, but Mr. Clissold was justifiably furious. He immediately went in to inform all and sundry to prepare for 'curtain-up'. Mr. Salberg, as my memory serves, just looked at us calmly as we stuttered our apologies and said, 'I gather you'll make sure you're in Town in the future when you have a show. We go up at 2. I'll see you afterwards.' Dashing into the dressing room, I could tell by the faces that this had caused a major upset. Nevertheless, my fellow actors had everything ready for me. They threw me into my Citizen's dress for the opening number and plopped a mob cap on my head as I slapped on some powder and lipstick. Then the knock on the door: 'Beginners please!' and I went out to take my place in the wings. I daren't look at anyone, I was so ashamed. The overture struck up, the babble from the audience died down, the tabs parted . . . and we were on! A happy, merry, band of citizens coming on in a Medieval conga line from stage right, then meeting and crossing with an identical line from stage left. Then we joined up and spun into a circle, singing with gusto… Unfortunately, I was at the end of the line, and my nerves must have compromised my usual ability to counter the whiplash effect. I went flying! But the Dance waiteth for no man, and I gathered myself off the floor as best I could, my dignity in shreds, and tried to incorporate a clutsy character into my persona so the audience would believe it was part of the fun. No wonder I don't remember much about playing the monkey - I was the monkey - perfect casting. After the show I apologized to everyone concerned, and was touched at how generous people were. Mr. Salberg had, of course, seen it all before - and worse! He knew I'd learnt my lesson and didn't labour the point. It was then that I realized the strength of the theatre family and the discipline that holds it together: a discipline that could put other businesses to shame.[140]

For this production, many of the cast once again had misgivings about blacking up and wearing the motley collection of brown and black bodystockings and Afro wigs. The Dame, Mrs Crusoe, is not one of the strongest comedy parts, and Geoffrey Brightman had less to work with than in the previous year's production. The cast was still very large, with 19 actors listed; not quite as many as in previous productions of this title, but still an expensive show to mount. David Beames was back again, this time as one of the Pirates, Barmy. He remembers the exhaustion of performing twice or even three times a day but despite the hard work he also remembers being helpless with laughter at times,

Robinson Crusoe 1973: Polly Perkins (Jill Baker) with the citizens of Hull

particularly when unrepeatable things were happening behind the stockade and out of view of the audience.[141]

The pit band was down to two, with Christopher Littlewood deciding not to have another year of teaching the music by ear to a bass guitarist who couldn't read music. Whether it was the casting difficulties, the unease about blacking up or the growing realisation that *Robinson Crusoe* didn't quite work – as it hadn't quite worked in 1955 – this was the last production of the title at Salisbury. It can't have helped that was the year of the three-day week, the miners strike and widespread power cuts, with some performances being given by the light of car headlamps in the auditorium.

By now, fund raising was under way for the new theatre. Christopher Littlewood and some of the company put on a series of *Songs from the Shows* performances on Sundays during the run of the pantomime, without pay. 'We managed to raise a lot of money for the new theatre,' Christopher remembers, 'and Reggie couldn't pay us but what he did was that in our wage packets on the weeks that we did the Sundays, he put a Timothy White's voucher in for £5, a lot of money in those days. He was so generous and kind in so many ways.' [142]

Forgiven for her late return Maria Heidler may have been, but her skin acting was also noted when it came to casting for the following year's production of *Babes in the Wood*. Maria takes up the tale.

I'd done my apprenticeship as an Acting ASM and was now a bona fide actor with some glorious parts. With the Panto coming up, I was convinced I'd be cast as befitting my new elevated status in the profession. The word spread through the dressing rooms that the cast list for Babes was finally up. Some played it cool and asked another thespian to let them know what they were playing. Others skulked until the corridor was free and they could review their fate in privacy. Gradually I noticed that everyone became very busy - and no-one was looking me in the face. People were assiduously scrubbing out their tea-stained mugs in the Green Room and/or offering to go into town to get a new tin of coffee or packet of biscuits. Others were rinsing out tights in sinks and others suddenly appeared to have an audition and had their heads buried in Shakespeare or Shaw. 'Anyone see what I'm playing?' I tossed out as coolly as I could manage. Negative mumbles were all I got back. I could stand it no more. I strolled down the corridor. At last I was in front of the typed sheet. 'Babes in the Wood'. I started at the top with the men and then the women: Maid Marian . . . .no, Babe 1 . . . .no, Babe 2 . . . .no . . . ..I was too big for a Babe anyway . . . ., The Fairy . . . ..no, Daisy Dimple . . . that was the Dame role . . . .where was I? . . . .Then . . . FIDO: Maria Heidler 'Oh no!' I yelled, 'I'm the bloody dog!' At that moment, Mr. Clissold came through the stage door - wouldn't he just! We looked at each other for a telling moment and he went on through. Heads started to poke out of doorways. What would she say next? A million thoughts screamed through my head, but I settled on . . . 'I'm working, I'm being paid . . . and I'd be wise to shut up!' Smirks were now appearing on those peeking faces so I said brightly, 'Well, I must have been one helluva monkey last year, and I'm not sure how I'll do the camel in Aladdin, but in the meantime I'll work on my begging skills.' Eventually it was wardrobe-call time. I made my way down Fisherton Street to Barbara Wilson's garret, wondering what on earth she was going to come up with. Barbara and her team did what I can only describe as miracles; supplying costumes for (by then) a three-weekly Repertory Company on, I'm sure, a vastly inadequate budget. (All departments were equally constrained.) Their wardrobe premises at that time were up a rusty old fire escape and in rooms that were too cold in winter and too hot in summer. Nevertheless they produced costumes that I remember to this day. I might be the 'bloody dog' but I was going to be the best-dressed 'bloody dog'. I knew Barbara would see to that: she didn't disappoint. She'd made me a wonderful suit of shaggy fur fabric. I was deep grey with flecks of white and had big soft paws. The head mask was a wonder. It was a huge head - but light and manageable; the effect of a cartoon dog. The wardrobe team went to no end of pains to ensure I could move easily and that I could see and hear and breathe through the enormous head. During the run, the coffee line-up at the interval was hilarious. There I was, trying not to shed into the sugar, with my head hanging from my belt! The interesting part about playing a dog is that it brings out the pooch-lover in everybody. Various members of the cast would regale me with stories of how their dog settled in its basket to sleep, or begged for a treat, or washed, or reacted to a strange noise. I soon realized that playing the 'bloody dog' was going to be fun, especially as I am a dog person myself. In spite of feeling a bit uncomfortable at having to lift my leg on the Big Bad Robbers who were disguised as trees, (it always got a huge laugh) I loved being Fido. People would come up to me afterwards and tell me how their dog went three times round their basket before settling - just like Fido did. Being a dog taught me a lot. I can highly recommend it...[143]

Babes in the Wood 1974. Derek Crewe and Alex Johnston (the Robbers) with the Sheriff of Nottingham (Jonathan Fryer)

The 1974 *Babes in the Wood* was the only time that Roger Heathcott played Dame. Christopher Littlewood remembers that he did not fit the conventional mould for the part. 'His Daisy Dimple was fascinating; I don't know where or how he found her, he must have gone back to Commedia dell' Arte or something. He was fine in the school scene, doing the schoolmistress stuff, but the frocks didn't hang on him right[144]'. Jonathan Fryer's Sheriff, however, was very much in the traditional mould, and Roger Leach joined the long line of male Principal Boys at Salisbury to play Robin Hood opposite Lally Percy's Maid Marian. Jill Graham took on the choreography as well as playing the Fairy, having also played Principal Boy and Dame in previous productions: surely the most varied set of roles of any of the Salisbury company. The programme also includes a new credit: Additional songs by Rex Walford. The song referred to was *The Banana Cantata*, and, says Christopher Littlewood, 'It worked, so I kept it in when I wrote the music for a later production. You could only sing *'Yes, we have no bananas'* and it went through every opera and oratorio. That was the additional song.' [145]

Much enjoyment took place offstage as well, with Christopher Littlewood also remembering that cast member Derek Crewe was responsible for one memorable evening. 'He was the first person that ever gave me so much alcohol that I couldn't get off the floor. It was the day Shostakovitch died. We were having a party in one of the theatre flats on Fisherton Street. He came in and said to me that Shostakovitch was dead and I had a glass of wine in my hand. He had a huge bottle of whisky and he poured some into my wine so that it was half whisky . . . I loved his Dame.'

Unusually, one cast member, Jane Quy, played the same part that she had in the 1968 production, once again appearing as a Babe but this time alongside Anne Rosenfeld. By this time, Oliver Gordon's comic role as Willie Whiskers was much reduced and played by Adrian Reynolds, while the robbers of Alex Johnston and Derek Crewe found their parts much enhanced and they showed themselves more than equal to that challenge.

Scene 5
The Fairy Godmother
Waves her Wand

B Y THE MID 1970s, the Henry Marshall pantomimes had become
firmly established at Salisbury over almost twenty years. Principal
Boys (male and female) remembered fondly by Reggie in the 1974
programme included Brigit Forsyth, Helen Dorward, Josephine
Tewson, Carolyn Moody, Chris Harris, Tim Meats, Brian Honeyball
and Elwyn Johnson. His memorable villains included Ian Mullins
(who frightened one little boy so much, according to Reggie, that Ian
had to invite the lad home to tea before he could sleep undisturbed at
nights once again) and Knight Mantell (who also later played Dame
– perhaps the only Salisbury actor to score that double). Of the many
graceful Fairies over the years, Reggie remembered in particular
Lynn Farleigh, Janet Hargreaves and Vivien Heilbron. The late 1960s
and early 1970s were the heyday of the Salisbury pantos, playing as
they always did to full houses throughout the run and to hundreds
of parties, many travelling a considerable distance. The opening of
the new theatre would greatly improve working conditions and
production possibilities, but the essential style and tradition of the
shows continued for many years.

The last pantomime at the old Salisbury Playhouse was
Aladdin, with Knight Mantell as Widow Twankey. Some remember
him slipping in jokes that were a little too naughty if he thought that

Aladdin 1975. Widow Twankey (Knight Mantell) and Abanazar (Roger Leach)

Roger Clissold was not in, and he was not known for his liking of children. He admits now that he was not good in the part as he was supposed to use all Oliver Gordon's material, but he overstepped the mark.

> Roger Clissold thought I would be good as Dame, but I was very blue by their standards and very badly behaved. Roger Leach as Abanazer had to produce rabbits, and they were the rabbits that Madame Barbara bred in the wardrobe and whose droppings were all over the costumes. You could see the rabbits, you could see the ears of the things sticking out of his costume. It used to make me hysterical, I used to think there's no mystery in this, we can actually see what you're doing. It was all a bit preposterous. I threw dough to the audience during the kitchen scene and it hit an old lady's glasses. I sent a message round in the interval via the usher but I ended up in Reggie's office again.[146]

Michael Stroud remembers that the rabbits had previously appeared in Dick Whittington, although not without incident.

> Dick Whittington was sitting on the milestone, 10 miles to London etc – and there was a little flap thing between her legs and at some stage the stage management used to shove a little bunny rabbit through and it used to pop out for the kids. This got bigger and bigger and eventually you just got to see its face coming through. The rabbits were kept in Madame Barbara's wardrobe. When you went for a fitting you would stand on a rug and there were all these rabbit droppings all over the place. Probably rats as well I dare say. [147]

Knight Mantell had worked at Salisbury for several years as an actor and would later return to direct in the new theatre. Although he was to cross swords with Reggie Salberg from time to time, he also recognises that he, like so many others, owes everything to Reggie. He has appeared in more than 35 pantomimes, in recent years often for commercial managements where, he says, 'They liked me because I was legit, which just meant you didn't get a microphone.' After leaving Manchester University and working at Liverpool Playhouse, Knight had been spotted by Reggie on one of his tours around the country looking for young actors for his company. In a meeting in the pub after the show, Knight was engaged for a season at Salisbury on £15 a week, and he went back again the next year. His Widow Twankey was certainly not in the traditional mould, and is remembered as a full-blown acting performance rather than a conventional pantomime portrayal. As Christopher Littlewood says now, 'He's got this voice so that wasn't going to change was it. I did like it. He definitely was a widow, there was definitely a bereavement in his Dame he acted that part. His Dame had that darkness inside it, and also that sense of loss, it was severe. It was a very, very true Dame but with rather more pathos than we were accustomed to.' [148]

Knight got on particularly well with Roger Clissold, and found him not only good to work with, but also, as many others have said, tremendously loyal to those in the company. Meanwhile, Reggie continued to select the actors, manage the finances and yet still be, as Christopher Littlewood described him, 'professional and yet human; I miss those days'. [149]

> He always went round switching all the lights off because he came from a background where he had to pay all the bills. But if you showed a profit – and it was the most successful regional theatre – he always gave the money away to the actors at Christmas, because if you made a profit, the Arts Council cut your grant for the next year.

Maria Heidler was in the last pantomime in the old theatre too, and finally graduated from monkey and dog to a human role.

I was cast as the Princess Badroulbadour in Aladdin, (I really was working on that camel . . . honest!) and I got to wear a beautiful crown and gowns and I got the boy in the end! How good does it get? Well, okay, I had the flu for the first few performances, but you can't have everything can you? I got to sing a poignant duet with the adorable, talented and funny Jeffery Perry as Aladdin who, together with his partner Patience Tomlinson, became two of my dearest and most supportive friends. Yet it hardly seems fair to single these two lovely people out when so many others in this cast helped me, encouraged me, made me laugh and formed me.[150]

Olivia Breeze returned for her first Salisbury pantomime in ten years, but this time as choreographer. She remembers the production as a very successful one, with which she was fully involved, from her first meetings about the set, to her discussions with Roger Clissold and Christopher Littlewood. She planned everything on paper before the read-through and the company worked long hours and took lunch breaks whenever they could. She also stood in for Roger on occasions during the run and had to put her foot down when she crept in to a performance and caught Knight Mantell being outrageously naughty. 'So many of us have stayed in touch from those days,' she says now, 'one felt safe there.'[151]

Roger Clissold directed the last five pantomimes at the old Playhouse and three at the new theatre, which opened in 1976. Two new pantos appeared during this time, as Henry Marshall wrote scripts for *Mother Goose* and *Puss in Boots*, but each was given only once before the familiar cycle of seven subjects returned. The first production at the new theatre, however, was *Cinderella*, and Jane Quy remembers it for what she thinks of as her favourite Dames to work with, Brian Ellis and John Branwell.

We all gathered in the wings every night to watch their slapstick washing up scene. Their timing was so good and they did something different every night. Brian was incredibly female and very composed, John was completely opposite, they were very good. John was the big one and Brian was very different. I played my regular part, Buttons' Fairy – that was my dream come true, being Fairy in the pantomime.[152]

Lionel Guyett returned for that production too, having appeared in the 1967 *Robinson Crusoe* at the old theatre. In all, he appeared in six of the ten Henry Marshall pantomimes at the new theatre, a record beaten only by Jane Quy. In *Cinderella* he played one of the Broker's Men and found some changes since his previous appearance more than ten years before. Although Roger Clissold was a very different director, he certainly maintained the tradition of the pantomimes. Lionel noticed that Henry Marshall was less involved by now, although he was unhappy if there was any attempt to update the script.

The technical possibilities of the new building were such that the transformation scene could be far more impressive than was previously possible, and then there was the pony... Those who were involved still remember the saga that ensued. Christopher Littlewood takes up the story.

Let's start with the pony shall we. Neville (Dewis, designer) was in his element. We had a pony. It wasn't a rabbit in Wardrobe with Barbara, it was a pony and we had a lot of problems about this, about where we were going to keep the pony. It was in a downstairs office, it had to be mucked out of course. It was brought in for the duration. I think it was Barbara who mucked out, with all the other chores of coming in to do laundry. Someone had to go and exercise it, walk it round. But it was very well behaved on stage.[153]

There were other problems in this production, with one performer not ideally cast for once, and this caused concerns for Henry and practical difficulties for Christopher Littlewood.

The band was large now, we were in the new theatre, we'd got a pit that was worth having. And we had sound, suddenly there was sound… We'd got a fly tower, we could do things at this theatre… so, as you can imagine, everybody round this person was going to have to overdo everything. Poor Elwyn (Elwyn Johnson as Prince Charming), I felt so sorry for him, he was always charming anyway. Brian (Ellis) and John (Branwell) as the Ugly Sisters were fabulous… Brian had broken his arm, and he'd had it reset and it hadn't worked quite right, so when he was Fifi he couldn't get his arm where he wanted to, so it made his performance quite different. I think he used a fan. And John Branwell was very good as the other Dame, very reminiscent of Geoffrey Brightman. Business got invented rather a lot in this show I remember. It looked gorgeous, it was stunning, absolutely stunning, and Derek's (Crewe) Buttons was played beautifully.[154]

Elwyn Johnson had played Dandini in the previous *Cinderella*, but his elevation to Prince Charming meant that once again, as in his two previous roles, he was required to rehearse some very effective fights.

It fell to me to carry the story as Principal Boy as energetically as I could in a period when chaps were allowed to don the tights and boots. Henry created traditional pantomimes, but the 1970s allowed what I think he might have thought of as an aberration. So whether as Charming, Dick or Dandini he, as Fight Director wanted to create spectacular sword-fights for his heroes. He was the Head of Stage Combat at RADA for many years and an authority on Fencing, so his choreography was straight out of Errol Flynn, no bish bash bosh for him. I managed a Fencing Bronze at Drama School which was a huge help, but those fights needed daily refreshment before performance to preserve safety. Those were happy days at Salisbury Playhouse, a truly excellent repertory theatre run by the legendary Reggie Salberg to whom I and others owe so much. The repertory system was a rock of civic benefit and cohesion for all ages at its best, and Henry Marshall underpinned that with his traditional pantomimes year after year. I was privileged to be a small part of that tradition.[155]

The following year was *Dick Whittington*, with the Henry Marshall script but with new music and lyrics by Christopher Littlewood. The change had been discussed between Roger Clissold and Christopher the previous year, when they agreed it was time to bring a different musical emphasis to Henry Marshall's scripts. To his delight, Christopher found that Henry was very ready to accept the change, and reprises were also included for the first time.

I said have you noticed that with the script the children are engaged, but when the music starts although we had brought in the band to make it more contemporary, it wasn't doing it. You can't do *Over the Hills and Far Away* now. We've got a new building, a new feel and the late seventies is quite different. I said I'm awfully sorry Roger, but we need a bit of pop, or they will go to commercial theatres. One of the regulars, Mrs Thornton who sat in the front row with her son, was quite shocked that it had a pop song to open it, but it worked. It wasn't vulgar, I didn't overstep Henry's tradition in any way, and he was thrilled by the way. I thought it was going to be awful, I was dreading his first visit. Henry's scripts – and I do mean this – were traditional panto at their best and I wouldn't have ever wanted to change that, but just occasionally there wasn't a reason for the song. Not just because there's got to be a scene change but because the characters have changed gear or one has found out something new about the other character. I am very proud of this collaboration, that happened here. I thought it worked a treat, and everything else seemed better this time. A new day dawned – and in fact the opening was called A New Day.[156]

Derek Crewe played the first of many Dames and Roger Clissold, in view of his many commitments running the new theatre, gave David Gilmore the chance to direct. The pastry scene involved gallons of water and dough and a steep learning curve for Derek, getting to grips with the timing of the role and the enormous physical demands and with limited technical rehearsal. Many remember this as the messiest of all the slosh scenes at Salisbury, a classic of a type all too rarely seen today. Gilbert Wynne as Alderman Fitzwarren was back after a five year gap, and this time he felt he was more successful in the part. 'David, the Director, put me wise. You have to play it big,' he said. It was not easy, being a lazy actor.'[157]

1978 saw the first appearance of *Mother Goose* at Salisbury Playhouse with a new Henry Marshall script set in and around the village of Odstock. Music and lyrics were by Christopher Littlewood and he feels this was his best score and Henry's best script. Each had taken on board the strengths and wishes of the other: 'we had a lovely script,' he remembers, 'and we had a ball. Derek Crewe had learnt the Dame part by now, and he was fabulous. The Pool of Beauty transformation scene was just stunning. Every stop was pulled out there, believe you me. We got Roger Clissold back and we really plotted and planned this panto properly. I promise you that's my best panto at Salisbury.' [158]

In a return to tradition, the pantomime began with an interchange between Demon Discontent and Fairy Goodheart, appearing on this occasion at Old Sarum.

Demon Discontent (Alex Johnston)
The sleeping town of Salisbury moans and sighs
'Tis well. I would not have it otherwise.
But still, tonight I feel in gen'rous mood
I'll send some gifts and ask no gratitude.
Famine! Hunger! Pestilence! Disease!
Poverty! Murder! Do all the ill you please
A merry Christmas to you all below
A glad New Year to you. Ho, ho, ho ho!

Fairy Goodheart (Christine Bishop)
Poor Sarum town, awaking with the dawn
Some waken to rejoice and some to mourn.
So many wretched, happy ones so few,
So little done to help, so much to do.
Descend, sweet health, your mission be to cure
And joy shall follow, precious bright and pure
A merry Christmas, and a New Year good
I'd give to all the world if I but could.

Mother Goose, who lives in Odstock Woods, gets rich from the golden eggs quite early in the story and also drives an impressive car, a stage effect which would not have been possible in the old theatre. Also showing off the facilities of the new Playhouse was the flight by balloon to Gooseland, after Mother Goose (Derek Crewe) has been persuaded by the Demon to transform herself in the magic lake. It is surprising that Oliver Gordon never played Mother Goose as it is often described as the pinnacle of the Dame's career, although this may have been because both he and his brother were unsure of the effectiveness of stories outside the traditional six that recurred. One wonders what they would have made of the current trend for titles such as *Snow White* and *Sleeping Beauty*, in an age when it is popularly believed that only stories familiar from animated films are likely to succeed as pantomimes.

Another new title followed in 1979 with *Puss in Boots*. Lionel Guyett was back, this time as one of the Miller's sons, and had the chance to do his first proper slapstick decorating scene with Stephen Hattersley in the Ogre Inn, and he remembers it working quite well. He found the attitude of locals to the actors was unchanged: 'You became part of the fabric of the town and they would tell you what they thought of each part.'[159] Henry Marshall had written scripts for *Puss in Boots* before, but not for Salisbury, and not for a long time. The script for Salisbury notes that it was written on 13th September 1979 and typed up ten days later, so the revision process was quite short in this case. Christopher Littlewood thought highly of the script again: 'if *Mother Goose* was the most spectacular and brilliant, this was the cleverest of them. It had lots of levels; so I enjoyed it for that reason. The chorus in this were like a commercial chorus, they looked good and they could move; and Liz Moscrop became another kind of Puss rather than Tiddles. There were some lovely things in this show; it was beautifully knitted, I didn't have to write any scene-change music. It felt more like a children's play. The designer was Richard Marks; it was red and black, there was nothing garish in it. We did start to think that panto was an art-form; perhaps that was the beginning of its downfall. I think we all felt we were doing art; it was not quite as boisterous. It was an absolute collector's piece and it should be done again.' ▨

Much of the story of *Puss in Boots* follows that in other Henry Marshall scripts, with a Miller and three sons living in the village of Dee. The main comic characters are King Rumtytum and Queen Bubblegum, with John Branwell playing Dame this time and Geoffrey Brightman forgoing the skirts to play King. The forces of Evil are divided between Rumble Grumble the Ogre and his assistant Hey Presto the Wizard. The names seem a little prosaic and there is more

Puss in Boots 1979: The walk-down, with in the front row the Good Fairy (Lynette Edwards), Sid (Stephen Hattersley), King Rumtytum III (Geoffrey Brightman), Charles (William Relton), Puss (Liz Moscrop), Princess Rosamund (Gillian Bevan), Queen Bubblegum (John Branwell) and Hey Presto (Marc Sinden)

of a child-like ring to this script than some of the earlier more literary titles. The immortals still quite correctly speak in verse when required however, as when the Good Fairy (Lynette Edwards) is required to use her magic to make the boots small enough for Puss.

> Behold a pair of tiny boots;
> So strange and rare these little boots,
> So finely made, so small and neat,
> And yet they fit no human feet.
> For they were made for furry paws
> To earn their wearer great applause.

They are untouched by human hand
For they are made in Fairyland.
My duty done, my leave I take,
The boots hang there till Puss shall wake.

As befits the title, there is a cat ballet, and much chasing of mice around the stage by Puss – presumably using the wuffenpoof device used in many other pantomimes by Henry Marshall but quite rarely seen these days. Sadly, the two new titles were not repeated, and the pattern set in the 1960s resumed apart from abandoning *Robinson Crusoe*, now largely considered unplayable in view of the plot (although it would be revived elsewhere in more recent times thanks to the popularity of Pirates of the Caribbean).

Lionel Guyett was back again in 1980 to play a robber in *Babes in the Wood,* and another regular performer from the old theatre, Peter

Babes in the Wood 1980: The full company at the walk-down, including Peter Robert Scott as Daisy Dimple

Robert Scott, played the first of two Dames. Christopher Littlewood remembers that he was very good in the role, if a little too sincere: 'he got quite hurt if the kids weren't quite there with him, as happened some days. And I'm not sure I contributed anything that was better than the original; I think I had peaked with *Mother Goose* and *Puss in Boots*. I do remember that the kids loved the song I wrote called *I Hate School*.' After one performance of that number, Henry was heard to say 'I think that's the best bit of anarchy I've heard in a long time.' Roger Clissold again decided that a change of director was needed and this time Graham Berown took over in the role. The actors playing Will Scarlett (Andrew Branch) and Maid Marion (Lyndsey Durant) were, says Christopher Littlewood, 'proper singers.'

The 1981 *Jack and the Beanstalk* was the last of the shows for which Christopher Littlewood wrote the music, although he was not Musical Director and did not see the show. 'I didn't do my usual score; I was writing this while I was doing *Underneath the Arches* at Chichester. I knew I wasn't going to be there so I did every number as a separate score. Obviously there were things going on in this show, because my score came back with stuff written on the back in large letters that could be held up from the pit for the cast to read. I will tell you something they would never have known. I was trained as a classical musician and I was going to be a concert pianist and when I finished college I found a composer that I had been denied there; this composer called Scriabin. I decided the finale to *Jack and the Beanstalk* was going to be the main melody from Scriabin's Piano Concerto. I think the lyric I wrote was *Now I'm Off to Do or Die*. I thought it was a suitable melody.' [160]

Peter Robert Scott was back as Dame however, playing a role which was an amalgam of the previous Dame Durden and Queen Iodine roles. The latest in a long line of male Principal Boys was Emlyn Harris, who was new to Salisbury audiences.

Jack and the Beanstalk 1981: Jack (Emlyn Harris) sells Tallulah the Cow (Charles Shaughnessy & Colin Hurley) to Abracadabra (Aaron Shirley)

In the summer of 1981, I had auditioned for Roger Clissold at Spotlight in London and he'd offered me a season at the Playhouse, to play 'as cast' in a programme of plays yet to be confirmed. I'd just ended a contract with the RSC and, having already spent a number of repertory seasons in the previous years in York I leapt at the chance to work for the first time in Salisbury. I had grown up in Basingstoke and the old Playhouse was the first repertory theatre I had ever visited as a schoolboy. Before I could start work at Salisbury it was announced that Roger was leaving to become Artistic Director at the Thorndike Theatre, Leatherhead. The caretaker director Graham Berown confirmed my roles for the season and I began work in August 1981. By the time the cast began rehearsals for the pantomime *Jack and the Beanstalk*, many of the actors in the company had worked together for three months and we were a happy crew. The season's productions had played to packed houses to enthusiastic and appreciative audiences and the pantomime tickets were soon sold out. Like me, a number of the actors were based in London so we were staying in digs in the City. A few were living in the theatre digs, a warren of rooms above a parade of shops in nearby Fisherton Street. These officially slept six, a mix of actors and stage management, and the residents had customised their basic rooms to make them as homely as possible. The digs remained freezing cold. That winter there was heavy snowfall and for a few days over Christmas Salisbury became cut off from the rest of the country. My digs were on the outskirts of the city and so the pantomime company, unable to get home for Christmas Day, decided to throw a party. I made it back to my digs, rather worse for wear, a few days later …

Early in the planning for the pantomime, the stage manager Ben resolved to make the beanstalk as spectacular as possible. The script called for the magic beans to be thrown down the well outside Dame Durden's house. Ben contacted the army and discovered that they had an extendible mast that, through a hydraulic system rose to more than a hundred feet. The mast and machinery was duly installed beneath the stage, a canvas sleeve painted to resemble a beanstalk was made to skin the mast and huge leaves attached to bamboo poles completed the magnificent edifice. At a flick of a switch, the beanstalk grew from the well, in the centre of the stage, its spring-loaded leaves flopping open as it grew, until it reached the full height of the stage. A rock-climbing ladder hidden at the rear of the beanstalk enabled me to climb the beanstalk for the Act One finale.

One of my fellow actors, who had also been engaged for the season, was Charles Shaughnessy, the son of Alfred Shaughnessy, the writer of the television series Upstairs Downstairs. Charles played one half of Talulah, the pantomime cow in the panto. He moved to the US shortly after the Salisbury season and found huge success playing Shane Donovan in the immensely popular American soap opera *Days of our Lives*. Charles inherited the title 5th Baron Shaughnessy in 2007. My main memory of Jack & the Beanstalk was the problem I had with my costume. Barbara Wilson, the costume designer, had created a leather jerkin with buckles up the front. The jerkin was designed to be a one-piece, to be worn with brown tights but without any trousers. Unfortunately, whenever I raised my arms, the sight of my brown tight-clad nether regions greeted the audience sitting in the front row stalls. Barbara refused to change the design saying, 'Don't raise your arms above your head then'. Not easy to do when you're climbing a beanstalk![161]

Jack and the Beanstalk 1981: Dame Durden (Peter Robert Scott), Jack (Emlyn Harris), Isabel (Mary Conlon) & King Cuthbert (Donald Pelmear)

Donald Pelmear returned for this production too, after a long interval; his last Salisbury panto had been in 1963. This time he was King Cuthbert, and his main memory is that Tom Fahy was such an appealing Giant Thunderclub that there were cries of dismay from the audience when he was toppled.[162]

Emlyn Harris returned as Principal Boy in 1982, this time to play Aladdin. 'It was the first time that the late Roger Leach had played a pantomime Dame but we had a great time. A couple of years later, when I was directing *Cinderella* at the Connaught Theatre, Worthing, Roger played one of the Ugly Sisters.'[163] Emlyn did begin to feel that the scripts were less effective than they had been, but he is quick to recognise their importance in pantomime history.

> Audiences expected more pizzazz and modern day references than Henry's shows could provide. I returned later to play Buttons in a version of *Cinderella* written by David Horlock, before I began to appear in commercial pantomimes, but the Salisbury Playhouse pantomimes, produced using Henry's scripts, remain in my memory as a perfect family show.[164]

By 1983 Lionel Guyett had graduated from Broker's Man to Buttons in *Cinderella*, although he remembers playing the role in the costume previously worn by Derek Crewe, which was made to fit him by strategically placed safety pins. Jack Chissick played Sister alongside Howard Attfield. This was Jack's first time in skirts, but he was to play the Dame role many times in the future. Jack – married to Jane Salberg – did not work at the Salisbury Playhouse while his father-in-law was General Manager, but by this time Reggie had retired. Jack had grown up seeing the Hackney Empire pantomimes each year, so he is another member of the Salisbury company to have been influenced by his childhood experiences of panto. He tried to carry on those traditions in the pantomimes in which he appeared and in those he would later write with David Horlock. The new Musical Director was Rob Mitchell and he introduced a number of new people to the company, which Lionel remembers as a happy one.

Cinderella 1983: Lionel Guyett as Buttons

Maria Heidler came back to appear at the new theatre, including the role of the Fairy in *Dick Whittington* in 1984, the last but one Henry Marshall pantomime at Salisbury. The only major change this time was the introduction of a mate for the cat to join up with at the finale. The songsheet was an old favourite, with plenty of opportunity for the audience to be active and join in with the animal noises.

> Oh the dogs go bow wow wow.
> And the ducks go quack quack quack.
> And the turkeys all go gobble gobble gobble.
> On the field out at the back.
> Oh the cows go moo moo moo!
> And it's anything but calm,
> With a bow wow, quack quack, gobble gobble, moo moo
> Down on the farm.

Dick's cat was back to being named Tomasina, not Tiddles, allowing the familiar strains of *'Come along Tomasina'* to be heard in the theatre, and which was also used for the walk-down.

Come along Tomasina,
You're so wrong Tomasina,
We have both got to see this thing through.
Oh get up Tomasina.
Don't give up Tomasina.
There's a new life waiting for you.
It's been rough Tomasina,
Now be tough Tomasina,
And remember we're always your friend.
Don't despair Tomasina,
Nearly there Tomasina,
Here you are, you have won in the end;
Here you are, you have won in the end.

Cinderella 1983: The Ugly Sisters (Jack Chissick and Howard Attfield) and the Broker's Men (Jonathan Howell and Jonathan Docker Drysdale)

It was during the run of that panto that Maria Heidler was shown once more the support and understanding of the theatre community.

Nearly a decade later and I'm back at Salisbury, in the stunning new Playhouse, and I'm back in Panto. This time it is *Dick Whittington*. I say I'm back - in fact I have by now made Salisbury my home and have my own house there. I was quite happy to play the Good Fairy lit by my special spot and to sing a challenge duet (*'There's a plot afoot'*) with my good friend, Alex Johnston. How was I to know that this Panto would prove, once again, the strength of the 'theatre family'? At this time my father was taken seriously ill and, as we all trundled off to the London train following the Christmas Eve matinee, everyone wished my family well. I managed to see my father in the hospital on Christmas Day, but had to return the next morning for the Boxing Day matinee. Everyone was so supportive during that next week. I remembered back to *Babes in the Wood* when Jill Graham played the Fairy. She had been going through a difficult time and, to cheer herself up, she taped some Christmas tinsel under her armpits. She really did perform sparkling magic that year and made us all laugh. I followed her example and it got me through the week.

My father died on the morning of Monday 31st December. I'd returned to London on Sunday (our day off) but had to get back to Salisbury for the New Year's Eve matinee. I was numb. I clearly remember walking into the Green Room; a couple of people were in there and Dominic Letts was pouring himself a coffee. I wasn't sure what to do, but I thought I'd better make an announcement because I wasn't sure how this shock would affect me. 'My father died this morning' I said to no-one in particular. 'I'm not sure how I'm feeling. You'd better keep an eye on me.' Dominic froze, then put the spoon down and walked out. 'Oh dear,' I thought, 'perhaps I shouldn't have said anything.' It was a difficult moment. It was as if my words just hung in the air searching for a resting place. Eventually someone spoke. Then, as suddenly as he had left, Dominic came back. He stood in front of me and put a glass of brandy in my hand. 'Drink that' he said. 'But I can't drink now, I've got a matinee,' I said. 'A sip won't hurt' he said, 'and take it into your dressing room and sip when you need it.' 'But I can't have alcohol backstage.' I said. 'It's OK' he said, 'I've cleared it with Alan [Alan Corkhill the Theatre Manager] and Stage Management. We'll look out for you.' Suddenly I knew I was going to be all right. I was back with my theatre family. I was safe. (To this day, I can't pour a cup of coffee without thinking of Dom and his kindness.) That is the strength and the power of being part of this wonderful profession. After the show that evening, at the 'walkdown', we traditionally held hands and joined with the audience singing 'Auld Lang Syne'. I nearly lost it at that moment, but I was held firmly by my actor buddies on either side and there, in the front, was the reason for it all - the audience. What an honour to be part of this world. How fortunate for me that I was nurtured by the good folks at Salisbury and by Henry Marshall's Pantomimes.[165]

In the 1985 *Babes in the Wood*, Lionel Guyett returned to the role of Robber Pete although he was the only member of the cast who was also in the earlier production. This turned out to be the last Henry Marshall pantomime at Salisbury, although it wasn't apparent to the cast at the time that this would be the case. It was also Lionel's last pantomime: 'That was when I decided I didn't want to do pantomime any more and I said goodbye at the last songsheet. I counted down the performances, the first time I did that.'[166] Jane Quy, meanwhile, had progressed to Fairy in what was her fifth *Babes in the Wood*, and was very impressed with herself for still being able to play the role en pointe. By this time, the long-term members of the company had got used to the new theatre, as Jane remembers: 'We all loved the old theatre, even though you had to go outside to get to SL, and you couldn't flush a loo without leaks everywhere. We dreaded going to the new one, but it was OK.' [167]

Jack Chissick was back as Dame too, and already beginning to develop Henry's scripts and add lines here and there, with the support of David Horlock who was directing. Jack remembers growling at Gary Blair as Fido and then, when asked what that was about, replying 'I speak doggerel' – a gag that Henry applauded. [168] When David Horlock took over as Artistic Director at Salisbury, he stopped using Henry Marshall's scripts after three years and began writing his own with Jack Chissick, although still very much in the traditional vein that Salisbury audiences had come to expect. Jack remembers it as a joyous time, cut short all too soon by the early and sudden death of David Horlock. [169] 'Our pantos were very moral' he explains, 'as well as being the world turned upside-down: that's what panto should be.' [170]

Henry Marshall's pantomimes were absolutely of their times and all the better for it: they represent a high point of repertory theatre achievement in the 1950s, 60s and 70s. If they did not quite work as well in the 1980s that may be as much to do with the changes in theatres and audiences as with anything in the scripts themselves. Lionel Guyett puts it this way:

> The pantomimes were of their age. Of their type, they were brilliant. They were tiny, they were tight and they were well directed. People think they know pantomime and they don't. I think the audiences after a while began to see that… the jokes were fairly old. I think Jack and David began to write their own and you needed a new influx of blood. [171]

In later years, the pantomimes at Salisbury began to change more radically and today they continue, although in a more modern vein and written by a range of authors; but there is still a pantomime at Salisbury Playhouse every December.

Scene 6
The Walk-Down

IN HIS 1981 book about pantomime, Derek Salberg admitted that there was something unique about repertory pantomime, even if it was very different to the style of show he had produced in Birmingham.

> Before the war there were only a handful [of repertory pantomimes]; they can now be counted in dozens, and many, such as Salisbury Playhouse, are... sold out before the opening performance. These pantomimes usually bear little or no resemblance to those of Harris, Wylie, the Littlers or Arnold, either in splendour or substance. Their general... pattern is to use either a specially written book or a standard one by say John Crocker, Henry Marshall or John Moffatt performed by the permanent or semi-permanent company with often the addition of local dancers... At comparatively small cost splendid results are achieved, the book is invariably beautifully acted and the actors for the most part enjoy the change from the more serious work, though on occasions some obviously begrudge every minute of it! [172]

He goes on to suggest that the repertory actors sometimes failed to cope with the demands of slapstick comic scenes as well as the more serious parts. This highlights one of the strengths of the Salisbury pantomimes: a repertory pantomime with comic expertise on the part of Oliver Gordon and others. Derek Salberg was also unconvinced that specially written numbers enhanced the show, and he kept to the commercial producer's belief in the need to insert current popular songs. Despite these reservations, it is interesting to note the high praise he has for this rival type of pantomime: they were, he said 'first class and intelligent… a huge improvement on the often indifferent pantomimes which were once to be seen in the now defunct theatres in many towns.' The Victorian diarist Leigh Hunt would have approved of Henry's pantomimes.

> He that says he does not like a pantomime, either says that he does not think, or is not so wise as he fancies himself. He should grow young again and get wiser.[173]

Roger Clissold died in 1998. Henry Marshall continued to advertise fencing and stage fighting lessons in *The Stage* until the late 1980s. He died on December 8th 2001 in Bath. Stephanie Cole in her *Stage* obituary of him wrote:

> Marshall was a great teacher, an eccentric who entertained while he taught and was much loved by those who worked with him. The continuing success

Roger Clissold

of the British Society of Fight Directors is a fitting memorial for a man who was passionate about the theatre and cared deeply about those working in it. He will be much missed by all who knew him.[174]

Reggie Salberg died on May 7th 2003 aged 87. He was, as Front of House Manager Mike Starke said, 'a manager respected and loved in equal measure throughout the theatrical world, with every justification.' Henry Marshall and Reggie Salberg were the last, with Oliver Gordon and Roger Clissold, of a breed of pantomime creators whose legacy will live on through the performances of those they trained, and those who saw and learned from the shows they produced.

Epilogue: The Harlequinade

THE HENRY MARSHALL pantomimes at Salisbury Playhouse may have come to an end in 1986 but their legacy lives on in so many ways: in current Dames that learned their craft at Salisbury like Chris Harris and Christopher Biggins; in the work of those directing pantomimes using knowledge acquired at Salisbury, like Richard Frost and Christopher Dunham; and in all those performers and creative personnel who have gone on to work in other areas but who have been touched, informed, enlightened and changed by the work of Henry Marshall, Oliver Gordon, Reginald Salberg and Roger Clissold.

Pantomime today is a different beast in many ways, but then pantomime is always changing. Henry Marshall's pantomimes are rooted strongly in the Victorian tradition of the Harlequinade, with its strong stories, stock characters, magical appearances and respect for tradition, with actors employed for their ability to play a role rather than as a name to bring in an audience. And Harlequinade, surprisingly, survives remarkably unchanged in Denmark of all places, at the Peacock Theatre at Tivoli, Copenhagen. In the summer of 2012 audiences could still see several of the surviving plays presented there.

The Unfortunate Suitor, for example, dates from 1855, but is by no means the oldest play still in the repertoire[175]. The characters are Columbine (Principal Girl), Harlequin (Principal Boy), Pierrot (a Clown), Cassander (an old man remarkably like Baron Hardup), a Suitor, a Customs Man, two quarreling Washerwomen (played by men), a barrel-organ man, a doctor and a fairy who at one point appears with other fairies in a tableau. Already, the similarities with Henry's pantomimes are clear.

Throughout the play, which is performed using mime and dance accompanied by a live orchestra, Harlequin uses magic to outwit the ridiculous suitor who wishes to marry the beautiful Columbine. The current theatre, built in 1874, is outdoors but with the stage under cover and fully equipped with all the traditional machinery of a wooden box theatre: traps (for people and costumes), sliding scenery and pyrotechnics.[176] There are no flies so tumblecloths are used alongside the sliding wing pieces. It takes five people to operate the peacock curtain so that the tail unfolds and the bird sinks out of sight; changing the sets during the performance, as happens very frequently, takes eight people in order that the changes, using traditional hemp lines, can happen in unison.

The performance begins with a loud tapping after which the peacock tail opens on the steeply-raked stage. In a prologue, Harlequin is given his magic powers by a mysterious wizard, whose book of spells rises in smoke through a trap. Leaving the forest behind, we find ourselves in a busy town, tumble-cloth and sliders providing an instant transition. Harlequin creates havoc with magic spells and his slapstick, the sound of which is provided by a stage hand operating a much larger pair of wooden blocks. Two washer-women played by men enter and although they do not play a large part in the action, they have much in common with the pantomime dame. Columbine's father Cassander, playing the Baron or Emperor role, is constantly outwitted with the help of a Doctor who carries extra large pantomime-size medical implements. The stories continues at a rapid pace, changing from forest to street to interiors, with fireworks, the sudden appearance of fairies and a supernatural tableau in front of a Greek temple.

At the end of the performance, when Harlequin has been united with Columbine and the suitor has been outwitted, Pierrot the clown in white face and costume comes forward and speaks to the audience. Still a much-loved and familiar figure in Denmark, Pierrot addresses his remarks in particular to the children as he asks them to thank the audience and performers and then raise three cheers for Tivoli – rejecting their first attempt, of course, as being not loud enough. To anyone brought up on traditional English pantomime, the whole event is remarkably familiar, and is to be recommended to any visitors to Copenhagen[177].

Like the Harlequin performers in the Prologue at Windsor stepping through the curtain from the past, or the Lupino family tumbling and appearing through traps, and current Danish performers at Tivoli, the Henry Marshall pantomimes at Salisbury were inexorably part of a noble and living tradition: the art of pantomime.

Notes

1   Clinton-Baddeley, V. C. (1963). *Some Pantomime Pedigrees*: p 7

2   Clinton-Baddeley, V. C. (1963). *Some Pantomime Pedigrees*: p 7

3   *The Stage*, 11th Nov 1887

4   *The Stage*, 3rd Jan 1895

5   *The Stage*, 26th Jan 1911

6   Sand, M. (1915) *The History of the Harlequinade*

7   See the Epilogue at the end of this book for more details

8   Clinton-Baddeley, V. C. (1963). *Some Pantomime Pedigrees*: pp 11, 12, 13

9   *The Stage*, 16th Nov 1944

10 *The Stage*, 26th Dec 1946

11 Transcribed in full as an appendix to this volume

12 Wilson, A. E. (1949). *The Story of Pantomime*. pp 120-121

13 *The Stage*, 9th Dec 1971

14 Email from Emma Battcock 27th Sep 2010

15 *The Stage*, 7th Oct 1937

16 *The Stage*, 29th Feb 1940

17 *The Stage*, 16th Nov 1944

18 See the Prologue

19 Counsell, J. (1963). *Counsell's Opinion*

20 Counsell, J. (1963). *Counsell's Opinion*.

21 Counsell, J. (1963). *Counsell's Opinion*

22 *The Stage*, 5th Aug 1937

23 *The Stage*, 30th Dec 1949

24 Transcribed in full in the appendices to this book

25 Interview with the author, 23rd Jan 2010

26 Interview with the author, 31st May 2012

27 Phone interview with the author, 20th July 2012

28 Interview with the author, 28th October 2010

29 Wisden, 1971

30 Salberg, D. (1981). *Once upon a pantomime.*

31 Programme, *Cinderella*, Salisbury Playhouse, 1983

32 Interview with the author, 26th Aug 2010

33 Interview with the author, 22nd Jan 2010

34 Interview with the author, 15th Jan 2011

35 Email to the author, 3rd Oct 2010

36 Email to the author, 5th Jan 2011

37 Interview with the author, 13th Dec 2009

38 Minutes of the Board of Directors, 22nd Nov 1955

39 The *Salisbury Times*, 30th Dec 1955

40 Email to the author, 15th April 2011

41 Interview with the author, 27th Sep 2010

42 Email to the author, 11th May 2011

43 *The Stage*, 3rd Jan 1957

44 Letter to the author, 17th Oct 2009

45 Emails to the author, 15th Oct to 4th Nov 2010

46 *Salisbury Times*, 28th Dec 1956

47 Email to the author, 13th June 2012

48 Email to the author, 26th Oct 2010

49 *Salisbury Times*, 27th Dec 1957

50 West, T. (2001). *A Moment Towards the End of the Play*

51 Biggins, C. (2008). *Just Biggins: My Story*

52 Interview with the author, 16th Aug 2010

53 *Salisbury Times*, 2nd Jan 1959

54 *Salisbury Times*, 2nd Jan 1959

55 Letter to the author, 17th Oct 2009

56 *Salisbury Times*, 1st Jan 1960

57 Minutes of the Board of Directors, 29th Jan 1960

58 *Salisbury Times*, 30th Dec 1960

59 Email to the author, 2nd Nov 2010

60 *Salisbury Times*, 30th Dec 1960

61 Clinton-Baddeley, V. C. (1963). *Some Pantomime Pedigrees*

62 Wilson, A. E. (1949). *The Story of Pantomime*

63 Interview with the author, 13th Dec 2009

64 Interview with the author, 28th Oct 2010

65 Email to the author, 3rd Oct 2010

66 Biggins, C. (2008) *Just Biggins: My Story*

67 Interview with the author, 16th Aug 2010

68 Interview with the author, 16th Aug 2010

69 Interview with the author, 16th Aug 2010

70 *Salisbury Times*, 28th Dec 1962

71 *Salisbury Times*, 27th Dec 1963

72 Letter to the author, 8th Oct 2010

73 Clinton-Baddeley, V. C. (1963). *Some Pantomime Pedigrees*. p 34, 36

74 Email to the author, 27th April 2012

75 Interview with the author, 16th Aug 2010

76 *Salisbury Times*, 27th Dec 1963

77 Interview with the author, 16th Aug 2010

78 Biggins, C. (2008) *Just Biggins: My Story*

79 Interview with the author, 7th Nov 2012

80 Interview with the author, 23rd Jan 2010

81 Email to the author, 3rd Oct 2010

82 Email to the author, 3rd Oct 2010

83 *Salisbury Times*, 1st Jan 1965

84 Interview with the author, 16th Aug 2010

85 Interview with the author, 16th Aug 2010

86 Interview with the author, 23rd Jan 2010

87 Interview with the author, 21st Oct 2009

88 Interview with the author, 1st Nov 2011

89 Letter to the author, 10th Feb 2010

90 Minutes of the Board of Directors, 15th Dec 1961

91 Interview with the author, 13th Dec 2009

91a Telephone interview with the author, 20th Aug 2012

92 Interview with the author, 13th May 2012

93 Email to the author, 3rd Oct 2010

94 *Salisbury Times*, 31st Dec 1965

95 Interview with the author, 22nd Jan 2010

96 Clinton-Baddeley, V. C. (1963). *Some Pantomime Pedigrees*. p 18

97 Interview with the author, 19th Oct 2010

98 Interview with the author, 28th Oct 2010

99 Email to the author, 10th May 2012

100 Interview with the author, 13th Dec 2009

101 Clinton-Baddeley, V. C. (1963). *Some Pantomime Pedigrees.* p 10

102 *Salisbury Times*, 29th Dec 1967

103 Email to the author, 24th Dec 2010

104 Interview with the author, 7th Nov 2010

105 Interview with the author, 15th Jan 2011

106 Interview with the author, 28th Oct 2010

107 Interview with the author, 26th July 2012

108 *Salisbury Times*, 27th Dec 1968

109 Email to the author, 3rd Oct 2010

110 Email to the author, 3rd Oct 2010

111 Email to the author, 16th Jan 2011

112 Interview with the author, 7th Nov 2010

113 Interview with the author, 16th Aug 2010

114 Interview with the author, 28th Oct 2010

115 *Salisbury Times*, 25th Dec 1970

116 Email to the author, 9th May 2012

117 Interview with the author, 16th Aug 2010

118 Interview with the author, 13th Dec 2009

119 Interview with the author, 25th Oct 2010

120 Email to the author, 20th Oct 2010

121 Email to the author, 16th Jan 2011

122 *The Stage*, 22nd Oct 1942

123 Email to the author, 26th Oct 2010

124 Interview with the author, 7th Nov 2010

125 Interview with the author, 26th Aug 2010

126 Interview with the author, 3rd May 2012

127 Interview with the author, 3rd May 2012

128 Interview with the author, 26th Aug 2010

129 *Salisbury Times*, 31st Dec 1971

130 *Salisbury Journal*, 31st Dec 1971

131 Letter to the author, 8th Oct 2010

132 Email to the author, 13th June 2012

133 *Salisbury Times*, 29th Dec 1972

134 Sadly, David Sadgrove later died following a cycling accident

135 *Salisbury Times*, 29th Dec 1972

136 Email to the author, 7th May 2012

137 Interview with the author, 26th July 2012

138 Interview with the author, 26th Aug 2010

139 Email to the author, 5th Jan 2011

140 Interview with the author, 26th July 2012

141 Interview with the author, 3rd May 2012

142 Email to the author, 5th Jan 2011

143 Interview with the author, 3rd May 2012

144 Interview with the author, 3rd May 2012

145 Interview with the author, 7th Nov 2010

146 Interview with the author, 28th Oct 2010

147 Interview with the author, 3rd May 2012

148 Interview with the author, 3rd May 2012

149 Email to the author, 5th Jan 2011

150 Interview with the author, 13th

May 2012

151 Interview with the author, 25th Oct 2010

152 Interview with the author, 3rd May 2012

153 Interview with the author, 3rd May 2012

154 Email to the author, 9th May 2012

155 Interview with the author, 3rd May 2012

156 Email to the author, 7th May 2012

157 Interview with the author, 3rd May 2012

158 Interview with the author, 15th Jan 2011

159 Interview with the author, 3rd May 2012

160 Interview with the author, 3rd May 2012

161 Email to the author, 8th May 2012

162 Letter to the author, 1st June 2012

163 Email to the author, 8th May 2012

164 Email to the author, 8th May 2012

165 Email to the author, 5th Jan 2011

166 Interview with the author, 15th Jan 2011

167 Interview with the author, 25th Oct 2010

168 Phone interview with the author, 20th July 2012

169 David Horlock died in a road accident in 1990

170 Phone interview with the author, 20th July 2012

171 Interview with the author, 15th Jan 2011

172 Salberg, D. (1981). *Once Upon a Pantomime.*

173 Hunt, L. (1828). *The Companion: A Miscellany for the Fields and Fireside*

174 *The Stage,* 20th Dec 2001

175 This description is of a performance on 19th May 2012

176 Ahrends, A. & Lyding, H. (2008). *The Pantomime Theatre.*

177 The pantomime plays are performed in the summer season only and not at other times when Tivoli is open, and are interspersed with ballet performances. The schedule of perfomances is available at www.tivoli.dk

Bibliography

Bavin J. (1976) *Heart of the City: The story of Salisbury Playhouse.* Salisbury: Salisbury Playhouse

Ahrends, A. & Lyding, H. (trans. P. Starbird). (2008) *The Pantomime Theatre – Life behind the peacock curtain in Tivoli.* Copenhagen: Forlaget Vankunsten

Biggins C. (2008) *Just Biggins: My Story.* London: John Blake

Clinton-Baddeley, V. C. (1963) *Some Pantomime Pedigrees.* London: Society for Theatre Research

Cole S. (1999) *A Passionate Life.* London: Hodder & Stoughton

Counsell J. (1963) *Counsell's Opinion.* London: Barrie & Rockliff

Frow G. (1985) *Oh Yes It Is: A history of pantomime.* UK: BBC/Crown Publications

Harris C. (2000) *The Alphabet of Pantomime.* UK: Chris Harris Publications

Harris K. (1998) *Exit Through the Fireplace: The great days of rep.* London: John Murray

Harris P. (1996) *The Pantomime Book.* UK: Peter Owen

Hunt, L. (1828). *The Companion: A Miscellany for the Fields and Fire-Side.* London: Hunt & Clarke

Lathan P. (2004) *It's Behind You: The story of panto.* UK: New Holland Publishers

Salberg D. (1980) *Ring down the curtain.* Luton: Cortney Publications

Salberg D. (1981) *Once upon a pantomime.* Luton: Cortney Publications

Salberg D. (1981) *My love affair with a theatre.* Luton: Cortney Publications

Sand, M. (1915) *The History of the Harlequinade.* 2 vols. London: Martin Secker

Stott A. M. (2009) *The Pantomime Life of Joseph Grimaldi.* Edinburgh: Canongate

Sullivan J. (2011) *The Politics of Pantomime.* Hatfield: University of Hertfordshire Press

Taylor M. (2007) *British Pantomime Performance.* Bristol: Intellect Books

West T. (2001) *A Moment Towards the End of the Play.* London: Nick Hern Books

Wilson A. E. (1946) *Pantomime Pageant.* London: Stanley Paul

Wilson A. E. (1949) *The Story of Pantomime.* London: Home and Van Thal

The Stage Archives

The Theatre Collection, University of Bristol (Henry Marshall Collection)

The British Library (Lord Chamberlain's Collection)

Appendix I: Cast lists
1955-1985

1955-1956
Robinson Crusoe
Book by Henry Marshall with additional dialogue and lyrics by Daniel Pettiward

Robinson Crusoe	Doreen Andrew
Mrs Crusoe	John Graham
Billy Crusoe	Ronald Harwood
Will Atkins	Kenneth Keeling
Bosun of the Saucy Sal	Brian Kent
Mate of the Saucy Sal	Francis Hall
Polly Perkins	Helen Jessop
Spirit of the Sea	Harriet Forbes
Man Friday	Frederick Peisley
Father Neptune	Kim Grant
Witch Doctor	Alison Wide

Sailors citizens of Hull savages etc:
Richard Hughes Jacqueline Cole Diana Coupe Regina Frankel Lily Freret Tina
      Matthews Alison Wide
Snake dance by Helen Jessop

Orchestra under the direction of	Sydney Carmen
Costumes designed by	Kate Servian
Choreography by	Anne Wide
Settings designed by	Jon Scoffield
Built by	Roberto Petrarca
The production directed by	John Barron

1956-1957
Babes in the Wood
Book and original music by Henry Marshall

Additional lyrics by Daniel Pettiward and Sydney Carmen

Robin Hood	Josephine Tewson
Maid Marian	Hermoine Gregory
The Sheriff of Nottingham	Ian Mullins
Peter his nephew	Michael Barnwell
Pauline his niece	Margaret Osborne
Dame Trot	Brian Kent
Ken a bad robber	Kenneth Firth
Len a not very bad robber	Leonard Rossiter
Will Scarlett	Geraldine Hagan
Friar Tuck	Sidney Burchall
Johnny Green	Frederick Peisley
Fairy Starlight	Janet Hargreaves
King Richard Coeur de Lion	Angus Mackay
Creepy (a gnome)	Frederick Peisley
Angostura	Geraldine Hagan

Men at arms crusaders Merry Men villagers etc
Richard Vaughan Angus Mackay Diana Fyfe Denyse Fox Diana Goodwin
Elizabeth Hearn Janet Lewis Thelma Marshall

The pantomime produced by	Terence Dudley
Dances and Ensembles arranged by	Margery Kent
Settings designed by	Jon Scoffield
Built in the theatre workshops by	Roberto Petrarca
Costumes by	Kate Servian
Music under the direction of	Sydney Carmen

1957-1958
Aladdin and his wonderful Lamp

Aladdin	Helen Dorward
Widow Twankey (his mother)	Ronald Magill
Abanazar	Ian Mullins
The Emperor of China	Sidney Burchall
Princess Badroulbadour	Elizabeth Howe
So-Shy (her maid)	Adrienne Stannard
The Grand Vizier	Brian Kent
Wishee-Washee	Oliver Gordon
Hi-Fi (a policeman)	Henry Manning
A Guard	Martin Fowler
Geni of the Ring	Zeph Gladstone

Geni of the Lamp	Timothy West
Citizens Arabian Dancers etc	

Carlotta Barrow Gillian Gale Dorothy Kingsmill Janet Lewis Judith Perkins
    Christine Rayner

The pantomime produced by	Oliver Gordon
Dances and Ensembles arranged by	Margery Field
Settings designed and painted by	Jean Adams
Built in the theatre workshops by	Roberto Petrarca
Costumes by	Kate Servian and Joan Salberg
Music under the direction of	Sidney Carmen

1958-1959
Cinderella

Fairy Godmother	Nancie Herrod
Hydro	Ian Mullins
Olive (Cinderella's sisters)	Ronald Magill
Baron Hardup	Geoffrey Lumsden
Cinderella	Mary Benning
Dandini	Helen Dorward
Prince Charming	Sonia Graham
Buttons	Graham Armitage
Broker's Man	Oliver Gordon
Jack Frost	Derek Smee
Major Domo	Timothy West
Minor Domo	Derek Smee
Domo Minimus	Martin Lisemore
Huntsmen Courtiers Villagers etc	

Ann Clark Tessa Bremmer Mary Farrer Penny Hind Ann Naylor Ann Robinson
    Valerie Seaman

Ponies by	Douglas George's Stables
The Pantomime produced by	Oliver Gordon
Dances & Ensembles arranged by	Jacqueline Boyer
Settings designed and painted by	Stanley Rixon
Built in the theatre workshops by	Roberto Petrarca
Costumes by	Kate Servian and Joan Salberg
Music under the direction of	Sidney Carmen

1959-1960
Dick Whittington and his Cat
Words and music by Henry Marshall

Town Crier	Philip Madoc
Tiddles (the Cat)	Nancie Herrod
Alice Fitzwarren	Doreen Metcalfe
Sarah (the Cook)	Ronald Magill
Alderman Fitzwarren	Michael Alexander
Idle Jack	Oliver Gordon
Dick Whittington	Josephine Tewson
Captain (of the good ship Unicorn)	Patrick Cavanagh
Mate	Raymond Bowers
King Rat	Ian Mullins
Good Fairy	Fredrica Nevill
Vizier	Patrick Kavanagh
Sultan of Morocco	Philip Madoc
Whirling Dervish	Michael Cleveland

Apprentices Townspeople Slaves etc
Avril Bebbington Elizabeth Downes Mary Farrer Joy Hamlett Celia Holmes and
Marjorie Smith

The Pantomime produced by	Oliver Gordon
Dances & Ensembles arranged by	Rosemary Rogers
The settings designed & painted by	Stanley Rixon
Built in the theatre workshop by	David Morrison
Costumes by	Joan Salberg
Additional costumes by	Yvonne Dunn
Music under the direction of	Sidney Carmen

1960-1961
Jack and the Beanstalk
Words and music by Henry Marshall

Slosh	Bryon O'Leary
Wallop (the King's Bailiffs)	Victor Carin
The King's Chamberlain	Ronald Magill
Dame Durden	Christopher Benjamin
Jack (her son)	Nancie Herrod
Isabel	Penelope Allen
Silly Sammy	Oliver Gordon
Tallulah (the Cow)	Patricia Brake & Elizabeth Harding

King Bertram	Raymond Bowers
Good Fairy	Cynthia Taylor
Miss Blood	Patricia Brake
Giant Thunderclub	Peter Cregeen
Villagers etc	

Mary Chirgwin David Monico David Daker Roger Stevens Delia Dermer
        Rosemary Gay Gay Holden Jennifer Hughes Lynne Robinson June Mitchell

Principal Dancer	Fiona McKean
The pantomime produced by	Oliver Gordon
Choreography by	Fiona McKean
The settings designed & painted by	Stanley Rixon
Built in the theatre workshops by	David Morrison
Music under the direction of	Reg Baker

1961-1962
Robinson Crusoe
Words and original music by Henry Marshall

Squeaky	Edmund Coulter
One Eye	David Daker
Barmy	Hugh Walters
Gash (Pirates)	Jolyon Booth
Will Atkins	Christopher Benjamin
Spirit of the Sea	Mary Chirgwin
Polly Perkins	Jennifer McNae
Robinson Crusoe	Beth Boyd
'Erb (Bow Street Runners)	David Monico
Montmorency	Tim Preece
Billy Crusoe	Oliver Gordon
Mrs Crusoe	Tony Steedman
King Neptune	Jolyon Booth
Nellie the Elephant	David Duke & Tim Preece
Witch Doctor	Fiona McKean
Cannibal King	Jolyon Booth
Man Friday	David Monico
Ermintrude the monkey	Hugh Walters
Citizens of Hull Sailors Animals Cannibals etc	

Isabel Brown Sally Cowdy Rosemary Gay Barbara Nichols Fay Werner Jenny
        Wright Richard Valentine Desmond O'Donovan David Duke

Principal Dancer	Fiona McKean

The pantomime produced by	Oliver Gordon
Choreography by	Fiona McKean
The scenery designed & painted by	Stanley Rixon
Animals designed and made by	Deirdre Deering assisted by Ruth
Grant	
Music under the direction of	Reg Baker

1962-1963
Robin Hood and the Babes in the Wood
Words and original music by Henry Marshall

Prince John	Hugh Walters
Robin Hood	Jill Graham
Will Scarlet	Christopher Dunham
Friar Tuck	Langton Jones
Little John	Graham Clayton Adams
The Sheriff of Nottingham	Jolyon Booth
Tina	Tina Spooner
Judy (The Babes)	Judy Spooner
Maid Marian	Ann Curthoys
Nurse Enos	June Watson
Willie Whiskers	Hugh Walters
Scruffy (the Babes' dog)	Fiona McKean
Dave	David Daker
Ollie (the Robbers)	Oliver Gordon
The Good Fairy	Lynn Farleigh
A Pilgrim	Anthony Healey
Captain of the Men at Arms	John Luckham

Outlaws Pupils Citizens Men at Arms Birds etc
Christopher Stephens Alan Daniel Jane Quy Marilyn Taylersen Rosemary Gay
      Anne Robinson Jane Robinson Vivien Roberts Cherylin Beswick
Tina and Judy Spooner are pupils of the Bellairs School of Dancing Guildford

The pantomime produced by	Oliver Gordon
Choreography by	Fiona McKean
The scenery designed & painted by	Stanley Rixon
Assisted by	Alan Daniel
Built in the theatre workshops by	John Scutt
Costumes designed and made by	Blanche Denton
Animals bird ballet and carnival heads designed and made by Deirdre Deering	
Assisted by	Ruth Grant
Music under the direction of	Reg Baker

1963-1964
Aladdin
Words and original music by Henry Marshall

Aladdin	Brigit Forsyth
Hi-Tee	Christopher Dunham
Lo-Pong (Chinese Constabulary)	June Watson
Grand Vizier	Lisle Jones
Mrs Twankey (Aladdin's mother)	Donald Pelmear
Abdulla (slave to Abanazer)	Oliver Gordon
Esmeralda the camel	Steven Mountstevens and Richard Gregson
Abanazer	Frank Barrie
Princess Baldroulbadour	Gillian Royale
Emperor of China	David Daker
Geni of the Ring	Joanna Brookes
Geni of the Lamp	Jonathan Newth

Citizens Slaves Guards etc
Eileen Bates Rosemary Bennion Jessica Benton Phillipa Dale Alan Daniel
Rosemary Gay Nicholas McArdle Rita Rhodes David Taylor

The pantomime produced by	Oliver Gordon
Choreography by	Felicity Gray
The scenery designed & painted by	Stanley Rixon
Assisted by	Alan Daniel
Built in the theatre workshops by	John Scutt
Costumes designed by	Audrey Bagot
And made by	Jill Annell
The Camel and the Dragon designed and made by Deirdre Deering	
Assisted by	Ruth Grant
At the Hammond Organ	Jimmy Berry
Percussion	David Nicoll

1964-1965
Cinderella
Words and original music by Henry Marshall

The Fox	Susan Salomon
John Peel	Desmond Gill
Dandini	Stephanie Cole
Mimi	David Daker

Fifi	Oliver Gordon
Prince Charming	Brigit Forsyth
Buttons	Christopher Dunham
Cinderella	Marilyn Taylerson
Hire	Michael Poole
Purchase (Brokers Men)	David Ryall
Fairy Godmother	Hilary Voisey
Fairy Cobbler	Christian Rodskjaer
Major Domo	Desmond Gill
Minor Domo	Christian Rodskjaer

Members of the Hunt Gentlemen of the Bodyguard Courtiers Villagers etc
Suzanne Beaumont Jessica Benton Kathleen Gardner Rita Rhodes Susan Salomon
Christian Rodskjaer Andrew Spedding

Principal Dancer	Susan Salomon
Cinderella's ponies trained by	Mrs Kathleen Grasby
The pantomime produced by	Oliver Gordon
Choreography by	Felicity Gray
The scenery designed & painted by	Stanley Rixon
Built in the theatre workshops by	John Scutt
Costumes designed and made by	Barbara Wilson
Ballroom costumes by	Judy Lloyd-Rogers
At the organ	Marie Phillips
Percussion	Jimmy Clarke

1965-1966
Dick Whittington and his Cat
Words and original music by Henry Marshall

Constable	Ralph Watson
Blackbeard	Michael Poole
Jack Stevens	Chris Harris
Dick Whittington	Carolyn Moody
Tomasina the cat	Jane Quy
Lady Fitzwarren	Oliver Gordon
Sir John Fitzwarren	Raymond Bowers
Alice Fitzwarren	Olivia Breeze
Margery the cook	Stephanie Cole
Landlord	Michael Stroud
Gypsy	Jenny Crews
Davy Jones	Ralph Watson
Vizier	Michael Stroud

Empress of Morocco	Stephanie Cole
King Rat	Jenny Crews
King Richard II	Roger Clissold

Apprentices Citizens Seamen Slaves and Rats
Chris Biggins Jessica Benton Elva Buck Richard Gregson Jenny Hall Josephine
    Johns Lesley Mould John Pickett Diana Warren

The pantomime produced by	Oliver Gordon
Choreography by	Felicity Gray
The scenery designed & painted by	Stanley Rixon
Built in the theatre workshops by	John Scutt
Original costumes	Barbara Wilson
Assisted by	Susan Starke
Other costumes by courtesy of the Alexandra Theatre Birmingham	
At the organ	Marie Phillips
Percussion	Andrew Spedding

1966-1967
Jack and the Beanstalk
Words and original music by Henry Marshall

Dame Durden	Stephanie Cole
Chamberlain	Michael Stroud
Jonathan	David Gooderson
Jenny Wren	Jessica Benton
Jack	Chris Harris
Tallulah	Alison Brown & Lynda Johns
Princess Isabel	Elisa Mitchell
Inspector Migraine	Raymond Bowers
PC Boggins	Christopher Biggins
Queen Iodine of Cornwall	Oliver Gordon
A Little Boy	Diana Warren
Abracadabra (a wicked wizard)	Howard Southern
The Fairy	Vivien Heilbron
Giant Thunderclub	John Swindells
Principal Dancer	Jessica Benton

Villagers Witches etc
Alison Brown Elizabeth Hardwick Lynda Johns Diana Warren Judy Booty Jemima
    Brignall Jenny Hall Peter Kellet Camilla Lumsden Paul Taylor Charles
    Waite Sonia Woolley

The pantomime produced by	Oliver Gordon
Choreographer & Assistant to the Producer	Felicity Gray

The scenery designed & painted by	Stanley Rixon
Built in the theatre workshops by	John Scutt
Costumes designed by	Barbara Wilson
And made in the theatre wardrobe	
Music under the direction of	Marie Phillips (organ)
Pianist	Suzanne Peveril
Percussion	Brian Robins
Guitar Brian Protheroe	

1967-1968
Robinson Crusoe
Words and original music by Henry Marshall

Polly Perkins	Joyce Rae
Beanpole	Roger Forbes
Bosun	David Gooderson
Barmy	Peter May
One-Eye	Frank Ellis
Robinson Crusoe	Norman Comer
Elisha Morgan	Knight Mantell
Billy Crusoe	Lionel Guyett
Will Atkins	James Tomlinson
Mrs Crusoe	Oliver Gordon
King Neptune	Michael Stroud
Miles the Crocodile	Roger Clissold
Nellie the Elephant	David Gooderson
	Roger Forbes
King Kong	Paul Haley
Witch Doctor	Alison Brown
Cannibal King	Michael Stroud
Man Friday	Howard Southern
Ermintrude the Monkey	Elaine Donnelly
Captain Woodes Rogers	Paul Haley
Citizens of Hull Sailors Cannibals	

Jane Breton Alison Brown Jenny Crews Jenny Hall Lynda Johns Paula Lansley
    Ruth Lewis Jennifer Pottage Sonia Woolley Paul Haley Ross Jennings
    Knight Mantell Jonathan Wright Miller David Weeks

The pantomime produced by	Oliver Gordon
Choreographer & Assistant to the Producer	Felicity Gray
Fights arranged by	Henry Marshall
Music under the direction of	Marie Phillips (organ)

Pianist	Stephen Banning
Costumes designed and made by	Barbara Wilson
Scenery designed and painted by	Stanley Rixon
Built in the theatre workshops by	John Scutt

1968-1969
Babes in the Wood
Word and original music by Henry Marshall

Prince John	Ross Jennings
Robin Hood	Ben Aris
Will Scarlet	Neil McLauchlan
Friar Tuck	Roger Hume
Little John	Cyril Appleton
The Sheriff of Nottingham	Knight Mantell
Tina	Anne Preus
Judy (The Babes)	Jane Quy
Maid Marian	Christine Edmonds
Willy Whiskers	Frank Ellis
Daisy Dimple	Oliver Gordon
Fido	Jennie Newport
Jim	James Tomlinson
Pete (The Robbers)	Peter Robert Scott
Angostura	Judith Paris
The Fairy	Sonia Woolley
The Herald	Christopher Scott
King Richard	Roger Clissold
Captain of the Guard	Ross Jennings

Outlaws Citizens Schoolchildren
David Beames Graham Davey Philip Reavey Christopher Scott Richard Wilkinson
Candace O'Connor Jennifer Pottage Tara Soppet Isobel Stuart

The pantomime produced by	Oliver Gordon
Choreographer	Judith Paris
Fights arranged by	Henry Marshall
Music under the direction of	Marie Phillips (organ)
Pianist	Suzanne Peveril
Percussion	Stephen Banning
Costumes designed and made by	Barbara Wilson
Additional costumes	Alexandra Theatre Birmingham
Scenery designed by	John Howden
Painted by	Maureen Ardren and John Howden

Built in theatre workshops by   John Scutt and Philip Reavey
Animals designed and made by   John Bartlett

1969-1970
Aladdin
Words and original music by Henry Marshall

Aladdin	Mark Christon
Hi-Tee	Robert Whelan
Lo-Pong (Chinese Policemen)	Frank Ellis
Grand Vizier	Christopher Dunham
Widow Twankey	Oliver Gordon
Wishee-Washee	Peter Robert Scott
Fatima	Charmian May
Esmerelda the Camel	Bernard Krichefski
	Charles Madge
Abanzar	Roger Hume
Princess Badroulbadour	Isobel Stuart
Soraya	Anne Preus
The Emperor of China	Robert Sessions
The Geni of the Ring	Sarah Taunton
The Geni of the Lamp	Cyril Appleton

Citizens slaves guards etc:
Philippa Eden Sally Muggeridge Gillian Rhind Jean Watson Jean Woollard Nick
  Greenbury Ian McNeice Ian Pool Steven St John

Directed by	Oliver Gordon
Dances and ensembles by	Christopher Dunham
Fights arranged by	Henry Marshall
Music under the direction of	Marie Phillips (organ)
Pianist	Jonathan King
Percussion	Stephen Banning
Costumes designed and made by	Barbara Wilson
Scenery designed by	Michael Seirton
Painted by	Michael Seirton and Philippa Eden
Built in theatre workshops by	John Scutt and James Bolton
Camel designed and made by	John Bartlett

1970-1971
Cinderella
Words and original music by Henry Marshall

Cinderella	Heather Bell
Fifi	Michael Stroud
Mimi	Roger Hume
Prince Charming	Tim Meats
Dandini	Elwyn Johnson
Buttons	Peter Robert Scott
Hire	Steven St John
Purchase (Broker's Men)	Michael Sanderson
Fairy Godmother	Christine Edmonds
John Peel	Christopher Ravenscroft
The Fox	Sylvia Carson
The Vicar	Ian McNiece
Major Domo	Christopher Ravenscroft

Members of the Hunt Courtiers

Sylvia Carson Gil Osborne Richard Derrington John Fleming Charles Madge Ian
McNeice Richard Perkins

Direction and Choreography by	Christopher Dunham
Fencing scene arranged by	Henry Marshall
Cinderella's Ponies trained by	Douglas George
Music under the direction of	Marie Phillips (organ)
Pianist	Jonathan King
Percussion	Stephen Banning
Costumes designed and made by	Barbara Wilson
Assisted by	Angela Wyatt
Scenery designed by	Michael Seirton
Painted by	Michael Seirton and Philippa Eden
Built in theatre workshops by	John Scutt and James Bolton

1971-1972
Dick Whittington and his Cat
Words and original music by Henry Marshall

Constable	Michael Sanderson
Blackbeard	Tim Meats
Jack Stevens	Richard Derrington
Dick Whittington	Elwyn Johnson
Tomasina the cat	Penelope Nice
Lady Fitzwarren	Derek Pollitt
Sir John Fitzwarren	Michael Stroud
Alice Fitzwarren	Marcia King
Margery the cook	Jill Graham

Landlord	Stephen Mallatratt
Ship's Mate	John Golder
Davy Jones	Richard Frost
Vizier	John Golder
Sultan of Morocco	Michael Sanderson
King Rat	Brian Honeyball
King Richard II	Richard Frost
Citizens	Helen Boggis Diana Waller
Directed by	Roger Clissold
Choreography by	Marcia King
Fights arranged by	Henry Marshall
Music under the direction of	Marie Phillips (organ)
Pianist	Christopher Littlewood
Percussion	Derek Brook
Costumes designed and made by	Barbara Wilson
Assisted by	Jane Quy and Lynn Creasey
Scenery designed by	Neville Dewis
Painted by	Neville Dewis and Margaret Meats
Built in theatre workshops by	John Scott and Stephen Wheeler

1972-1973
Jack and the Beanstalk
Words and original music by Henry Marshall

Jack	Brian Honeyball
Princess Isabel	Rosamund Shelley
Dame Durden	Geoffrey Brightman
King Cuthbert	Gilbert Wynne
PC Rafter	David Beames
Lord Chamberlain	Frank Ellis
Simon	David Grout
Abracadabra	Richard Frost
Fairy	Liz Moscrop
Giant Thunderclub	David Sadgrove
Tallulah the cow	Jenny Burke
	Amanda Boxer
Jenny Wren	Christine Absalom
Kitty	Penny Jones
Bobby	Robert Richards
Amy	Sara Coward

Directed by	Roger Clissold
Choreography by	Liz Moscrop
Music under the direction of	Christopher Littlewood (piano)
Drummer	Derek Brook
Bass Guitar	Graham Beazley
Costumes designed and made by	Barbara Wilson
Assisted by	Judith Hackett
Scenery designed by	Neville Dewis
Fight directed by	Henry Marshall

1973-1974
Robinson Crusoe
Words and original music by Henry Marshall

Polly Perkins	Jill Baker
Bosun	David Sadgrove
Barmy	David Beames
Beanpole	Lloyd Johnston
One-Eye	David Grout
Will Atkins	Lee Donald
Robinson Crusoe	Neil Phillips
Elisha Morgan an old seaman	Adrian Reynolds
'Erb	Peter Clark
Montmorency (Bow St Runners)	Graham Richards
Billy Crusoe	Michael Tudor Barnes
Mrs Crusoe	Geoffrey Brightman
King Neptune	Adrian Reynolds
Ermintrude the monkey	Maria Heidler
Miles the crocodile	Peter Clark
Nellie the elephant	David Sadgrove
	Lloyd Johnston
Witch Doctor	Jenny Burke
Cannibal King	Adrian Reynolds
Man Friday	Frank Ellis
Speciality Dancers	Penny Jones
	Marcia King
	Anne Rosenfeld
Directed by	Roger Clissold
Choreography by	Marcia King
Scenery designed by	Neville Dewis
Costumes designed by	Barbara Wilson

Lighting designed by	Stanley Osborne White
Music under the direction of	Christopher Littlewood (piano)
Drummer	Derek Brook
Fights directed by	Henry Marshall

1974-1975
Babes in the Wood
Words and original music by Henry Marshall
Additional songs by Rex Walford

The Sheriff of Nottingham	Jonathan Fryer
Robin Hood	Roger Leach
Will Scarlett	David Grout
Friar Tuck	Lee Donald
Little John	Daniel Gerroll
Tina	Anne Rosenfeld
Judy (the Babes)	Jane Quy
Maid Marian	Lally Percy
Willie Whiskers	Adrian Reynolds
Daisy Dimple	Roger Heathcott
Fido	Maria Heidler
Jim	Alex Johnston
Pete (the Robbers)	Derek Crewe
The Fairy	Jill Graham
King Richard	Jeffery Perry
Speciality dancers	Catherine Lock Tricia Thorns
	Patience Tomlinson

Directed by	Roger Clissold
Choreography by	Jill Graham
Scenery designed by	Neville Dewis
Scenery built by	John Scutt
Costumes designed by	Barbara Wilson
Lighting designed by	Alan O'Toole
Music under the direction of	Christopher Littlewood (piano)
Drummer	Derek Brook
Fights directed by	Henry Marshall

1975-1976
Aladdin
Words and original music by Henry Marshall

Aladdin	Jeffery Perry
Hi-Tee	Stephen Boswell
Lo-Pong (Police)	Jill Graham
The Vizier	James Charlton
Mrs Twankey	Knight Mantell
Wishee-Washee	Derek Crewe
Abanazer the African magician	Roger Leach
Esmeralda the camel	Michael Ames
	Christopher Reeks
Princess Badroulbadour	Maria Heidler
Soraya her slave	Mary Keegan
The Emperor	Alex Johnston
Geni of the Ring	Adrian Reynolds
Geni of the Lamp	Graham Sinclair
Citizens slaves jewels etc	

Sally Ann Goodman Maya Kemp Jane Quy Patience Tomlinson & members of the
company

Directed by	Roger Clissold
Choreography by	Olivia Breeze
Scenery designed by	Neville Dewis
Scenery built by	John Scutt
Costumes designed by	Barbara Wilson
Lighting designed by	John Beecroft
Music under the direction of	Christopher Littlewood (piano)
Drummer	Derek Brook
Guitarist	Myke Reid
Fights arranged by	Henry Marshall

1976-1977
Cinderella
Words and original music by Henry Marshall

Cinderella	Jane Argyle
Fifi	Brian Ellis
Mimi	John Branwell
Prince Charming	Elwyn Johnson
Dandini	David Shaughnessy
Buttons	Derek Crewe
Hire	Graham Sinclair
Purchase	Lionel Guyett
Fairy Godmother	Jill Graham

John Peel/Major Domo	Graeme Malcolm
Buttons' Fairy	Jane Quy
The Fox	Lionel Guyett

Members of the Hunt Courtiers etc:
Helena Breck Richard Clews Brian Cutler Mary Keegan Graeme Malcolm Neil
    Martin Jane Quy Patience Tomlinson Rebecca Wright
Musicians (Lynx): Steve Harris / Chris Littlewood / Myke Reid / Rob Wilford

Directed by	Roger Clissold
Musical Direction by	Christopher Littlewood
Choreography by	Paul Mead
Scenery designed by	Neville Dewis
Costume designed by	Barbara Wilson
Lighting designed by	Kevin Flynn
Fencing arranged by	Henry Marshall
Cinderella's coach and all scenery built by	John Scutt

1977-1978
Dick Whittington
Book by Henry Marshall
Music and Lyrics by Christopher Littlewood

Town Crier	James Wardroper
Tiddles the Cat	Liz Moscrop
Butcher	Clive Hornby
Alice Fitzwarren	Helena Breck
Sarah the Cook	Derek Crewe
Alderman Fitzwarren	Gilbert Wynne
Idle Jack	Lionel Guyett
Dick Whittington	Simon Shepherd
Captain	Roger Leach
Mate	Richard Clews
King Rat	Alex Johnston
Good Fairy	Mary Keegan
Vizier	Donald Maciver
Sultan of Morocco	Roger Leach
Whirling Dervish	James Wardroper
King Richard	Richard Clews

Citizens Sailors Dervishes Concubines etc
Amanda Bell Selina Cadell Mary Keegan Jane Quy Richard Clews Clive Hornby
    Alex Johnston Roger Leach Donald Maciver James Wardroper

The Musicians
Keyboards	Christopher Littlewood
Percussion	Derek Brook
Bass	Steve Harris
Directed by	David Gilmore
Musical Direction by	Christopher Littlewood
Choreography by	Liz Moscrop
Scenery designed by	Neville Dewis and Joan Wadge
Costumes designed by	Barbara Wilson
Lighting designed by	Kevin Flynn
Scenery built by	John Scutt

1978-1979
Mother Goose
Book by Henry Marshall
Music and Lyrics by Christopher Littlewood

Demon Discontent	Alex Johnston
Fairy Goodheart	Christine Bishop
Colin the Squire's son	Peter Birch
Jill Mother Goose's daughter	Monique de Sain
Dora a Country Girl	Catherine Owen
Jack Mother Goose's son	Edward Arthur
Mother Goose	Derek Crewe
1st cyclist	Berny Richards
2nd cyclist	Sam Naylor
Priscilla the Goose	Maya Kemp
Squire Bugle	Brian Tully
The Laird of Borderland	Ray Mariner
Policeman	Charles Baillie
The King of Gooseland	Ray Mariner
Villagers dancers etc	

Gillian Barber Lynette Edwards Marcia Gresham Ellie Haddington

The action takes place many years ago near Salisbury and in Gooseland
Keyboards	Christopher Littlewood
Percussion	Derek Brook
Bass	Steve Harris
Directed by	Roger Clissold
Musical Direction by	Christopher Littlewood
Choreography by	Sam Naylor

Scenery designed by	Neville Dewis
Costumes designed by	Barbara Wilson
Lighting designed by	Kevin Flynn

1979-1980
Puss in Boots
Book by Henry Marshall
Music and Lyrics by Christopher Littlewood

Sid	Stephen Hattersley
Simon) the Miller's sons	Lionel Guyett
Charles	William Relton
Princess Rosamund	Gillian Bevan
Puss	Liz Moscrop
Archibald a Flunkey	Mark Perry
King Rumtytum III	Geoffrey Brightman
Queen Bubblegum	John Branwell
Hey Presto	Marc Sinden
The Cobbler	Trevor Nichols
Good Fairy	Lynette Edwards
Mr Rumble Grumble an Ogre	Trevor Nichols

Villagers Courtiers Guards Animals:
Lynn Clayton Leigh Conroy Rupert Farley Susan Seager Jonathan Warren

Keyboards	Christopher Littlewood
Percussion	Derek Brook
Bass	Steve Harris
Directed by	Roger Clissold
Musical direction by	Christopher Littlewood
Choreography by	Rae Landor
Scenery designed by	Richard Marks
Scenery built by	John Scutt
Costumes designed by	Barbara Wilson
Lighting designed by	Kevin Flynn

1980-1981
Babes in the Wood
Book by Henry Marshall
Music and Lyrics by Christopher Littlewood

The Sheriff of Nottingham	Michael Henry

Robin Hood	Keith Woodhams
Will Scarlet	Andrew Branch
Friar Tuck	Mark Scrimshaw
Little John	Troy Foster
Tina	Karen McMullen
Judy) the Babes	Marion Owen-Smith
Maid Marian	Lyndsey Durant
Willie Whiskers	Alex Johnston
Daisy Dimple	Peter Robert Scott
Fido	Richard Platt
Jim	Michael St John
Pete) the Robbers	Lionel Guyett
The Fairy	Lynette Edwards
King Richard	Edward Halsted

Citizens Bowmen Loyal Subjects Schoolchildren and Toys:
Karen Davies Annie St John Cecilia Richards

Keyboards	Christopher Littlewood
Percussion	Derek Brook
Bass	Steve Harris
Directed by	Graham Berown
Musical direction by	Christopher Littlewood
Choreography	Judy Gridley
Scenery designed by	Richard Marks
Costumes designed by	Barbara Wilson
Lighting designed by	Peter Hunter

1981-1982
Jack and the Beanstalk
Book by Henry Marshall
Music and Lyrics by Christopher Littlewood

Jack	Emlyn Harris
Isabel	Mary Conlon
Dame Durden	Peter Robert Scott
King Cuthbert	Donald Pelmear
PC Boggins	John Michie
Chamberlain	Patrick Carter
Abracadabra	Aaron Shirley
Simon	Mark Caven
Giant Thunderclub	Tom Fahy
Tallulah	Charles Shaughnessy

	and Colin Hurley
The Fairy	Victoria Burton
Jenny Wren	Deborah Snook
Kitty	Karen McMullen
Bobby	Kelvin Omard
Amy	Sarah Cremer
Villagers Witches and Clouds	

Piano	Dominic Barlow
Bass	Anthony Houska
Drums	Ray Linquist
Directed by	Graham Berown
Musical direction by	Dominic Barlow
Choreography	Karen Rabinowitz
Scenery designed by	Richard Marks
Scenery built by	John Scutt
Costumes designed by	Barbara Wilson
Lighting designed by	Peter Hunter
Sound by	Stephen Huttly

1982-1983
Aladdin
by Henry Marshall

Aladdin	Emlyn Harris
Princess Baldroubadour	Christina Barryk
Mrs Twankey	Roger Leach
Abanazer	Graham Rees
Wishee-Washee	Billy Fellows
Hi-Tee	Gary Willis
Lo-Pong	Colin Hurley
The Emperor	Bernard Finch
Soraya	Franchine Morgan
Geni of the Ring	Junior A Walker
Geni of the Lamp	John Michie
Esmeralda the Camel	Nicola Begg
	and Charlotte Strevens

Citizens Slaves Jewels Launderette Assistants Caroline Swift Michael Lunts

Directed by	Graham Berown
Musical Director & Arranger	Rob Mitchell
Choreographer	Gary Willis

Set designed by	Richard Marks
Set built by	John Scutt
Lighting by	Peter Hunter
Sound by	Stephen Huttly
On the Book	Gillian Farr
ALADDIN Band	
Keyboards	Rob Mitchell
Bass	Paul Power
Percussion	Jim Matthews

1983-1984
Cinderella
by Henry Marshall

Cinderella	Julia Chambers
Prince Charming	Lisa Bloor
Dandini	Jenny Michelmore
Fifi	Howard Attfield
Mimi	Jack Chissick
Buttons	Lionel Guyett
Hire	Jonathan Howell
Purchase	Jonathan Docker Drysdale
The Fairy Godmother	Venetia Barrett
John Peel	Philip Aldridge
The Fox	Lynn Wyfe
Major Domo	Tony Chambers
Buttons' Fairy Godmother	Jane Quy

Hunt Members Courtiers Villagers:
Philip Aldridge Tony Chambers Sian Howard Roy Leighton Michael Lunts Jane
    Quy Lynn Wyfe Richard Gay Josh Marriott Steven Gerry Peter Smith

Directed by	David Horlock
Musical Director	Rob Mitchell
Choreography by	Jonathan Howell
Set designed by	Stephen Howell
Set built by	Garth Reid
Costumes designed by	Barbara Wilson
Lighting by	Peter Hunter
Sound by	Chris McLean
On the Book	Caroline Burchill
Keyboards	Rob Mitchell
Alto Saxophone	Pete Burt

Percussion	James Matthews

1984-1985
Dick Whittington
Book and Music by Henry Marshall

Dick Whittington	Helen Gemmell
Alice Fitzwarren	Sara Weymouth
Tomasina the Cat	Lynn Wyfe
Sarah the Cook	Howard Attfield
Idle Jack	Colin Hurley
Alderman Fitzwarren	Jonathan Wyatt
Captain	Stifyn Parri
Mate	Dominic Letts
Sultan of Morocco	Stifyn Parri
Vizier	Steven Elliott
Town Crier	Sam Graham
Butcher	Steven Elliott
Whirling Dervish	Robert Beach
King Richard II	Sam Graham
Tom Cat	Stephanie Simm
Good Fairy	Maria Heidler
King Rat	Alex Johnston

Citizens Apprentices Slaves Rats and sellers in the Golden City:
Steven Elliott Sam Graham Maria Heidler Dominic Letts Camilla Lumsden Jane
    Quy Robert Beach Stephanie Simm

Directed by	David Horlock
Musical Director	Rob Mitchell
Choreography by	Jonathan Howell
Set designed by	Bill Crutcher
Set built by	Garth Reid
Costumes designed by	Barbara Wilson
Lighting by	Peter Hunter
Sound by	Chris McLean
Dance Captain	Jane Quy
On the Book	Marie Curtin

1985-1986
Babes in the Wood
by Henry Marshall

The Sheriff of Nottingham	Steven Elliott
Robin Hood	Lisa Bloor
Will Scarlet	Bill Deamer
Friar Tuck	Roy Leighton
Little John	Geoffrey Abbott
The Babes - Tina	Stephanie Simm
Judy	Jeanne Downs
Maid Marian	Tracey Halsey
Willie Whiskers	Christopher Reeks
Daisy Dimple	Jack Chissick
Fido	Gary Blair
The robbers - Jim	Jonathan Howell
Pete	Lionel Guyett
The Fairy	Jane Quy
King Richard	Dermot McLaughlin

Outlaws citizens children toys
Lynn Wyfe Caroline Mander Linda May Harris

Directed by	David Horlock
Musical Director	Rob Mitchell
Choreographer	Jonathan Howell
Scenery designed by	Bill Crutcher
Scenery built by	Garth Reid
Costumes designed by	Barbara Wilson
Lighting by	Chris McLean
Sound by	Nick Hunt
Dance Captain	Bill Deamer
On the Book	Merril Dalton
Panto Band	
Keyboards	Campbell Simpson
Bass and Acoustic Guitar	Jo Meacham
Percussion	James Matthews

Appendix II: Actor Database

Geoffrey Abbott 1985
Christine Absalom 1972
Philip Aldridge 1983
Michael Alexander 1959
Penelope Allen 1960
Michael Ames 1975
Doreen Andrew 1955
Cyril Appleton 1968 1969
Jane Argyle 1976
Ben Aris 1968
Graham Armitage 1958
Edward Arthur 1978
Howard Attfield 1983 1984
Charles Baillie 1978
Jill Baker 1972
Gillian Barber 1978
Michael Barnwell 1956
Venetia Barrett 1983
Frank Barrie 1963
Carlotta Barrow 1957
Christina Barryk 1982
Eileen Bates 1963
Robert Beach 1984
David Beames 1968 1972 1973
Suzanne Beaumont 1964
Avril Bebbington 1959
Nicola Begg 1982
Heather Bell 1970

Amanda Bell 1977
Christopher Benjamin 1960 1961
Mary Benning 1958
Rosemary Bennion 1963
Jessica Benton 1963 1964 1965 1966
Cherylin Beswick 1962
Gillian Bevan 1979
Chris(topher) Biggins 1965 1966
Peter Birch 1978
Christine Bishop 1978
Gary Blair 1985
Lisa Bloor 1983 1985
Helen Boggis 1971
Jolyon Booth 1961 1962
Judy Booty 1966
Stephen Boswell 1975
Raymond Bowers 1959 1965 1966
Amanda Boxer 1972
Beth Boyd 1961
Jacqueline Boyer 1958
Patricia Brake 1960
Andrew Branch 1980
John Branwell 1976 1979
Helena Breck 1976 1977
Olivia Breeze 1965 1975
Tessa Bremmer 1958
Jane Breton 1967

Geoffrey Brightman 1972 1973 1979
Jemima Brignall 1966
Joanna Brookes 1963
Alison Brown 1966 1967
Isabel Brown 1961
Elva Buck 1965
Sidney Burchall 1956 1957
Jenny Burke 1972 1973
Victoria Burton 1981
Selina Cadell 1977
Victor Carin 1960
Sylvia Carson 1970
Patrick Carter 1981
Patrick Cavanagh 1959
Mark Caven 1981
Julia Chambers 1983
Tony Chambers 1983
James Charlton 1975
Mary Chirgwin 1960 1961
Jack Chissick 1983 1985
Mark Christon 1969
Ann Clark 1958
Peter Clark 1973
Lynn Clayton 1979
Graham Clayton Adams 1962
Michael Cleveland 1959
Richard Clews 1976 1977

Roger Clissold 1965 1967
  1968 1971 1972 1973
  1974 1975
Stephanie Cole 1964
  1965 1966
Jacqueline Cole 1955
Edmund Colter 1961
Norman Comer 1967
Mary Conlon 1981
Leigh Conroy 1979
Diana Coupe 1955
Sara Coward 1972
Sally Cowdy 1961
Peter Cregeen 1960
Sarah Cremer 1981
Derek Crewe 1974 1975
  1976 1977 1978
Jenny Crews 1965 1967
Ann Curthoys 1962
Brian Cutler 1976
David Daker 1960 1961
  1962 1963 1964
Phillipa Dale 1963
Alan Daniel 1962 1963
Graham Davey 1968
Karen Davies 1980
Monique de Sain 1978
Bill Deamer 1985
Delia Dermer 1960
Richard Derrington 1970
  1971
Jonathan Docker
  Drysdale 1983
Lee Donald 1973 1974
Elaine Donnelly 1967
Helen Dorward 1957
  1958
Elizabeth Downs 1959
Jeanne Downs 1985
David Duke 1961
Christopher Dunham
  1962 1963 1964 1969
  1970
Lyndsey Durant 1980
Phillipa Eden 1969

Christine Edmonds 1968
  1970
Lynette Edwards 1978
  1979 1980
Steven Elliott 1984 1985
Frank Ellis 1967 1968
  1969 1972 1973
Brian Ellis 1976
Tom Fahy 1981
Lynn Farleigh 1962
Rupert Farley 1979
Mary Farrer 1958 1959
Billy Fellows 1982
Margery Field 1957
Bernard Finch 1982
Kenneth Firth 1956
John Fleming 1970
Roger Forbes 1967
Harriet Forbes 1955
Brigit Forsyth 1963 1964
Troy Foster 1980
Martin Fowler 1957
Denyse Fox 1956
Regina Frankel 1955
Lily Freret 1955
Richard Frost 1971 1972
Jonathan Fryer 1974
Diana Fyfe 1956
Gillian Gale 1957
Kathleen Gardner 1964
Rosemary Gay 1960 1961
  1962 1963
Richard Gay 1983
Helen Gemmell 1984
Daniel Gerroll 1974
Steven Gerry 1983
Desmond Gill 1964
Zeph Gladstone 1957
John Golder 1971
David Gooderson 1966
  1967
Sally Ann Goodman
  1975
Diana Goodwin 1956
Oliver Gordon 1957 1958

  1959 1960 1961 1962
  1963 1964 1965 1966
  1967 1968 1969
Sonia Graham 1958
Jill Graham 1962 1971
  1974 1975 1976
John Graham 1955
Sam Graham 1984
Kim Grant 1955
Felicity Gray 1963 1964
  1965 1966 1967
Nick Greenbury 1969
Hermoine Gregory 1956
Richard Gregson 1963
  1965
Marcia Gresham 1978
David Grout 1972 1973
  1974
Lionel Guyett 1967 1976
  1977 1979 1980 1983
  1985
Ellis Haddington 1978
Geraldine Hagan 1956
Paul Haley 1967
Jenny Hall 1965 1966
  1967
Francis Hall 1955
Tracey Halsey 1985
Edward Halsted 1980
Joy Hamlett 1959
Elizabeth Harding 1960
Elizabeth Hardwick 1966
Janet Hargreaves 1956
Chris Harris 1965 1966
Emlyn Harris 1981 1982
Linda May Harris 1985
Ronald Harwood 1955
Stephen Hattersley 1979
Anthony Healey 1962
Elizabeth Hearn 1956
Roger Heathcott 1974
Maria Heidler 1973 1974
  1975 1984
Vivien Heilbron 1966
Michael Henry 1980

Nancie Herrod 1958 1959 1960
Penny Hind 1958
Gay Holden 1960
Celia Holmes 1959
Brian Honeyball 1971 1972
Clive Hornby 1977
Sian Howard 1983
Elizabeth Howe 1957
Jonathan Howell 1983 1985
Jennifer Hughes 1960
Richard Hughes 1955
Roger Hume 1968 1969 1970
Colin Hurley 1981 1982 1983
Ross Jennings 1967 1968
Helen Jessop 1955
Josephine Johns 1965
Lynda Johns 1966 1967
Elwyn Johnson 1970 1971 1976
Lloyd Johnston 1973
Alex Johnston 1974 1975 1977 1978 1980 1984
Langton Jones 1962
Lisle Jones 1963
Penny Jones 1972 1973
Mary Keegan 1975 1976 1977
Kenneth Keeling 1955
Peter Kellet 1966
Maya Kemp 1975 1978
Brian Kent 1955 1956 1957
Marcia King 1971 1973
Dorothy Kingsmill 1957
Bernard Krichefski 1969
Paula Lansley 1967
Roger Leach 1974 1975 1977 1982
Roy Leighton 1983 1985
Dominic Letts 1984

Janet Lewis 1956 1957
Ruth Lewis 1967
Martin Lisemore 1958
Catherine Lock 1974
John Luckham 1962
Camilla Lumsden 1966 1984
Geoffrey Lumsden 1958
Michael Lunts 1982 1983
Donald MacIver 1977
Angus Mackay 1956
Charles Madge 1969 1970
Philip Madoc 1959
Ronald Magill 1957 1958 1959 1960
Graeme Malcolm 1976
Stephen Mallatratt 1971
Caroline Mander 1985
Henry Manning 1957
Knight Mantell 1967 1968 1975
Ray Mariner 1978
Josh Marriott 1983
Thelma Marshall 1956
Neil Martin 1976
Tina Matthews 1955
Peter May 1967
Charmian May 1969
Nicholas McArdle 1963
Fiona McKean 1960 1961 1962
Neil McLauchlan 1968
Dermot McLaughlin 1985
Karen McMullen 1980 1981
Jennifer McNae 1961
Ian McNeice 1969 1970
Tim Meats 1970 1971
Doreen Metcalfe 1959
Jenny Michelmore 1983
John Michie 1981 1982
Elisa Mitchell 1966
June Mitchell 1960

David Monico 1960 1961
Carolyn Moody 1965
Franchine Morgan 1982
Liz Moscrop 1972 1977 1979
Lesley Mould 1965
Steven Mountstevens 1963
Sally Muggeridge 1969
Ian Mullins 1956 1957 1958 1959
Ann Naylor 1958
Sam Naylor 1978
Fredrica Nevill 1959
Jennie Newport 1968
Jonathan Newth 1963
Penelope Nice 1971
Barbara Nichols 1961
Trevor Nichols 1979
Candace O'Connor 1968
Desmond O'Donovan 1961
Bryon O'Leary 1960
Kelvin Omard 1981
Margaret Osborne 1956
Gil Osborne 1970
Catherine Owen 1978
Marion Owen-Smith 1980
Judith Paris 1968
Stifyn Parri 1984
Frederick Peisley 1955 1956
Donald Pelmear 1963 1981
Lally Percy 1974
Judith Perkins 1957
Richard Perkins 1970
Jeffery Perry 1974 1975
Mark Perry 1979
Neil Phillips 1973
John Pickett 1965
Richard Platt 1980
Derek Pollitt 1971
Ian Pool 1969

Michael Poole 1964 1965
Jennifer Pottage 1967
 1968
Tim Preece 1961
Anne Preus 1968 1969
Jane Quy 1962 1965
 1968 1974 1975 1976
 1977 1983 1984 1985
Joyce Rae 1967
Christopher Ravenscroft
 1970
Christine Rayner 1957
Philip Reavey 1968
Christopher Reeks 1975
 1985
Graham Rees 1982
William Relton 1979
Adrian Reynolds 1973
 1974 1975
Gillian Rhind 1969
Rita Rhodes 1963 1964
Graham (Robert)
 Richards 1972 1973
Berny Richards 1978
Cecilia Richards 1980
Peter Robert Scott 1968
 1969 1980 1981
Vivien Roberts 1962
Ann Robinson 1958 1962
Lynne Robinson 1960
Jane Robinson 1962
Christian Rodskjaer
 1964
Rosemary Rogers 1959
Ann Rosenfeld 1974
Leonard Rossiter 1956
Gillian Royale 1963
David Ryall 1964
David Sadgrove 1972
 1973
Susan Salomon 1964
Michael Sanderson 1970
 1971
Christopher Scott 1968
Mark Scrimshaw 1980

Susan Seager 1979
Valerie Seaman 1958
Robert Sessions 1969
David Shaughnessy 1976
Charles Shaughnessy
 1981
Rosamund Shelley 1972
Simon Shepherd 1977
Aaron Shirley 1981
Stephanie Simm 1984
 1985
Graham Sinclair 1975
 1976
Marc Sinden 1979
Derek Smee 1958
Marjorie Smith 1959
Peter Smith 1983
Deborah Snook 1981
Tara Soppet 1968
Howard Southern 1966
 1967
Andrew Spedding 1964
Judy Spooner 1962
Tina Spooner 1962
Steven St John 1969 1970
Michael St John 1980
Annie St John 1980
Adrienne Stannard 1957
Tony Steedman 1961
Christopher Stevens
 1962
Roger Stevens 1960
Charlotte Strevens 1982
Michael Stroud 1965
 1966 1967 1970 1971
Isobel Stuart 1968 1969
Caroline Swift 1982
John Swindells 1966
Sarah Taunton 1969
Marilyn Taylersen 1962
 1964
Paul Taylor 1966
David Taylor 1963
Cynthia Taylor 1960
Josephine Tewson 1956

 1959
Tricia Thorns 1974
James Tomlinson 1967
 1968
Patience Tomlinson 1974
 1975 1976
Michael Tudor Barnes
 1973
Brian Tully 1978
Richard Valentine 1961
Richard Vaughan 1956
Hilary Voisey 1964
Charles Waite 1966
Junior A Walker 1982
Diana Waller 1971
Hugh Walters 1961 1962
James Wardroper 1977
Diana Warren 1965 1966
Jonathan Warren 1979
Jean Watson 1969
June Watson 1962 1963
Ralph Watson 1965
David Weeks 1967
Fay Werner 1961
Timothy West 1957 1958
Sara Weymouth 1984
Robert Whelan 1969
Alison Wide 1955
Richard Wilkinson 1968
Gary Willis 1982
Keith Woodhams 1980
Jean Woollard 1969
Sonia Woolley 1966 1967
 1968
Jenny Wright 1961
Rebecca Wright 1976
Jonathan Wright Miller
 1967
Jonathan Wyatt 1984
Lynn Wyfe 1983 1984
 1985
Gilbert Wynne 1972
 1977

Appendix III
Henry Marshall's Gag Book

The Henry Marshall gagbook (contents © Emma Battcock) is a hard-covered exercise book in which all the gags and routines have been typed out and then sellotaped in place. Each of these is then ticked in

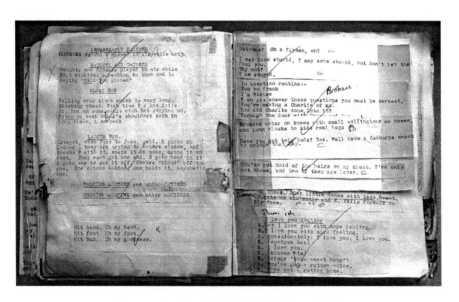

Some pages from Henry Marshall's gag book
Copyright Chris Abbott

pencil when they are used in a script. The gag book is marked: Property of Henry Marshall, 54 Belsize Park, Hampstead NW3 and is tabbed by section: Routines; Animals; Illegible; Comic and Entrance. The gag book has been deposited in the Theatre Collection of the University of Bristol, where it forms part of the Henry Marshall collection, five boxes of scripts, programmes and other papers. The following transcript is verbatim using the abbreviations in the original, although bus has been expanded to business throughout to aid clarity.

Henry Marshall's gag book

A: You pay for your hobbies you know.
        If you play golf you lose your balls
        If you fish you lose your flies
B: It's a good thing he doesn't keep poultry

He's a fine upstanding figure of a man
Someone's starched my underwear

He's going to get rid of the gas cooker and get me a griller
I don't know what I shall do with one of those big hairy things in my kitchen

I hate children. I especially hate the ones out there
(At one point) I'll poison your ice cream in the interval

I got out of bed one day and couldn't walk. I went to the doctor like this (demonstrates). I came out like this (demonstrates). I had both legs in one knicker.

(To audience) You look like a lovely garden of flowers. One or two old weeds out there.

I was riding a bicycle but it wouldn't move
It was too tired (two tyred)
I was holding the bicycle over my head when I was stopped by a policeman. The officer said "What are you doing?" I said "I'm sorry, officer, I'm holding a rally" (Raleigh)

Shopping routine
I bought a dear little water otter. Would you like to see my water otter? (build-up) produces hot

water bottle

What's tall and pointed, got snow on the top, and got ears?
A mountain
A mountain hasn't got ears
You've heard of mountaineers haven't you?

Why did the skinhead go to Timothy White's?
He didn't want to bovver Boots

Additions to the kitchen scene
Putting tablecloth on table, two get it twisted
One lifts other right round to untwist it
Doling out porridge, two on plates, one on A's hat
A turns it onto plate then puts some onto B's hat
Mutual preparation. Flicks some to start with
Shall I? B ducks, C gets it
One is bending over, legs apart. A pushes it through legs onto face, then rest of it onto bum. A about to sit on cake which is on chair. Audience may tell him? He keeps stopping from actually sitting down. Eventually sits in it

Routines

Ghost in double bed
Two little lambs which have gone astray
(on seeing ghost between them) Baa!
Spider down - shoot it (sink ship in picture)
Bed spread goes. Sheet goes.
Blanket unrolls to bottom
Bang on head of one of them with bag on rope
Each accuses the other
You hit me on the head
I didn't, did I?
What a funny woman
You struck me
I didn't did I?
Ghost crosses bed. They get out (then lamb song)
Back to bed, ask audience to tell them if ghost comes in

Deep freeze etc routine
Sausages put in limp. Taken out almost at once stiff.
Chicken put in oven. Is it high? I'll see. Bell rings
Cooked large turkey taken out.
Start cooking. Two thirds of a cup of something.
Have you got two thirds of a cup? I have now (hammer used)
Nuts. I haven't got any nuts. I'll use bolts.
Chicken stock. Stringy chicken. It's alive. Shoot it, then take chef's hat off in mourning for dead chicken.
Pastry makes complete jacket. B puts it on. A pats him hard with apron. A takes yellow liquid. Shall I? Brushes hands flicking it on A's face.
Cake stand, large with compartments and notice sticking out. Twirls round hitting face of same person each time. Extra man comes in. Can I have it now? Shall we let him have it? But he ducks

and it hits same person again.

Laundry
Partition with two holes on one side. On other side Bath, mangle iron. A outside B inside. C tells A there is no one in there only machinery. A puts Jack in. B gives it treatment, wash in bath, through mangle and ironed. Puts it into second hole. Out of second hole comes identical jacket, dry in cellophane wrapper. A puts in trousers, same business. Complains "these are not my trousers." B takes off own trousers puts them in second hole and they come out dry in cellophane. From time/time A says sure there is someone in there. B makes noise like machinery. A puts in whole suit of clothes. B works frantically, tie gets caught on mangle, iron on cord etc. A insists on someone in there, looks in hole. B pulls him through gives him treatment. Steam from iron when A is ironed.

Cooking routine following radio instructions

Buttons	Now we'll get our instructions from the BBC (turns on radio)
Radio	Pip pip pip pip
B	One more pip
R	Pip
B	That's right
R	This is the six o'clock news
All	Ah (sound of shot from radio)
B	Someone's shot Alvar Liddell (twirls knob)
Kissem	Hurray (others subdue him)
R	Here is tonight's Cookery Talk
All	Ah
R	How to make a Cabinet Pudding
All	Oo
R	First of all, get a bowl
All	Bowl, right
(Pinch bats at one end of table with a rolling pin. Buttons bowls with apple. Kissem prepares to field)	
R	No, no, no. Not that sort of bowl. Get a basin.
B	Oh, get a basin
R	Now get some grease
B	Grease - ah, the crease in my trousers (lifts leg on table)
R	No, not the crease in your trousers. Lard.
B	Oh lard, I see. Here we are.
R	Now line the basin with grease.
B	We've got to get the basin in line with the grease
	(They align basin and lard on the table taking sight along table with eyes)
Kissem	(Army fashion) Up no 2, no 3. Right
R	Now get some flour
B	Flowers, here we are (vase of flowers)
R	Put it in the basin
B	(putting the flowers in basin) In the basin
R	Add a pinch of soda
	(Kissem gets soda syphon and squirts water into basin)
R	Just a pinch more
	(Kissem squirts himself)
R	Now get some yeast
(Buttons gets Pinch's watch and chain, whirls them round and sends them flying with loud crash off)	
B	That's yeast

Pinch	Why?
B	They've gone west
R	Now take a little thyme
B	A little time (Kissem throws in large clock. It rings loudly in basin)
R	Add some dates
	(Buttons gets calendar off wall and puts it in basin)
R	Take three eggs
B	One two three. Three eggs (puts them in)
Pinch	Four eggs
B	Three eggs (to Radio) Which did you say - three eggs or four?
R	I said three (Buttons puts tongue out at Pinch)
R	And some figs
B	Jigs. We must dance some jigs (they do so)
R	Now get some whipped cream (Kissem gets some) Find a mug
B	(indicating Pinch) Here's a mug
R	Put the cream in the mug
B	Put the cream on the mug
	(They put cream on Pinch's face)
R	Finally, watch it rise (they all do. Pudding actually rises from the basin)
B	Here, it's going to burst

(Gets pistol and shoots it. Pudding subsides. Then Hydrophobia's head appears, the entire contents of pudding basin on her head. Hole in table and a bottomless pudding basin. The pudding now appears like a hat. Hydro is under table from start of scene.)

Parcel gag

A has expensive parcel he will register at Post Office. It has ninety seven piece dinner service and costs vast sum of money. Rattles parcel. Has Fragile on it. He relates this to B and C. B takes parcel from him and shows him what they will do in Post Office. First of all nice and register it, then when he has gone bang it down, push it about and say "This isn't for us it's for Jack. Oy Jack" Parcel thrown to C who catches it and says "That isn't all." When Jack gets it he - kicking business by accident in passing, bang about throw down and hurl at feet. A picks it up and say "You mean to say they'll..." - does what they have done only more so and jumps on it, bangs it with mallet etc. "That's dangerous isn't it? I mean you might chip one of the cups." "I won't send it by post, I'll deliver it by hand." B "Who's it for?" A reads name. B "That's me" Exit in tears with parcel. A gives C a huge tube marked GLUE "Help him to stick it together again with that."

Cooking routine 2

Props - three jugs, basin, ladle, tin of flour, saucepan with big egg in it, small table
French chef with big moustaches on to teach comics to cook a pudding. Takes bowl, takes flour, puts flour in basin. A puts too much flour in, it goes everywhere. A sneezes twice into bowl and the flour is scattered. Is about to sneeze third time - big preparation then does not. B sneezes instead. Water in flour, out through hole held in front as though peeing. Attempts to stop it with hand. Water on floor. Falling over business. Jug of water poured in face of chef who is on floor. A holding on to table to stop falling with legs working. B puts mop between A's legs to stop him falling. Take egg, break big egg into basin. Green liquid comes out. Policeman on point duty business for smell of egg. Chef falls down. Green liquid poured in face. Wash liquid from face by pouring jug of water on him. A does sliding business "Out of the way" Slides for fun. "Spotted Dog pudding" Real spotted dog comes out of oven.

Dough Routine

Two long rolls of dough from butter churn as butter. Put on table and roll in comic's hat with feather on it. Use roll as shawl, swing round shoulders and hit comic in face. Hit dough with cricket bats - Anvil Chorus. Cricket game, dough into audience. Fold the cloth round it and say "Put it on the bed as an eiderdown."

Cooking routine 3
Radio says "how to make a steak and kidney pudding without the stea k and without the kidney." Comic adds "and without the pudding." Brylcreem put in it. Fried egg in pan thrown at picture on wall, egg comes out on picture. "Stir well" stare well at audience. Soda syphon squirted on either side of bowl, never getting bowl in right position, eventually use syphon on comic. Lump of dough emerges. Iron dough with iron. Drop iron on feet. Dough with feet. Wipe table with dough. Wipe legs and under table with dough. "Knead well" dough with knees. Both knees get stuck. Argument about steak. "Are you a whale steak?" Spout of water from steak. "The meat's in" (skit on Fleet's in number) Sit on dough. Dough sticks to bum.

Cooking routine 4
Making a pie with dough. "Make a short crust" How? "Make it long, then cut a bit off." "So that's the dough" (throwing it on the table) "yes that's the dough and don't do that to it" Repeat with bang each time from both. Rolling dough. Pounding dough. Hit with rolling pin. Box with it. Pulling it in half. Each throw half down. Roll it on floor. Mop floor with it. Use bucket and dough to wash floor. Wring it out in bucket. Clean table with it. Paste it. Pepper and sneezing business Dough over face. Place for mouth, place for eyes. Shooting business rabbit down from ceiling. Rabbit into pie.

Crooning machine
Machine has "Learn to Croon" on it. Buttons sings White Christmas gets snow in face. Persuades Pinch to use it saying "Wouldn't you like to croon like Crosby" Sings Singing in the Rain and gets water in the face. Baron on, "I know I'm going to get a big surprise" etc. Baron sings "Smoke gets in your Eyes" and smoke pours out and chokes him. Kissem on, sings "Just the touch of your hand" Hand with mallet comes out and hits him on head. Two of them get Buttons to have a go. Sings Dance Little Lady. Beautiful girl appears and he dances out with her.

Proposal scene 2
Dame will show Sammy how to propose. Sammy puts on bonnet and sits on chair. "That's back to front you fool. Now sit like a girl" "I said like a girl not an ostrich" (sitting business) Your legs are all wrong (pulls legs right) Sammy balances in position for a minute then falls over. Dame says will come in.

D	Bonsoir, bonsoir, bonsoir
S	Bonsoir, bonsoir, bonsoir. What does that mean?
D	I don't know. That's how you start anyway. Now I'm going to woo you. Would you like to be wooed?
S	Oh I woo'd
D	Goo'd (climbs over him and he leans back) Your eyes darling, your eyes are like winkles on waddin'. Your lips, your lips are like petals - bicycle pedals. Your ears, your ears are like flowers - cauliflowers. How I'd love to be alone on a desert island with you. Just you and me and a palm tree.
S	What's the palm tree for?
D	I've got a dog. Tell me, who do you love?
S	Tis you, tis you, tis you
D	What a nasty cold you've got (she swings him right off chair in her arms)

Tell me that you care. Oh God she doesn't care (seizes him wrong way up and addresses his bum) Answer me. Answer me.

S	Ow
D	Oh she's answered, she cares, she cares
S	Are we engaged yet?

Proposal scene 1

Buttons practises proposal to Cinders on Ugly Sister

B	Cinders, I think you're ripping
Olive	Slipping? What's slipping
B	No, ripping not slipping. Cinders, dear, give me a kiss
O	On an empty stomach?
B	No, on your face. Will you?
O	Nay, nay
B	Nay, nay? Was your mother frightened by a horse? Cinders, I want to get a kick out of loving you
O	That's easy (kicks him)
B	If you marry me, the whole earth will be at your feet
O	It always has been
B	I will go even further
O	You would. That's not the way to propose. That's all eyewash. Eyewash, eyewash
B	Well what do you think I do? Wipe myself down with an oily rag?
O	I'll show you how to propose. You be Cinders and I'll be you
B	Right I'm Cinders (simpers, Olive goes down on one knee)
O	(moaning) Oh, oh, oh
B	Have you got a pain?
O	No, that's love
B	Oh, I see. Oh, oh, oh (they moan away together)
O	Could I kiss the tip of that shell-pink ear (takes nose in hand, pulls ear down and bites it) Do you love me?
B	(through nose) Just a little bit
	(She tries to embrace him. They fall over, Olive crawls to him and holds up his head)
O	Will you be mine?
B	No, no
	(Olive bangs his head on the ground)
O	Now will you be mine?
B	Yes, yes
O	Then come to my arms (picks him up and lays him face upwards across her knee as she kneels. She plays on him with her fingers as though playing instrument)

Comedy love scene

(Enter Dame gorgeously dressed)

D	How do you like my new dress? I call it my Mills Bomb dress. You take out the pin and it's every man for himself. How do you like my built-up area? Here comes Idle Jack. This is my chance to get him to propose to me

(Enter Jack)

J	Blimey, you must have won a football pool
D	Oh Jack, when you see me in this dress, don't you feel something inside you?
J	Yes. Nausea
D	Tell me, Jack, have you ever been in love?
J	No, but I've felt round the edges
D	Oh the night is young and I'm so beautiful
J	Eh?
D	Well, the night is young.
J	Here, what are getting at?
D	Marriage
J	What about it?

D	Well I'm going spare
J	Look here, Sarah, I'm in love with Alice Fitzwarren
D	And I'm in love with you (seizing him) Your eyes, Jack, your eyes are like winkles on wadding. Your lips - your lips are like petals - bicycle pedals. Your ears - your ears are like flowers - cauliflowers.
J	Mum!
D	Those lips, those eyes, those nose. Jack, kiss me!
J	If I kiss you, will you let me go?
D	Yes (Jack gives her a peck on the cheek)
D	(releasing him) I'll never wash that spot again
J	Good morning (tries to go but Dame seizes him by coat)
D	Jack, look at me, aren't I disgusting? Look at me, look at my face?
J	Make a good door-knocker wouldn't it?
D	If you marry me, we'll live together in my pre-flabbergasted house
J	Mum!
D	If you marry me, I'll sell all my jewels to buy you a trousseau. You'll wallow in riches.
J	Blimey, I thought you said I'd swallow my breeches
	(Dame swings Jack right round in her arms and holds him lovingly)
D	Tell me, tell me, tell me that you care
J	Help!
D	(dropping him with a bang) He doesn't care. I shall commit suicide
J	(on floor) You can't!
D	I can. I've done it before and I'll do it again (cries)
J	(rising to knees) Don't take on so, Sarah
D	(with a gesture that knocks him flat) It's all over
J	(rising) But Sarah -
D	(knocking him flat with another grand gesture) It's all over (she kneels down and holds him by the hair) Do you love me?
J	No
	(Dame bangs head on floor several times)
D	Now, do you love me?
J	(faintly) Yes
D	(clutching him to her bosom) Jack, my hero!

(Into Duet)

Comedy Love Scene
Comic and girl. Girl goes and Horse comes in and sits in her place. It rubs comic. "Give me thy lilywhite hand" Horse gives hoof. Horse laughs. "Give me thy lips" Horse bites him. He turns and horse opens mouth wide at him and chases him off.

Magic powder routine
"Blow a little of this powder onto anyone and they'll love you for evermore" King gets it first. Tries it on passing lovely. "Oh what a wonderful feeling. I've never felt like this before. It's as though I were on a barge floating down still waters with my loved one beside me" King blows more powder onto her. She gives him big kiss, exits, after come hither with head. Sammy comes in and after disbelieving blows it onto King. King repeats lines and says "Darling" leaps on Sammy. Sammy alone. Dame on behind parasol, looking like smasher. Jack blows powder onto her. She leaps on him and chases him.

Imaginary instrument gag
Four comics. One starts to yell and complain to imaginary man. "You come in here, riding your bicycle and don't even ring your bell" (to others) "Are you all right?" Did he hurt you?" Takes

imaginary bicycle of imaginary man, asks Figgs to hold it.

Figgs I've burned my hand. I didn't know lamp was alight. Isn't it a nice bike?

Ammonia I don't like the mudguards very much

Syrup They're all made like that nowadays

Riding business. Pickles persuaded to ride. "Don't scratch the paint" Gingerly getting on. Touches bell which rings. Riding round stage. Gives man back bike because on way to music lesson but man loans violin. Taking violin out of case. Syrup plays to pizzicato notes. Figgs plays one and rushes away terrified. Syrup plays note. Pickles look under skirt. Syrup plays phrase. All look everywhere. Pickles given instrument. "You'll need to bow" "Oh how silly of me" "It's round the wrong way" throw up and catch bow. Plop on drum. Pickles plays quick phrase. "Never had a lesson in my life"

Syrup Oh what a wonderful cello (picks it up and plays a note) Would you care to try this?

Pickles I'd love to. I hope it's as easy as the violin (plays phrase) Let's have a concert

Figgs told to get piano. "Which one, the upright or the Baby Grand?" "Silly girl, she's seeing things, there's only one" The baby grand.

Figga gets imaginary piano. Stool business arpeggio. Note in treble gets stuck. Finger gets stuck in note. Piano lid down on other hand.

You'd better sit down to play that cello

Get me that chair dear, will you

This one

No, not that one. The chaise longue, it's more comfortable (imaginary chair sat on)

Syrup breaks fiddle string, gets piccolo. They all play. Record of Rigoletto is used. Ammonia singing. Eventually piano falls over. All bow and do cod musicians exit.

Drilling routine

March round. Halt. Each collide with one in front. Left turn. One turns R. Order arms. Bang muskets on toe of next person. Slope arms. Comic's musket goes over shoulder and on ground. Present arms. Music. Enter 1st comic as general with medals

Pickles Men

Dames Where?

Pickles I'm now going to address you

Figgs I've got a good address here

Pickles ...and I will now display my medals. Here is Kings Cross, pinned on me by Victoria at Waterloo, Here is Queens Cross pinned on me by Miss Tull at Paddington. And here is Order of Bath Bun pinned on me by ... at the White Hart

Ammonia What's that one?

Pickles That's to hide a soup stain (indicating medals) Won at Maidenhead, won at Slough, won at Woolworths, won on the frontier and one on the back-ear. Now inspection. Head up, chest out, stomach in, feet together. (various comic contortions) I said feet together (Cat falls over) What's your name?

Ammonia Phillips

Pickles Get among the F's. What's yours?

Figgs Gin and lime

Pickles Your rank?

Syrup I know, but I have no hot water (Pickles blows whistle. Syrup gurks)

Pickles I see you're in the Gurkhas

     Close up (all pull skirts up)

     Number (Rumba)

     (They number going ten Jack Queen King Ace)

Pickles Left turn (all but Syrup) I said Left turn

Syrup Well actually I wasn't interested. I have a confession to make

Pickles What is it

Syrup I love you. Have a suck of my lolly

Pickles	Thanks very much. I like it
Syrup	I didn't
Pickles	Left turn
Figgs	We've done that
Pickles	We'll do it again
Figgs	It gets boring if you do it more than once
Pickles	All right, we'll do something different. Present arms

        (All throw muskets at him)
        As you were. Right turn
        (All but Cat march right away. Cat waves to audience, marches into pros arch)
        Left wheel. Jump to it (All jump)
        Shake a leg there (All shake legs)
        Look alive (all scratch) Double time, march

(All double, singing Boys and Girls and kicking each other. Pickles blows whistle. Cat knocks his helmet off and they play hockey with it. After goal they march off.)

Singing competition (or reciting competition)
A B C D. A announces will give prizes for singing. B C D all sing together, are told to sing one by one. B coughing business "I've got a frog in my throat" "Well keep quiet dear and let the frog sing" B sings hot number. C and D dance. B gets first prize which is jug. C sings lively number and collapses and gets second prize which is basin to match jug. D ponders on these two prizes "I don't think I'll bother" D forced to compete, is given hatbox as third prize. "Come on, open it" "It's not so much the prize as the thought behind it" D looking into hatbox says "It's not big enough for me" "It's a little boy's hat" Takes out. Puts it on

Singing competition 2
First competitor gloomy looking at stooge called One Lung. Wishee "How many prizes" "Three" (starts to exit) "I'll go and see if the tide's in" (to No 2) "What are you going to (obscured) I do?" "Shall I tell him?" (Wishee) China should be old fashioned, definite pattern some kind. Wishee "I passed by your window this morning at three. Come tell me what was it you emptied on me"(on looking in box) I don't use these. Anyway it's too big for me. Exit with bowler hat much too big on head.

Short white-washing scene
Pickles Look at your wallpaper. It's disgraceful. Get some paint and the ladder, we must fix this at once
(Syrup gets ladder and Figgs bucket with whitewash and two brushes. Syrup goes up ladder, splashing Pickles as she does so and slipping down)
Pickles   You don't understand this at all. I'll do it
(Goes up ladder, splashing himself. Syrup roars with laughter. Pickles comes down and plasters her face. Figgs laughs. Syrup plasters her face. Pickles laughs. Syrup and Figgs plaster Pickles face. Exit with ladder and bucket as in advertisement to drum thump)

Kitchen routine
Sausages go off first, having been brought in. Hit at them with rolling pin. Running gag "I like cleanliness in my kitchen" B wipes hands on flour. "Wipe that up" referring to water. B wipes it up with dough. "All covered in fluff" Give it a brush. B dusts it with dustpan and brush. A "I'm sure I've got a cold coming on" wipes nose with dough. "Kills all known germs" hits dough with back of brush. When sausages come up in tin, fire at them with pistols. Slow fall. "Make fancy pastry at the edge" A does it with false teeth. "As my husband said with these very teeth" (Teeth move up and down) "What's he saying now" "Mammy" Policeman comes on. Whizz door, chaser and chasee meet either side, back to back. Three concealed flap doors. Comics just walk in. Keep

hitting policeman with tin (baking tin) Birds whistle when policemen is hit so often. Put him through mangle at end. Cardboard cutout

By hand on your way home
Olive, Hydro, Buttons
Hydro   We want you to deliver some parcels for us on your way home tonight (wheel in lots of parcels on porter's trolley)
Buttons   Who do you think I am, C Paterson?
(Hydro reads out addresses as Olive gives him parcels. Funny names and addresses each one further away. "By hand on your way home" repeated each time. Interpolations "I say I still live at Datchet" "I say, can I take a tram" etc. Finally a great big parcel for Mrs Porridge, John o Groats.
Hydro   Now off you go and be here bright and early in the morning.
Exit Buttons and re-enter immediately. "I went jet-propelled"

Tacks on chairs
Large chair with large tack on it. P sits on it first when alone. Enter Syrup
Pickles   Tell me what do you think of the state of the country? (Answer) Do you approve of tax on furniture? leading to tax on chairs?
Syrup   Yes I approve of tax on chairs
Pickles   Well sit down and let's talk it over (Syrup sits down. Business)
            There you are, tax on chairs (Exit)
            (Enter Ammonia) "State of the country"
Syrup   What do you think of taxes?
Ammonia   You can't get one?
Leading to Ammonia not approving of tax on chairs. Syrup gets audience to agree she ought to approve of tax on chairs. She does and business as before. Figgs enters and into routine with Ammonia. Business. Finally Pickles. Ammonia and Figgs do it on him. Pickles agrees to everything. Sits down, no effect. They press him down, eventually getting on him. Pickles rises.
Pickles Yes, I believe in tax on chairs but I also believe in self-protection (turns round and shows cushion on him)

Kitchen scene
Sausages coming up. One sees it. The other doesn't. Playing draughts with pastry balls to get into batting balls with audience.

Take boiled shirt front to driller from inside jacket. "Here's a message from the front"

Limping business with rifle on shoulder in front of others.

One goes to sleep leaning backward, rifle on shoulder. Another props up sleeper with own rifle wedged on floor and in back. Later kick rifle away.

Mop drill scene
Dame Jack Mate and Stooge being drilled by Bosun
Bosun   Squad, shun. Right dress
Dame   This is the right dress
Bosun   Squad, shoulder arms (They all do so. Dame's mop goes over her shoulder) Pick it up,
            pick it up
(Dame picks it up and forms up again. Jack rests his chin on the end of his mop. Dame kicks Jack's
            mop away and he falls on his face)
Bosun   What are you doing down there?
Jack   Getting up again

Bosun (referring to scrubbing brush in Jack's trousers) What's that sticking out of your trousers?
Jack My toothbrush
Bosun Give it to me (taking it) You mean to tell me that you can get this great big brush inside
       your mouth to clean your teeth?
Jack No, but I can take my teeth out can't I?
Bosun On the command order arms I want you to slap them down. Squad, order arms
       (Dame throws her mop on the deck)
Bosun Pick it up, pick it up
Dame You said slap it down (picks it up again)
Bosun Squad, shoulder arms
(They do so. Dame's goes over shoulder again. General business of passing and re-passing mops to
       each other. Eventually they get their mops in the shoulder arms position)
Bosun Squad, order arms
(They do so. Dame bangs her mop on Jack's foot. Jack hops around. Dance business. Dame and
       Jack)
       Get fell in
Dame Get fell in? Isn't he common?
Bosun Don't you realise that you'll soon be in the Pacific?
Dame How terrific. The Pacific.
Bosun And when you get there it will be very hot
Dame Hotter than... on a Saturday night?
Bosun Where were you up brought up?
Dame (splashing Bosun) Paddington Station
Stooge Where?
Dame (splashing Stooge) Paddington Station
Jack Where?
       (Dame turns to splash him but Jack ducks and Mate gets splash)
Dame Paddington Station
All Oh she means Paddington Station (they all splash her. Dame falls over and then gets up
       again)
Bosun Get into line. Close up (Dame lifts up skirt. General scream. Dame walks away) Where
       are you going?
Dame I'm going home. I'm not in the mood.
       (Band plays In the Mood. General dance until stopped by Bosun)
Bosun Fall into line there. Shuffle
(General shuffling business Dame zigzagging in and out of line between each person ending up at
       opposite end to Bosun where she makes faces at Bosun from behind her mop. Bosun
       moves round to beside her. Dame suddenly sees him and falls down. Bosun moves
       back to his original position)
       Left turn
(Dame turns left and bangs mop on her foot. Limping business. Jack turns right at other end of
       line)
       About turn (Jack and Dame turn inward again) As you were
Dame How were we? (they all stand to attention again)
Bosun Left turn. Quick March
       (They all march to British Grenadiers)
Bosun Left wheel. Left wheel. Left wheel (Jack marches into proscenium in passing)
(They approach footlights Stooge and Mate lift up Dame from either side. Jack throws away his
       mop and lifts from behind)
Dame Say something, if it's only goodbye
Bosun Get into line (they do so) This time, follow me. Right turn. By the left quick march.
(They all march off. Final gag as arranged)

Band routine (1)
Sousaphone, cymbals, triangle (triangle player has bananas hanging between legs and one foot bandaged enormously, also trumpet, bass drum. Drum Major leads march in. Drum Major has no trousers. March in and stop. All stop except Bass Drum which goes on, eventually stops. One last bang suddenly, all jump. Cymbal player holds cymbals wide and looks up. Drum Major looks up too. Music is played by orchestra. Bang on cymbals out of time. Drum out of time on rept. When starting again cymbals dropped with bang. Jumping over bunion business. Hitting bunion with Bass Drum stick Bass Drum mimes permission to hit it just once, then only very lightly. Triangle is looking out front in dream. Eventually Bass Drum drops stick on bunion. Play waltz, Bass Drum bangs after beat. Second time one ting on triangle. Bass Drum hits him on bum. To audience "Shall I" All say Yes. Repeat this. Cymbal crash in pause. Tap of baton echoed by Bass Drum. Rude noise on trumpet. Goose thrown up on stage. Drum Major plays it as bagpipe and all march off to Scottish music.

Band routine (2)
4 x Harp, Triangle, Sousa, Drum. Open posed as for photo Chamber of Horrors. "Follow me" turns to go and all follow. "One two go" all go. "Go with stick" drummer exits with stick. Tap tap with stick - "Come in" Start with Pizzicato from Sylvia. Ting, ting on tri. Conductor and triangle bow to each other. Second time bang bang. Conductor and drum bow to each other. Drummer goes to sit down and falls. All off but conductor who takes cornet and triangle who takes cello. "I'll get you under my chin" violin business with cello. Tuning business. Screw up cello with noises. "Me, me" "And me too" Oiling cello. Right, right. At start drop cello bow, break string and bridge. Bring out three little fiddles and exit with them and cello. "Poet and Peas" Drummer getting ready. Roll over drum. Type on valves of euphonium. Music sticking to hands. Drumbeat rhythm after end of phrase. Waltz, two dance. Drummer goes to sleep on couch, and couch is pulled off. Duel between drumsticks and baton. Drummer changes places with conductor. Prepare to start. Swaying business all fall over. Hit self on bum with stick. March off.

Additional gags
Cymbals held outwards. Conductor inspects player and music then puts music other way up. Balloon out of trumpet. Blown till it bursts.

Song interruption business
First deviation "Daisy" no notice taken first time. Second time "You're taking a liberty aren't you" then "Pack up your Troubles" mouthing business. Hanky down front "Well, where do you keep yours" "Good King Wenceslas" "What do you keep knocking for, can't you go?" "You ought to see his trousers" Conductor "Relax" "Oh that chocolate stuff"

Choking routine
A B C. B choking C. A says "I bet I can choke better than you" Bet 5s. "Who shall we choke?" "Him" (C) "Who shall be referee?" "Him" (C) Business How's that? Not bad. How's that? Oh that's much better. "It's a draw" C tries himself and eventually kills self. "He's won" Carry off C as dead.

Wireless routine (for 2)
This is the Home Service programme
The what?
The Home Service, fathead
Here is a talk on poultry
Who wants to listen to a talk on poetry
(Gets up and walks away)
Sit down

Now to commence at the beginning
I bet he finishes at the end
Now you all know what a hen is -
Yes, the wife of an old cock
Be quiet
Now we are going to ask our listeners to produce an egg
(Comic points to Dame. Business)
Now how to blow an egg
You go and blow your brains out
Hold the egg in the left hand, I said the left hand fathead
Take a pin (business: Dame looks for one. Com points to D's drawers. D makes him look away while she finds one in drawers)
Make a small hole or aperture in the apex of the egg
The what?
The top fathead
Now one in the base
The bass fiddle
Place the egg on your lips (they do) Then - suck it and see

Washing routine
Comic throws things from line to Dame who mangles them. Comics hands go through mangle then whole body. Cardboard cutout comes from mangle. Dame says to audience "He wants a bath, doesn't he" Wishee says no. Work up this. Meanwhile Dame gets bath, can etc. Shy business. Taking off clothes. Squeak with trousers. "Have you got ants in your pants?" "Come on Gandhi" Tests bath water with toe. Dame "Park it" Slow lowering of body into bath. Scrubbing with big lavatory brush. Towel on knees. Powder, lots of it, into face of Wishee. Sneezing business. Huge comb. Nappy business Huge safety pin. Eventually puts nappy round neck. Nightie. "What about my Guinness" Dame gives it to him. He drains it. Dame sings lullaby "Goodnight and God Bless You." Wishee curled up asleep. Dame carries Wishee off with watering can hitched to foot.

Hiking routine
Dame and Wishee with poles and appropriate dress. Wishee goes on with hiking business to drums. Dame "When you've quite finished, Montgomery" "There's a nail in my foot" "Why not take it out?" "It's a toenail" (re Dame's stocking) "What are those two pink tapes hanging down from your dress?" Those are me legs" "You ought to wear two pairs of stockings" "I'm wearing four pairs as it is" "I bet you there's no other stocking like this in the whole country" Wishee lifts Dame's skirt to show other stocking. Wishee does business ending in "I wear odd stockings" shows them

Laundry routine 1
Just had the laundry from a nudist colony (large fig leaf on stocking) And they want them starched (confetti) Looks as though there's been a wedding. (Producing baby clothes) There has been a wedding. Three threes are ten. Argument with Dame. Counting with socks. Business. These must be an MP's trousers. Why. Something's been contesting the seat.

Laundry routine 2
Comic pulled on in laundry basket by kids. "That's me and that's the basket" Don't get mixed up. I hate the so and so. (3 times) and three hates make 24. "Good old Buttons" Don't stress the old. Tell 'em not to starch the shirt, they starched 'em last week and I was walking round like this (business) Combinations and nightshirt come out of basket, both enormous. Bedsocks - riding boots. Trousers with holes. Dancing cheek to cheek. Business with trousers.

Blown-up routine

One policeman falls in copper. "He must be done by now" Pull policeman out. Huge balloon under jacket on tum. He lies on floor. Scratch tummy. Rub tummy (noises for each business) Press tummy (motor horn) "It won't be long now" Machine gun business on top of tum with broom with noises. Wave white flag. About to hit tum with broom. Get pump and put pipe in mouth. Pump water into mouth and balloon gradually deflates.

Baths routine
W sitting doing pools as a bath attendant. "That's a draw and that's a draw, and that's a bloomer. That's two drawers and one pair of bloomers" Gives each customer a towel, soap etc. Peppers soap. One customer says "These little things are sent to dry us" (re towel). Soap ration business cutting out coupons with big scissors. "I need a bath" "You're telling me" "What sort of bath do you suggest?" "A sheep dip" Put life belt round neck. "There's your soap" "What sort of soap is this?" "Life Buoy" "I want some salts" (hands customer big box of Epsoms) "I want some soap" (wet soap all over face) "I want a shower" (squirts water in face from garden syringe)

Ghost routine
This laundry is haunted (three on bench)
Man had throat cut from ear to ear
From where to where?
From 'ere to 'ere
Ghost walks every night at 12 o'clock
What time is it now?
Five to twelve
(Two get up to walk away)
Body was found just here
(Three scream and move bench to other side)
When his head fell off it rolled and rolled (drum) and we found it just here
(Scream and move, putting bench up, one falls off)

Washing and weighing routine
Dame rubbing business on rubbing board. Holds up tiny vest. Pants with motor light colour in circular patches. Holes in back.
Oh dear he's been sliding down the banisters again
Washing up. Plates, potato peeling, washing hands all in the same water. Where to put water. Going to throw it at audience. King might like a drop of soup. Pours it into drawer and it goes on floor. Mops it up, singing
There's a man outside with a funny face (says King entering)
Tell him we've got one
Weighing machine speaks weight. A goes on it.
Nine stone, eleven pounds
How much?
You 'eard
B goes on it
Four and a half pounds
Dame won't go each time, eventually is persuaded and jumps on.
You haven't put your penny in.
Oh, aren't I a naughty girl?
We girls get nothing unless we put our pennies in
Now then, one at a time, one at a time
Butcher on phone. Into One Meat Ball dance and sing. King puts hands round Queen's tum and does finger business
Can you play In a Monastery Garden

Mirror gag (variation)
Large empty mirror facing downstage. First time comic goes, someone similarly dressed appears and does all the same things, ending with slap. Second time reflection appears with shawl and red nose and puts out tongue. Third time comic takes parasol from reflection. Reflection disappears and returns with syphon and squirts comic. Returns with syphon and squirt fainting Dame later.

Tripping routine
A sits at table with vase of flowers. B walking up and down and talking, keeps on tripping over something imaginary in front of him. A bangs table, vase jumps. Eventually B removes what A trips on, then B trips on something else.

Counting up to nine
Three irons on table. Three threes are ten. A counts them each three times, holding up two at seven, making it come to ten. Children in audience count with comics. B does it, holds up two at seven and eight, making it come to eleven.

Fight routine
Comic and Principal Boy
Don't hold me back
I'm not
I know you're not
Comic comes over on Pr Boy's side
What are you doing over here?
I'm on your side
Principal Boy hits comic
Comic exits calling Mum

Revolver routine
To see if it loaded. A clicks it at B's earhole. Then at head. Then clicks all over head like Barber's clippers. Finally at bottom. Big bang. All scared.

Walking routine
Just keep quiet. B walks round with block noises. A reprimands him Says "Look at me, I don't make a noise when I walk" Demonstrates. Then saying "look here" makes enormous bang

Busy bee routine
A and B. A to run round collecting honey then B asks A to give it to him. Buzzing noise. Water in face. King Bees and Queen Bees. A and B do it on C but A whispers to C and both fill mouths. So does B. B trips and spills water. "Aren't you going to ask me to give it to you?" C gives B water in face then he gets it from A as well.

Without saying ooh. Jack and the Beanstalk

Kissing scene from Jack and the Beanstalk

Wasp scene from Jack and the Beanstalk

Additional gags (school)
Milk bottle wooden in two halves. Quarrel over whose it is. Divided by teacher and half given to each. Ethics? I was born in Thuthes. Picture taken down. 3 beetles crawl up wall.

Undressing
Blouse made of towel with British Railways on back. No parking on one pair of pants. Stick no bills. Frying tonight. The end.

Audience song
Start with short balloon dance - Dame and Billy. Guess who's coming? Dame shuts eyes. Elephant enters. She feels it. "A leather piano."
What's got four legs etc etc
That's irrelevant
That's right
Divide up or competition. Dame does second go. At end of first go with Billy, Dame: when are you going to start? Billy: we've done it, weren't you listening? Dame: sorry I just dozed off. After Dame has go they work with audience. "Oh yes we were, oh no you weren't" re who was louder. Draw (pair of drawers gag?) Once all together. Exit with elephant.

Busy Bee
A to B "Busy Bee, Busy Bee, give me the present you have for me" B to C. C forgets it. B has to swallow. Audience reminds him. Both fill mouths offstage no water seen. Not coming back to A again.

Sack of flour
Comic on alone. Sings A little Bit of Heaven. Gets bags of flour lowered from the flies which hits him on head at certain cue. Comic does it to B. Gets him to sing an Irish song. Puts him in position, stand away from him. But at cue Comic gets it again. Comic and B do it to C. "Stood here" business They put him between them. C sings various other Irish songs. When sings the right one, bag comes down, is suspended over C's head for a time then goes up. They tell C to sing higher. They lift C on B's shoulders and eventually C gets it. Dame enters.
We're having a conference. Meet my colleagues - Mr Strachey, Mr Bevin and I'm Clement Attlee
Who are you?
I'm Dr Summerskill
They get Dame to sing promising her she'll get a little present (use this phrase throughout) She sings. A basket of fruit and bottle of drink comes down instead of sack. Finish

In rocker scene Dame undresses to reveal two sou'westers sewn onto tape as brassiere, takes them off and puts them on as hat

Rocker scene with bunk
Bunk with double berth. Porthole over top berth and door L. Dame enters on stage level, pulls down steps from cabin to get herself up. Undressing business on lower berth. Undies etc. Throws clothes out of porthole. Puts on nighty and nightcap. Spider from roof of cabin. She gets into bunk and closes curtain. A enters in pyjamas gets into bunk and rolls through back out of site then through flap below bunk. Flap routine using top bunk as well then add more people up to entrance of comic in funny clothes ready for bed. Peers round door. Now four men on top bunk with spider. Dame and comic on lower berth. Roll rocker. Green line. Sea serpent thro' porthole. They all descend. Another serpent comes from rocker level. No finish

Proposal scene with comments
Dame and Baron with Comic doing football pools. I want a wife of my own. One home and two away. We'll go to Gretna Green tonight. And Sheffield Wednesday. Who wants to go to Sheffield on a Wednesday? We'll have children. An easy six. My hand in (...) treble chance, ...remind me of Grimsby etc. ...myself at your feet and what...

Drilling gags
I'm giving the orders. I'll have a gin. Comic talks on and on in spite of driller. (re rifle) What's this?
That's my pistol. Comic talking to driller keeps rubbing his hand on face of A. Put that rifle on your
shoulder. Where? On here. Comic puts it on A's shoulder. A has collapsible rifle which breaks every
time. Comic hits it with his rifle.

Sea-sick scene
Take a good turn on deck.
I'm having a good turn down here.
Get the cook to bring up some food
I can bring up my own food

Recitation routine
Under the mistletoe buff
Bow
I haven't finished yet.
Repeat with bow
Stood a boy with a hacking cow
Cough
(Comic does so)
Cough spelling business
His mother gave him lots of doff
D O U G H spells dough
Oh
Start again
Under the mistletoe boff etc
His mother gives him lots of dough
Until he says he has enow

Magic wand
One tap you turn to stone. Two taps you come alive again. Three taps you become mechanical.
Comic works it with four coming on one by one and gets them as statues in row. They come on
and work into good comedy positions for turning to stone. Mechanical business to exit. May be
possible to work this up into good routine.

Interruption gags
Sudden applause and spot on Dame in box.
What are you doing up there?
I'm the audience
I come from Dublin
What part?
All of me
What do you think you look like sitting up there
The last rose of summer
What would you give to have hair my colour?
I don't know, what did you give?
Eats chocolates from box on rail of box, presumably belonging to people in box

Love scene with balloon effects
King   My little French fern. My little bit of swansdown. I'm a lonely man (keeps putting hand
           on Dame's knee)
Dame   (taking hand away) They all start that way

King	There's something about you that I like
Dame	You try and get it
King	You make me feel all gaga
Dame	You make me feel all unnecessary
King	I'm on fire
Dame	Put yourself out. What's your name?
King	...
Dame	(pushing hand away) It ought to be Handy Andy (hand business kept up throughout)
King	You're trifling with my affections
Dame	You're trifling with my skirt

(Dame feels faint. King brings in trolley with two large bottles and bowl of goldfish. He gives her drink from first bottle Waters of Strength)

Dame	I can feel it going through my veins. I'm all of a glow (She is sitting on bench down R by leg and adjust balloons at ankle)

Her arms swell up enormously with balloons for muscles. She staggers about. "Come up and see me sometime" Dame returns to bench DR. King gives her bowl of goldfish. She eats fish and swallows water. Her body swells up enormously with balloons in her front / two balloons. Stagger about. Business with swollen tummy, noises. She lies on bench and pulls cover like cover of roll-top desk to hide herself

King	What have I done? I know, I'll give her the water of youth

(He puts down bottle by bench. Goes to look at book. Dame unrolls cover, drinks whole bottle, pulls cover down again)

King	Take one teaspoonful to take back a thousand years (looks at bottle) She's drunk the lot. I wonder what the result will be.
	(Unrolls cover. Large monkey (doll) is revealed)

Cricket routine (details from OG)
Comic. Who's going to bat? Entrance of wicket keeper after first gag, plays very well off. Going down business when batting. Caps, blazers, running gag "well, they're my things" Statue business with two fielders. Comic fields, then bowls, then bats, finally wicket keeps. At end is hit by batsman when keeping wicket.

Football story and match gag (details OG)

William Tell
Ugly Sisters enter in comedy Archery costumes. Tall one with tiny bow and arrow and vice versa. Baron joins them with Shh gag. Buttons crosses with gun and shooting hat.
Where are you going Buttons?
Fishing
Exit Buttons
He must be after flying fish
Bang off. Re-enter Buttons carrying haddock with hole in it. Smelling business. He's shot a humming bird. Shooting practice business leading into putting apple on Buttons head. He objects. Cowardy Custard business sung by others. Buttons is afraid. Coy business by Buttons when soothed by Ugly Sister. Shaking business by Buttons with drum noises. Bow and arrow too dangerous.
Let's get the blunderbuss
Buttons takes bite from apple during getting of blunderbuss. They sight the blunderbuss, see something wrong, walk to Buttons, take apple off head, examine it, then walk back. Business with small Ugly Sister in hobble skirt. Buttons takes another bite, frozen into position when Ugly Sisters turn round. They sight weapon again. See something wrong. Examine apple. Ugly Sister and the Baron both take bite, start to walk back, turn twice freezing Buttons each time as he eats, catch him the third time, his mouth full, go up to him. Ugly Sister hits his cheek and he spits apple over other

US's face. They put apple back and start again. "I cannot move, I cannot move" Buttons repeats it imitating US's funny voice. Waggly pistol, duelling pistol. US fire and miss, Baron shoots "That's funny, that's the first time I've missed" Cloud of poultry fall from flies.

One from two
Are you married
Yes
Any children
One
You and your wife are one
And your child is one
One from one makes three
A and B to Buttons
Are you married
No
Have you a sister? (splashing gag)
Is your sister married?
Yes
Any children?
Five
Have you a brother?
Brother married, one child
One from two makes three
You're wrong - they adopted the child

Headline Gags
Woman in Kilburn has twenty-first child - Husband applies for Marshall Aid
Post Office pulls down a hundred telegraph poles - Gag re dogs
Someone has quintuplets - Churchill blames Attlee

End to baths scene
Each of various characters enter from bath doors saying "Look what I found in my bath" with various props - rat etc. Emperor ends with same line and entrance, undressed Dame

Interruption scene
Straight man singing Bedouin love song. Applause too soon. "I do not want any applause till I've finished"
You have it while you can get it
You're too soon
Too soon business
On line "Fire" Dame (in box) puts on fire helmet and turns syphon on straight man from box. "Pom pom" from Dame on orchestral interlude. "Understa-a-a-and" imitated by Dame and Wishee. "My cry" Mizow business rat thrown onto stage. Veil business from Dame. Dame escorted out by male attendant. Returns wearing his cap "This way for the one and ninepennies"

From Band routine
Dame   (with triangle) When do I tinkle?
Feed   Not yet
Comic   (crossing to her) I'll settle this. Do you want to tinkle?
Dame   I've wanted to tinkle all day
Comic   Have a tinkle (she does) (to feed / conductor) You see, there's no need for all this unpleasantness.

Interruption Scene
(Enter Fitzwarren)
Fitz   Ladies and gentlemen, in honour of the marriage of my daughter Alice to Dick Whittington, I will now recite Gray's Elegy.
         (Spot comes up on box in which Dame and Jack appear clapping loudly)
Fitz   (bowing to them) Thank you.
         (he starts to recite dramatically)
         The curfew tolls the knell of parting day,
         The lowing herd winds slowly o'er the lea –
(Dame and Jack moo lugubriously)
Fitz   I beg your pardon?
Dame   That was the lowing herd.
Fitz   Thank you very much. (Dame and Jack get up and bow to him)
         The ploughman homeward plods his weary way,
         And leaves the world to darkness and to me.
Both   (clapping) Hurray, jolly good. Well done, sir.
Fitz   (coldly) I have <u>not</u> finished.
Jack   That's a pity
Fitz   Now fades the glimmering landscape on the sight,
         And all the air a solemn stillness holds,
         Save where the beetle wheels his droning flight,
         And drowsy tinklings lull the distant folds.
Both   (playing pat-a-cake and singing) Jingle Bells, Jingle Bells, Jingle all the way
Fitz   Madam, would you and your friend mind keeping quiet, I am reciting.
         Save where from yonder ivy-mantled tower –
Jack   I say, I know a much better poem than that
Fitz   Indeed? Perhaps you would like to recite it.
Jack   Thanks, old cock (gets up)
         Santa Claus came down the spout
         He was big and strong and tall.
         He had a sack all full of goods,
         And presents for one and all.
         He gave my sis a great big kiss.
         He gave me a great big drum.
         And then he took his whiskers off
         And popped into bed with Mum. (Bows)
         It's all right – they were married.
Fitz   And now, with your permission, I will continue. I will repeat.
Dame   Pardon?
Fitz   Repeat
Jack   Hic
Dame   Granted
Fitz   The curfew tolls the knell of parting day –
Dame   We've had all that once
Fitz   Well, you're going to have it again.
         The curfew tolls the knell of parting day –
Both   Ding dong bell. Pussy's in the well
Fitz   For the last time, I insist on silence.
         Thank you
         The curfew tolls the knell of parting day –
Dame   There was an old lady of Cippenham

	Whose pants had a great big rip in 'em
	She rode into Slough
	On the back of a cow
	And never came back to Cippenham
Fitz	The curfew tolls the knell of passing day –
Jack	There was a man in Farnham Royal
	Who bought a saucepan to the boil
	There was a girl in Eton Wick
	Who hit her mother with a stick
	(he and Dame shake hands)
Fitz	Ladies and gentlemen, owing to circumstances beyond my control, I shall abandon my recitation
Both	Hurray
Fitz	Instead I shall render an aria entitled "Oh Sole Mio" (bows)
Dame	Oh Sole Whatto?
Fitz	Mio (orchestra plays introduction)
Jack	Get on with it. When are you going to start?
Fitz	That was my introduction
Dame	Oh I see. How are you?
Fitz	I'm all right. How are you?
Dame	I'm quite well. How's your father?
Fitz	He's doing fine. How's your mother?
Dame	She's all right. How's little Ernie?
Fitz	Oh little Ernie's all right. But Claribel – she's got a pimple on her – Look here, I'm here for a purpose
Jack	Well get on with your purpose, and keep it clean
(Fitz prepares to sing)	
Dame	Where's your horse?
Fitz	Look here, I've had enough of this. Whatever you do I'm going to sing – willy nilly.
Jack	Never 'eard of it. (Fitz gestures to band to start again)
Dame	It's a put-up job
Fitz	What is?
Dame	Paper-hanging (Band starts again. Fitz throws head back)
Jack	I can see right up your nostrils
	(Fitz turns back on them and sings. They sing with him, making an awful noise)
Dame	Don't worry, we'll fix him

(They leave box, re-appear on stage with wheelbarrow, push Fitz into wheelbarrow and wheel him off, still singing)

Riddle Routine

What is the difference between a weasel, a stoat and a monkey? (A to Dame)

A weasel is weasily distinguished, a stoat is stoatally different

Where does the monkey come in?

He doesn't. You've been here all the time.

Dame repeats this to B, but says "I've been here all the time" Oh, I've said it wrong, haven't I?"

Tree of Truth Routine (Dame and Squire)

S	Do you see that tree?
D	Of course I see it, I'm not deaf.
S	That is the tree of truth. If you tell a lie when sitting under that tree, the fruit of falsehood falls upon your head
D	Well, you'd better not sit there had you? (They sit under tree)

D	I've been married four times. Twice for love and twice for revenge.
S	I've had the good sense to remain single (fruit on head) I've got nothing to hide (f)
D	I'm just a simple girl (f)
S	Go on, you can trust me (f)
D	(re drink) I know when to stop (f)
S	That's why I admire you (f)
D	No man apart from my husband has ever kissed and cuddled me (shower of fruit – blackout)

Magic sleeping hat
When you wear it you can't hear a sound, when you take it off, you can hear normally. Squire demonstrates to Simon. Simon puts it on. Squire talks in dumb show, winking at audience etc while Simon tries to hear. Simon says he will try it while Squire sings. Jealousy. Who is? You are (or who's lousy?) Oh you mean <u>jea</u>lousy. While he sings Simon takes hat on and off and Squire cuts off sound and brings up sound according to position of hat. Do this on long held note with sound cut on and off. S almost catches Squire out on ee – sound. Simon agrees to buy hat for ten pounds but when Squire asks for money Simon says "Sorry, I can't hear a word you say with this magic hat on" and exits.

Bills
We'll never pay the baker
Let's boycott the baker
How?
Eat fish and chips
As for beef, I ask you, when was beef higher?
When the cow jumped over the moon.

A fat girl and thin girl were smoking a cigarette. Who finished first? Fat girl, she took bigger drawers.

For Laundry Routine
Corsets. Accordion business Comic puts them on and struts round. Red pants. "These belong to Mrs Braddock" (patch) "She must have been having an all-night sitting." Comic and Dame do washing in flicker wheels – Old Silent Film effect with jangly piano. Very quick to start with, then in slow motion.

Blinds Routine
Three blinds worked from right to left. When third is down first two go up. Third up when first two pulled down. All three go up. Pulls them down one by one from left to right but third ie No 1 comes down by itself. All three up. All three pulled down. Third (no 3) is held down by foot. Shh to audience and creep away. All three up at end.

Undressing scene
Put on golf green socks to get into bed with. Tiny screen for putting on nighty. Washing business with jug and basin and real water. Just dip hands in water and damp slightly behind ears. Pour water in drawer. Look under bed, produce hatbox, get out nightcap. Pummelling pillow, noise of rattling when shaken. Candle blown out then comes on again. "Nighty, nighty."

Animals

Horse and cart Routine
Handcart. One comic riding, one walking. Comic riding starts spiel interrupted by horse neighing.

To make it shut up he hits it on rear and it falls down bringing cart with it and comic. After business getting horse up again, middle of skin gets twisted, then it closes right up with backside pointing down. Build up that horse is going to jump tiny hurdle. Music. Stops at last minute. Laughs when argued with. Second attempt it rears up. Then falls with legs spread out front and back. Snorts flour. Attenshun. Business Eventually runs off pushing cart like handcart

(This is pants with three legs)
This is an angel's coat.
How do you know?
It's got St Michael on it
One pair of stockings with no feet
Sandie Shaw
One long hair net
Mick Jagger

Horse Routine
Jumping over small hurdle. Gallop. Knocks it over first time. Second time stops, then steps over it. Picks up hat with teeth. Comic bends down to show him and Horse kicks him. Sentimental stuff, horse rejected. "I've brought you up from the time you were a little rocking horse." (shows with hand how high horse was. Horse looks down to height of hand) "Sorry" Reunited, Army routine. Shun. Stand at ease. Form fours. March off with semi-limp.

Scene with Dog
Comic reads out bill. Monday one lb of steak taken by Bonzo. B shakes head. No? (Bonzo hits floor twice) <u>Two</u> pounds steak by Bonzo. Goes on itemizing B's steals and B starts to creep away, brought back twice. Cod liver oil taken by B. Ends (in Humpty) by comic sending B away. I sent you for a bite in the kitchen and you bit Mother in the pantry.

Cab Routine
Complete cab. Roof has paper pasted over so head comes through. Floor gives way when they get in. Door comes off. Rabbit and stocking found inside. Back gives way and comic somersaults out. Step is on a spring. Comic as cabman, comedy horse, two comics in cab. Routine: Open door, door off. Running gag: "The door's come right off." Cleaning out cab. "Stocking's come right off." Bottom of cab gives way. Cabby mends it. Wood through legs of comic but he doesn't realize it. "You've got a splinter" "Where" "Right through the middle of your Thames Valley." Cab rocks as Dame gets on step. Phone business to Cabby, picks up phone. Dame puts head through roof and says hullo. Two inside lean back and back gives way and they fall out. "Mrs Winterbottom" "I'm not Mrs Winterbottom, I'm Mrs Summerup" They go into pub. Horse follows them. Re-enter from pub and horse sits down wrong way in shafts and is reversed by Cabby. "Excuse me" "Why, what have you done?" "Is your name ____?" "no" "Then you must have a double" "Thanks I will" All into pub again. Re-enter tight, horse tight.

Cat Scene 1
Cat told not to touch saucer of milk. Left alone on stage with it. Asks audience not to tell on it, drinks milk. Comic returns and asks audience if cat has drunk milk. Audience does not tell

Cat Scene 2
Stray cat appears. Welcomed, told to keep watch while comic reads paper. Cat sits on watch for a moment, then comes and looks over comic's shoulder, follows line of print with eyes quickly. Comic sees him looking and holds paper for him. "There's a bit there you missed out" Told naughty pussy and must keep watch. Pussy cries. "If you go on like this, I'll have to get the plumber in." Don't cry Pussy. Reconciliation. "He's trying to get round me" "He has got round me" (after cat has

circled him) Pussy shows hunger, comic tries to pour milk but pussy walks to and fro through legs and stops him by insistence. Cat looks at poured milk with head on one side then drinks it. Given tiny drop more. Refused more. Cat gets cross, bangs saucer on ground, then knocks it across floor and scratches itself. Comic says will beat cat. Tells Pussy to come. Pussy coy, comic does miaoux. Comic lures Pussy to him. "Shall I beat him?" to audience "Shall we kiss and make up?" Puts out lips for cat to kiss, closing eyes. Cat takes face in paws and looks at it from several different angles, finally spits in it. Comic falls over, cat runs to entrance, looks at comic through legs and runs off chased by comic.

Shoeing horse bus
Horse laughs. Bald blacksmith laughs till Dame puts hot shoe on his bald head. Kicking business all around. Horse sits down. Horse sings.

Cat Scene III
Enter to Big Bad Wolf with blue bow. Cat miaows "hullo" and holds paw up to shake hands. Cat has mouse. Plays with mouse. Crouches down and hisses, pats it etc. "Do you want to give it to me?" Cat shakes head. Cinders puts mouse away for cat until wanted again. "Are you going out tonight? I believe you're in love. Is it Blackie? Is it Ginger? Is it Tabby?" Cat acts coy. "What's he got that the others haven't got? If you're going to be late tonight I'd better give you a key." Large key given cat. Exit with cat.

Horse Bus
Horse does Scotch number.
I thought so, he's been on the Scotch
Horse does wanting to go to lav business with front legs

Cow Scene
Approach cow to milk her. Tail switches. Cow shakes head. Cow kicks milker and stool over. Sits down on stool itself and twirls round. Second comic on shows first how to milk, gets kicked over etc. Little boy shows them how one on stool, one on tail, take your time from me. "Anvil Chorus" routine. Other business for cow, standing with two right feet wrapped over two left feet. All horse bus

Introduction of Cook to Cat
Cook not knowing it is cat. "You silly kipper" Cat behind cook. Cook thinking it is Fitz. Cat while drinking milk stroked and lifts whole body up in ecstasy.

Cat Routine IV
Cat tells how old it is by tapping on floor with paw. "Three months?" Cat shakes head and touches ears with paw three times. "Oh I see, three years" Funny story-telling business: laugh and push, comic bending down to cat. Work up to cat laughing and pushing comic so hard that he falls over.

Cow Routine
On back of cow a notice saying "Register with me" Cow kisses Dame. Brush cow with broom, comb hair with big comb. Make up cow's lips with lipstick which cow eats. Powder cow's nose. Cow bites Dame's bottom when she is bent down. Put pail and stool in position for milking but cow moves. Repeat. Put stool under cow and sit on bucket, kick bucket away knocking it over. Milk cow by raising tail. Tinned milk comes out. "For export only" Pair of shows "Real cow hide" Bottle of beer, cow takes this in teeth. Exit to Volga Boat Song.

Horse routine
Enter on horse "Come this side" Horse goes other side. Horse wants to bite him. Asks audience to

warn him if horse comes in by calling horse's name. Horse comes on side, cut-out of horse comes from other side. Both sides at once? Blotto chases him. Crying business from horse on sentimental speech by comic. Drilling business with audience shouting words of command. Form fours etc. Horse kicks self. Smacking of horse's bottom. Exit as camel with Eastern music.

Cow scene with cow dancing better than comics and them trying to do dances cow doesn't know. End with polka and cow twisted up. Running line – "Who did it best, us or the cow?"

Simple Simon aint here yet
Dame repeats this. Where's your grammar?
Gone to the pictures with Granpa
You mustn't say Simple Simon aint here
You must say Simple Simon aint here yet.

If I gave you six apples and then six more apples, what would you have?
Tummyache

Dame stops football gag with whistle then takes cap (ball) from them and throws it in herself

You juvenile detergents

Dame about to hit with nap but doesn't. Victim cries enormously

"Stop laughing" to gloomy boy and knock him over. Repeat several times. Eventually hits another boy and both he and original boy fall over.

I know I'm a foolish woman to give way to feminine emotions

What's that scar on your neck?
That's my appendix
It's the first time I ever heard of an appendix being taken out of the neck
They had to in my case because I'm ticklish down here

We'll go to Vienna and sail down the waters of the Danube in a gorgonzola
Gorgonzola? You are a fool. You mean a Chaffoniere

You held my hand (in the picture house)
And you held both mine
I had to

Large file used to file toenails

I'm the pretty one
No, I am

Taking long cummerbund off one US exit other with one end. It goes on unrolling. Other enters on other side with end of cummerbund marked "The End"

When the Prince sees my figure I've got two things in my favour. I'll overwhelm him. Not when I've finished with you (bursts two balloons)

Bra with three breasts. This is my Brook Bond Tea Bra. Two cups, two lumps and one for the pot.

Captain Birdseye (man with beard)

Fox fur thrown out of laundry basket. Goes off on string.

A bit of a draught round the Marble Arch (re dress)

Perfume called Sudden Surrender. They warn you not to wear it if you're bluffing.

Throwing away tangerines, then eggs (dummy) from egg carton

He's our type too
Under ninety and breathing

A galaxy of talent
Positively galaxative

(When approaching man) I'll think of something on the way over. I may even try the subtle approach. (falls into his arms) Hullo Cheeky

Ladies of such culture
And it's all physical I'm glad to say

Together we'll tie the marriage knot. Together we'll get knotted

She was so fat that when she fell over she rocked herself to sleep trying to get up

Twelve children. A baker's dozen eh?
Well two of 'em were the baker's. The others were the milkman's

Are you a grass widower? Yes
Splendid. I'm a vegetarian

Re bum (over knee) You get cheekier every day

Windmill Pie. Windmill Pie?
Yes, if it goes round you can have some

What's the time when a Chinese goes to the dentist?
2.30 (Tooth hurty)

Ugly Sisters exit. "Back to the Nunnery"

Don't be common
Shut your face

She's never been the same since she saw the Virgin Soldiers

Oh the Diddy Men from Knotty Ash
We've been hoodwinked
Yes, they winked our hoods

You chunky flunky

(To Prince) Can I take Corgis for walkies?

I think I'm going to have one of my turns (turns round) It's all right, I've had it.

Costume: jug on head. Basin round neck as collar. "I'm sure there's a third piece to this set"

I'll get the Prince to put a ring on my finger or bust.
Well, make your mind up which.

I'm sorry I'm late. I've been three and a half hours trying to stuff a turkey. I could have killed it.

A gift of precious stones from General de Gaulle
General de Gaulle?
Yes de Gaulle stones

A sad book
Name of sexy book Lady Chatterley's Lover
That's not a sad book
It is when you're my age

Order given. Three cups of tea and a bit of crumpet.
You know you haven't got any crumpet
Three cups of tea and a muffin

GB on license plate
I got that from George Brown
What does GB stand for?
Gone Boozing

He said I haven't had a bite for a week
What did you do?
I bit him

I'm so hungry I could eat a horse
Well don't look at me

She's been playing tiddly winks with the Duchess. Oh that match was over hours ago. The Duchess tiddled when she should have winked

Sound of bells on tannoy
What's that?
Me wringing my hands

Three chimes
Oh dear, one o'clock three times

Lovely to be back here in Peyton Place

Tea poured out. Only water. "I like it weak"
How many lumps? Nine

Dame pours tea into sugar basin and gives it to him as cup

Americans. You know what they're like. They've got the statue over there and they take their liberties over here

I've got a lovely room in Paddington and she's got a flat behind

I appeal to you on my bended knees
You don't appeal to me in any position

Two beautiful diamonds on ring given to Dame
What changed your mind?
A double diamond

Little corgi. I call her Bessie Braddock
Bessie Braddock? Why?
She does little motions around the house

Alarm clock with string.
That's my potato clock. I set it at night and in the morning you get up at eight o'clock

You've got so many bags under your eyes your nose looks like a saddle

Made it (money) out of the fat of the land.
Fat of the land?
Yes he makes corsets for Elizabeth Taylor

Difference between C sharp and B flat
The difference etc is a banana skin lying on the pavement
What has a banana skin lying on the pavement got to do with it?
If you don't see sharp you'll be flat

I am sorry
Am you?

You can always tell a widow
Yes, but you can't tell 'em much

Bill for piano. If I don't pay for the piano they'll come and take it away.
Water rates. If I don't pay water rates they'll come and cut water off
If I don't pay for grandfather's funeral they'll dig him up tomorrow

To Cinderella. Get upstairs and clean the carpet and catch the dust before it settles

With other in bread costume. US enters with frying pan complete with bacon and eggs painted on it and chops for ear-rings

Very short Tartan dress

We are the Baron's little girls

Your magistrate

Lift can-can skirt. Ooh La La on inside

The Virgin Soldiers

Not a pot washed, not a sausage pricked.

I wish I was ten years younger.
How long?

I saw a lady come out of a swimming pool and give a penny to the attendant. She was very honest. She found it on the bottom of the pool.

Fancy me being related to royalty. From now on you'll always find me in the King's Arms.

My little hot cross bun

(Before actually seeing Genie)
There's a funny smell of gorgonzola
Aladdin: He's the Genie
I thought he was a pickled gherkin
I want my washing done and up on the line
(Genie makes this happen – line on wire with three pairs of pants on it)
We've won the pool. Three draws."

(to Emperor) I see you grow your own bootlaces

What could be better than a piano in the parlour?
A fiddle in the passage (coy business)

All the sopranos, contraltos, basses and Guinesses

Let me think. I've got it.
He's thunk

Dame to Comic "Smacky botty"

(re chicken) Look at this, twelve and six he asked. I got him down to ninepence.

(re supper) Any afters?
Yes, the washing up

Dame and Mayor on sofa (re Dame's dress) Can I share the bedspread? Girlie? Do you mind if I call you girlie or am I too late? Sneezing business Blowing wigs off footmen

Dame's son "I'll be good for a shilling"
Dame "At your age I was good for nothing"

Everything's going up. Something came down last week but that was only owing to bad elastic

Shall I ring for tea?
(Presses nipple on naked chest (half naked chest). Bell rings loudly. Feed brings out cup of tea and

saucer from back of torn shirt.

Have you a long pedigree?
Why, is it showing?

Enter with cat on hat
I put the Sheriff's cat out two days ago and I haven't seen her since. (work to audience reaction)

Fascinated
Vaccinated?

I like an old man. They don't yell, they don't tell and they're ever so grateful

You've got something the others haven't got
You're telling me

Moustache business Kiss and Dame comes up with moustache on

Have you ever run after a man
No, but I may have walked a bit quick

He took me into the woods to pick bluebells.
There were so many people we had to pick bluebells

Business moving cow out of way. Sit down. Oh I've sat right in it

Your father was not my first love
No, I had a bicycle when I was younger

A stamps foot twice
Dame: How dare you tell everyone your father was a business conductor

You've had every tunyoperty

You remind me of Nero
You will keep fiddling

(hand on knee)
I'll give you two hours to take your hand away

I've got to go down to the Police Court. I may be away about fourteen days

I want a husband who'll love me when I'm old and fat
Oh they don't do that. They say they'll love you for better or for worse, not through thick and thin

You – you –
So you're calling me a yu-yu

The night is young and I'm so beautiful
Well, the night is young

I shall never wash that spot again (after kiss)

You'll wallow in riches
I thought you said I'd swallow me breeches

He treats me with distemper
You want a Bob Martins

Did your first husband leave you much when he died?
No, but he left me pretty often when he was alive

I've got the lamp mother
It's no good, you can't get the paraffin

He's magic
He's mouldy

Isn't my face familiar? (puts arm around Dame)
No, but your actions are

Look at my face
Make a good door-knocker, wouldn't it?

Diamond tiaras
Diamond pyjamas

I wish you had a photograph of what I'm thinking

My husband stood nine foot six in his stockinged feet and there was snow on his hat all year round

In the cinema there was a man molesting women. I had to change my seat fourteen times.
Did you get molested?
(happily) Eventually

(to one wearing chain of office) If I pull your chain will you flush?

(to one going near breast) Careful, there's less in there than meets the eye

I can't go to the banquet. I've been on a diet of nuts and bananas for six months.
Have you lost any weight?
No, but I can't half climb trees

Corsets scene – Ugly Sisters. Get audience to shout "Pull

I'll give them Andrews Liver Salts
What good will that do them?
None, but at least I'll know where they are

Name business Forgets it. Have you got amnesia?
I had some this morning. Milk of Amnesia

I drank twenty four cups of tea this morning

It keeps me going. I won't say where to

I was using the royal we
There's one in the palace
(separate gag) Going out for a wee while
This castle must be as high as Everest
I beg your pardon?
Everest
(starts to have a rest) I think I will

How old is Granny? Well put it this way. You know that Phyllosan fortifies the over forties? She's been taking it for twenty five years.

First flush of womanhood
If that's your first flush, there's something wrong with your plumbing

Over my dead body
That can be arranged

Shall I pour coffee on the terrace?
Yes. We can all paddle in it

Thirty six pound turkey. Thirty six pounds! I couldn't get it in the oven. I got so mad I could have killed it.

Why do cows wear bells round their necks?
Because their horns don't work

Short skirt. It's about three inches below sea level

With (about to say name) Schhh you know who

What's reindeer?
That stuff from the sky darling

I used to have a living bra, but it died from lack of nourishment

He had a terrible end
He came down a ladder three weeks after they'd taken it away

If you're not careful I'll take down your trousers and box your ears

(re Abanazer) I'm sure I've seen his face on twenty Players

(re Slave) How Wilfred Pickles has altered

This is my Mills Bomb dress. Take the pin out and it's every man for himself

How do you like my built-up area?

Reference to bosom. I do admire your contours.
I can assure you they're entirely supported by voluntary contributions

(to Dame who has feather in her hat)
I don't like the feather. I think you should wear it where the ostrich wears it.
Where's that?
In South Africa

How were you married?
In a hurry

You know what a miser is?
Yes. A man who catches mice

Don't speak in inverted commas

When I look at your face time stops still
Do you mean my face would stop a clock?

I'm pure as driven snow
I bet you're longing to drift

Boys will be boys and aren't we girls glad of it

Aren't you then old woman who lived in a shoe?
No, I'm the other one. I did know what to do

I'm going spare

What shall I do with this?
Sorry, but I must stick to the script

If you tickle me I come over all unnecessary

Here's mud in your eye
Here's holes in your socks
Skin off your nose
Water on your knee
Happy days
Glamorous nights

(after taking off corsets)
My tummy looked like a golf ball
I had the maker's name right round here
Think of it… (local shop name)

Have you seen your son by chance?
What do you mean by chance? He's legitimate

My husband had a head eight inches round
Good thing it isn't twelve inches round or it would be a foot

Give the baby onions and you'll find it in the dark

I love Paris
You dirty old so-and-so

I will go even further
You would

£5 kiss from young man. Build to Dame's exit to go blackberrying

My daughter's a debutante. She's coming out next year. She looks just like me.
In that case hadn't you better keep her in?

Pursue me (jumping bus)

I think I shall wed again
Well, two weds are better than one

My eyes are watering. One of my pupils didn't have time to put his hand up

You're only young once
I was young three times

You're one in a million
You look to me as though you'd been won in a raffle

Let me be your faithful swine
There was an old farmer had an old sow

Does he come up to scratch?
No, he goes down to tickle

We'll play Air Mail
What's that?
Post Office on a higher plane

Dame's Undressing Scene
Music – Goodnight Sweetheart
Takes off hat, which she hands to someone offstage. Cleans teeth with large brush and toothpaste tube. Drops them in box. Picks up large framed mirror with glass and comb. Hair combing business Puts all props in same box. Puts two bulldog clips from box onto hair. Takes off dress, puts it in box. Takes off brassiere which is really two chip-frying pans tied together. Takes off long roll dress which is helped off by Cat running on and pulling end of dress till it is off. Picks up Vim tin and powders herself. Takes off girdle made of hot water bottles. Takes off trunks with Save Fuel on them. Takes off trunks advertising local beer. All these in box. Takes off trunks with the utility markings. Takes off trunks Export Only. Takes off trunks with Union Jack and Rule Britannia on them. Takes off corsets which are locked with large padlock, by undoing same with large key on chain hanging from her neck. Puts all in box. She is now dressed in striped pants only. She steps into nightdress which is arranged by box. Picks up large electric candle of wobble variety. Waves goodnight to audience. Candle wobbles violently. She eventually gets it straight and exits with it.

I shall recite The Flea – a little thing out of my own head

There was a young man called Vickers

Who took his best girl to the flickers
He saw some pink wool
So he started to pull
And that's how the girl lost her – jumper

I'm Rita Haybag
And who is this?
That's my mother

My name's Gertrude. I'm called Gert for short. Yes, I cut out the rude part

I was in a business the other day and a man said to me "Would you like my seat?" I looked him straight in the eye and said "No thank you, there's still plenty of wear left in mine."

My first husband's name was Robinson
I had such fun buying Robinson Truseau

My new perfume – California Skunk. Anyway, it gives you that "bite me" feeling

I do envy you
Why?
The thrill of meeting me for the first time

At the moment they're USA
USA in America?
No USA. Upstairs in the attic

I'm sure we're going to be such friends, perhaps even something deeper
Like Romeo and Juliet?
Yes, or Huntley and Palmer

Our alarm clock was set for six
Well?
There's seven in our family

This is an American frock, yes American. One Yank and it's off

Only one drawback to riding. It may not affect you in the beginning, but it certainly gets you in the end.

I love this part of the country. I stay down here quite often.
Are your stays long?

You know the Savoy of course?
Of course, the Savoy is a cabbage with a permanent wave

My nephew in the army's doing awfully well. He's only been in a week and he's been promoted to a Court Martial already. I think he's growing tomatoes now. Something like that. Anyway, he's in the Glasshouse.

Bust bodice
What made it bust?

The business was so crowded even the men were standing

Writ
Who wrote it?

You're only a subject
You're not even an object

Yes and No
What do you mean yes and no. You sound like a government department

On Pants
No entry
Rinse and return
The end

I've got this watch from the Squire.
(listening to it) It doesn't work.
Oh no, he's giving me the works tonight

I've been in bed with flu
Well that's better than being under the bed with fluff

I can't have any lunch today, I've lost my corkscrew

Don't you call _me_ a good woman
You know best

I shall go to the Rent Tribunal about you

Re veil. Standing there with that birdcage on
That's not a birdcage. That's a barbed wire entanglement to protect me from you.

I can't help being poor. I'm not a politician

She doesn't know any of the answers.
I know _all_ the answers but no-one asks me any of the questions

Just as I reached your front door someone shouted "They're coming down" and they were

Do you file your nails?
I always throw mine away

I'm using flour for powder. Every time I blow my nose I break out in biscuits

Ammonia, I appeal to you
Appeal dismissed, six months

(to Dame) Do you know something? (pat cheek) You haven't shaved this morning

A game. You chase me under the table and then I chase you under the table.

Where does the fun come in?
Under the table

I'm going to take some M and B
Yes, Mild and Bitter (or Mitchell and Butlers)

I'm all aflame
I'll get a bucket of water and put you out
Come closer, closer, closer (Dame does so)
If I come any closer, I'll be behind you
Let me pluck the nectar from your lips
I'd rather have a gin and vermouth
You're a basket of flowers
Don't you call me a basket
Do you sing? Do you sing?
I don't sing, no. I hum a bit (into number)

Tar, ever so tar

Letter from Town Hall. They're coming to cut my water off on Monday

What's that on your neck?
A mole
A mole. How funny, it's moving

Don't shush in my face
You shouldn't have such a face to be shushed in

You're nothing but an old haybag
Haybag?
Haybag your pardon

Whispering business He didn't. He did. Repeat several times. He did. And he hasn't come back from America yet.

Nighty, nighty
Pyjama, pyjama

Would you say I looked Regal?
Oh yes. In fact, you look Marble Arch too

You're like a goddess
Burst my bodice, how dare you?

Romantic patter
It was a wonderful sunset just after closing time, then he appeared – my hero. He picked himself up (romantic build-up to what he said) "What's cooking, kid?" In meadow we dallied etc. he was so kind, so attentive. He moved a cow so we'd have a warm spot to sit down.

All men are cast in the same mould. Only some are more mouldy than others

I'm five foot two

With heels?
With anybody

Corset business On floor. My big end's gone. Something's gone. Can't pick up purse from ground. Ratchet noise every time bends down.

Umbrella
Dropped on ground. Hole in stage. Umbrella dances. Dame dances too

Ugly Sister: Cinderella, to the sink

Was there something? (To Dame. Dame looks behind her)

Can I cook? Can I cook? (scornfully)
No!

Re small man. Look, Gordon Richards. I didn't recognize you without your horse.

He said "haven't we met before?" I said "no." He said "You must have a double" I said "I don't mind if I do."

I stood in a queue for two hours for a sausage

When I was young everybody was after me, dogs and all

As Shakespeare said, "As surely as the sun sets in the West." "Yes?" "So will the bread rise in the yeast."

Did he love me? Many's the time I've sat holding his hand for hours. If I'd let him go, he'd have killed me.

I've been a good mother to you, a better mother than your father ever was.

Shaking mat with powder on it by Dame in face of Broker's Men

Broom business by Dame to King at eviction various positions with broom ending with drill business and march off

If I had a face like yours I'd put it on a wall and throw a brick at it.
If I had a face like yours I'd put it on a brick and throw a wall at it.

Have you had tea yet?
No
What a shame, I've had mine

Picture of cow on wall. They sing goodbye to it. Eyes move. Dame mops those eyes.

Clean chair with own bum for guest

Description of husband with bag of tools
Plane. Saw. Level. Hammer. Rule. Square. File. Screw. Awl. Nail. (Bag of bass) no good finish

Smell that. Cote Sheep
Smell that. Barney's Bull

You don't a bath. You want a rub down with an oily rag

I was flat-chested but my young man didn't mind.
What he lost on the swings he gained on the roundabouts

Kathleen West
Crying business Frontcloths "If this isn't love" "That lovely weekend"
Imitation of ventriloquist's doll

Oh Prince you couldn't lend me a couple of bob till Friday.

Haddock Finnan
Take it away and bring a thick 'un

(in mirror) God, who's that. It frightened my life out

Ugly Sisters
(looking in mirror) Oh. What's that?
(Gives mirror to other US who looks in it) That's me
Oh, I thought it was me
Bell chimes on the hangings from corset

Love… it starts when you sink in his arms and it ends with your arms in his sink

Present of garters to Dame. "Now I can give back the Council their red tape" (takes red tape from bloomers)

(Fainting bus) Oh, I've gone all semolina

(to Principal Boy) You, my little boy I used to bath every night in the pudding basin

Don't cry mother
I like it, it makes me thirsty

I shall marry the Emperor and be the Empress and we'll have lots of little empties

You don't know me, do you?
No, I don't think I've had that horror

(jewellery) I've gone all Marks and Spencers

I know a cave
I daresay, but I'm not that kind of a girl

Splashing gag with "lamp – p"

Bill comes to one ping, two pongs and a whiff

I was married. At the moment, I'm redundant

Hitting Gag
A (hitting C with club) Hullo
B Don't do that
A What?
B (hitting C to show him) That
A I didn't do that. I did that.
B You didn't. You did that.
A I did not. I did that.
(Work up business to hail of blows)

Sawing the Pole
If I had a pole three feet long and I want to make it two feet long, what do I do?
Saw a foot off
That's where you're wrong
Why?
I've lost my saw
Ah, but I'm not wrong. You can borrow mine.
No I can't
Why not?
It was your saw I lost

Pushing gag
Three people. Push passed on. No 3 falls down each time.

Entrance
Two men with noise and yells thrown out of house by child. Men first, then child dusting hands. "Let that be a lesson to you" Child raises hand to them. They retreat together.

Rum-A-Tum-Tum
Mention this as town. One starts singing with orchestra. Other elaborates it. Into exit

Noughts and crosses
Noughts and crosses played in air while No 3 explains something to them and is saying "<u>Will</u> you listen"

Cloak bus
Falling over cloak which is very long. Knocking chest. Each time B's hat falls off. End on somersault with hat staying on. Enter on each other's shoulders each in long cloak. L on back

Ladder bus
Creep on, when face to face, yell. A picks up ladder – they are trying to enter window, and knocks B with it. Snaps it on nose, drops it on feet. They each get one end. B gets head in it. A gets saw to saw it off. Shakes "blood" off the saw. One climbs ladder, one holds it. Acrobatic bus

Hit hand. Oh my foot
Hit foot. Oh my foot
Hit bum. Oh my goodness

Buttons? Oh a flyman, eh?

I may look stupid, I may act stupid, but don't let that fool you

Why not?
I am stupid

In question routine:
You be frank
I'm Wishee
When you answer these questions you must be earnest
You're making a Charlie of me
How did Charlie come into it?
Through the door with Frank and Earnest

Brokers enter on knees with small Wellingtons and long cloaks to hide real legs.

Have you got twin beds?
Yes
Well, have a Cadbury's Snack to bridge that gap

You've got hold of the hairs on my chest. I've only got three and two of them are loose.

Keep quiet, keep quiet. Don't shout.
Who's shouting?
You are

Routine
They shake hands. Their hands get stuck together and they pull apart in vain. Pinch puts one foot over hands. They strain to get apart again. Pinch puts foot right down to floor so that their hands are low down. They pull again. They twist round so that their hands are back to back, bending down. More pulls but in vain. They bring their free hands into play but these get stuck too. They twist round so that Kissem's head is stuck between Pinch's legs. With a final effort, Pinch is stretched on floor with legs to audience, with Kissem sitting on his stomach, his own legs back out of sight. It now looks like a dwarf with Kissem's body and Pinch's legs. Kissem is surprised at finding such long legs. Stretches legs. Knees give way suddenly. K sits with elbow on knee. Does little dance with legs. Event. Pinch gets up violently and K falls forward on his face.

I love you Routine
A	Say I love you with more feeling
B	I love you with more feeling
A	(passionately) I love you, I love you
B	(eyebrow bus)
A	I love you
B	(kisses him)
B	(sings Home Sweet Home)
A	You've got a rotten voice
B	I've got a rotten home

Echo Gag
Bosun	Now I've got an easy way to make some money. When Idle Jack comes along I'll bet him there's an echo round here, and you'll be the echo
Mate	What do I do?
Bosun	You go and hide over there and repeat everything that Idle Jack says. Now let's have a rehearsal. You go over there and everything I say – you say after me
Mate	Repeat everything you say. Right. (hides)

Bosun   Are you ready?
Mate   Are you ready?
Bosun   No, no, we haven't started yet
Mate   No, no, we haven't started yet
Bosun   Will you shut up?
Mate   Will you shut up?
(Bosun goes to him and kicks him)
Bosun   Shut up
Mate   (kicking him back) Shut up
Bosun   Here comes Idle Jack now. You hide here and repeat everything he says – but <u>not</u> until I
        give you the sign
Mate   Right
(Mate stays hidden. Bosun goes to meet Idle Jack)
Bosun   Hullo Jack, I bet you five quid there's an echo round here
Jack   I bet you five quid there isn't
Bosun   Here's my money (puts money on floor)
Jack   And here's mine
Bosun   Now then, let's see if there's an echo (signs to Mate)
Jack   Hullo, hullo
Mate   Hullo, hullo
Jack   Hullo, hullo, hullo
Mate   Hullo, hullo, hullo
Jack   Are you there?
Mate   Are you there?
Jack   I'm a silly twerp
Mate   You're a silly twerp
Jack   Eh?
Mate   Eh?
Jack   That's funny
Mate   That's funny
(Jack sings phrase of a popular song. Mate sings next phrase)
Jack   I know where I can get a bottle of whisky for ten and six
Mate   (appearing) Where's that?
(Jack picks up money and exits. Bosun chases Mate off)

One-handed beer Gag
Bottle of beer, glass on tray. One condition that beer drunk with one hand. Beer poured out into
glass by person making condition and he then turns glass upside down onto plate. A takes glass
and plate and rests them on his forehead, bending back. Then takes them off again so he can put
them on tray right side up this time. A "There you are, one hand." B drinks beer and says "One
hand"

Broker's men Scene
Frontcloth. Door with flap in grill. Window opening outward. Two shutters dividing in middle.
Cellar entrance below window. Knock on door by Broker's Men. Buttons opens flap from within.
"No cigarettes" Second knock. "No matches" Knock again. Shutter of window is open and knocks
one of B Men sideways. B Men get clubs, one waits by door and one by window to club Buttons.
He opens cellar entrance and hits one of them on foot. Then comes out of door and hits them both
on bum with long club. Exits through door which now works on a swivel. Brokers enter through
swivel then come out again. They peer in through window. Buttons comes out with red hot poker
and burns them on bum. Then takes hold of wrong end himself. Knock on door later "We're not
frying tonight."

Routine
One challenges other to defy laws of gravity and stand here, jump in the air, turn a complete somersault and come down on same spot. Spot marked with hat. First time B does it, A moves hat. Second time same business "Did he move it?" Audience: "Yes" "I didn't" "You did" "Oh no I didn't" "Oh yes I did" (twice) "I didn't" (quick) "You did" (quick) A: "Tell me if he moves it" B prepares to move it, then pretends not to when audience shout. One, two, two and a half etc. Business of B moving backwards etc when caught in act. A does business and finds B moving hat so kicks him on backside, they put hands on each other's shoulders rock to and fro, exit one under other, changing round (upside down) before exiting.

Broker's men
Run on from different sides and swing round on arms and fall
Same entrance, swing round on legs being entangled and fall
Exit one on other's back

Bush scene with safe
There's someone here
Who?
Me
There's someone else here
Who?
You
Anvil chorus business with hammers on safe. Shooting business either side of safe with hammers, making noises with mouth only, pausing to reload etc. Sh Sh business into train noise effect, also with mouth only. Combination of safe, should go click, click, click. They turn it, two clicks on mike, third click spoken on mike. BBC announcement business Safe opens, voice over mike. "Yoo hoo boys I'm open." Treasure in safe. Dame on and takes coal out of it or egg etc

Baron   I've got two words to say to you
Brokers Men   And we've got two words to say to you
Baron   Yes?
Brokers Men   We're going

There or four going in circle kicking each other

I'm it (repeat)
If you're it, I'm that
What's that?
That's it

Takes snuff. Several preparations to sneeze during scene, stopped each time. Finally sneezes knocks other over and floats flash

Duelling with two carrots finally up bum from behind with carrot

Hats gag
A and B talking C gagging. Each gag A takes C's hat throws it on floor and shouts "Silence!" Eventually C does it himself. All get wrong hats

One drinks
One gargles

One spits out

Crockery smashing scene
Don't make a mess and don't break any of the china
Start by breaking single pieces from dresser full of china. Throw over head when counting. (They are searching for something) Four thrown down but joined together. Some put away in bottomless drawer but fall through and break (impression is of many breaking but only a few do) One broken overhead of A by B

Join the Navy and see the world
I've seen it. I've been to Dudley Port twice

Come here, that stupid-looking one (all step forward)
Smith   Aye aye sir
Brown   Aye aye sir
Nelson One eye sir

(One character bending over side being sick)
Look, a Rear Admiral

Song by Boris Gudonov
Thank you, Boris (first two chords of accompaniment)
That's good enough

A comes in to shake hands with B and puts hands through C's legs, so when they shake, they lift B right up. B very small man

Dog with two heads (false head tied on tail)

(re red nose) Cherry Ripe
Warm hands at nose, light cigarettes at nose

What's your name?
Worthington
Any relation to the beer people?
Yes. Customers

Able bodied seamen
I can see the bodies but you don't look able
I've sailed twice round the world and once to Smethwick

If you give me a shilling, I'll give you eighteen pence.
(Counts out pennies up to eight)
There you are, eight in pence. Not bad is it?
No, but the shilling was

Telephone call
Auntie. You have left water running in the bathroom. (Water comes out of phone into face)

Watch your tongue
I can't. My nose is in the way

Eeny meeny miny mo. We stamp our feet and away we go. (Exit dancing with block effect)

Furniture scene
Various articles of furniture outside, to be taken in. Wardrobe. "Put it on my back" Falls down. "To me, to me" from another. Turn with wardrobe and knock down others. Tickle with feather duster and make hysterical. "Hold up your arm" tickle under arm. Give me three chairs. Three cheers. All loaded onto smallest man. Two chairs on arms, one with back round his neck. Basin on this chair seat. Table on basin. Wardrobe on table.

Flabbergasted
Have you ever had your flabber gasted?

Knead it (the dough)
Kneel on it on table
Use your head
Put head on it

Bread and jam eating business Fall and get jam on face. "Put it there" on other's hand

Feel like dancing. Shall I show you some steps? Yes. There you are (real steps) Snapping them shut on hand. Photo business with cloth on top of steps

Whistle. Dinner. One takes out carrot. One does knitting. Dancing, knocks sandwich out of mouth. Don't you know an antique when you see one?
Yes. How do you do?
Picking up big clock, turning to hit others with it

This is my trick with the ball
(ping pong ball on thread)
This is my trick with the scissors
Do you mind? Comic told to shut up
Feed does business with ball on thread (supposed to be invisible) Then My trick with the ball. Comic severs ball from thread My trick with the scissors

Flowers presented to Dame
Dame takes them, bloom comes off in Comic's hand, leaving Dame with stalk

Tall ghost (one man on another)
Comic fires pistol, head falls off
Comic throws head to other comics who pass it on. Exit ghost

Enter from opposite sides, hook arms and fall down

Delayed pain. Kick drum in temper and hurt foot. Pulled out still banging drum.

You are his mother
Well his father said so

Any children?
That's my business
How's business?
Lousy

I can see what you've got in that bag
Well you're not going to get any
I can see through anything
I'm going. This is no place for a girl in a thin print dress

On your chin, on your chin (sentence leading to)
You said that twice
You've got a double chin

You've got big eyes like saucers and you've got the cups to go under them

I'm all dizzy
That's how I like them. Let's go to the woods
You've won me
Has there been a raffle?
Take me while I'm warm

A is about to throw flour bag at Dame.
B   Don't you dare throw a bag of flour at poor C
Oy, Damey (she calls – he pitches it at her. Scream. A bigger bag comes from other side or same
side? And knocks down A)

Here's my card
(Punched in puncher) Change at Brixton

I can trace my ancestry back to the family tree
What are you, the sap?

(Kick) Oh, I've got such earache

There's enough water in your head to fill a kettle
There's enough gas in yours to boil it

Spell Mug
MG
There's something missing
U

You said what I heard me

Cat that lived in a chemists
Yes. Puss in Boots

The pee is silent, as in swimming

Can you scream (little oh)
Come for a walk

My father was a conjuror
What are you, one of his tricks?

It was Christmas Eve at the Flanagans
The hour was growing late
Down the chimney came Santa Claus
And landed plonk in the grate
He gave brother Billy some soldiers
And he gave me a great big drum
And then he took his whiskers off
And jumped into bed with Mum.
(it's all right – they were married)

Two worms were digging in earnest
Poor Ernest

…hairy Pyrenees
My mother suffered from that
What?
Hairy knees

Hot water bottle sewn inside fur coat

Rigoletto
If she wants to wriggle, let her

Wet water. Any other kind of water?
Yes. Beer.

What did the brassiere say to the hat?
You go on ahead while I give these two a lift

I've been reading a book called How to Diet by a Swedish doctor
Was it any good?
Yes, it won the No Belly Prize

When a laddie meets a lassie
Coming through the rye
Both of them must wear thick knickers
Cos the thistles are mighty high

A terrible accident in the bakers. A woman was electrocuted.
Electrocuted?
Yes, she trod on a bun and the current ran right up her leg

Build up re when I'm rich
Coat trimmed with vermin, and lackeys standing there in their liver

One day you will have pearls and jewels at your feet
Why, what are you going to do?
I'm going to trip up Elizabeth Taylor

It's too late. I've chalked it up all over the Palace walls. BBC. Buttons bags Cinders

I'm not crying. My eyes are leaking

Re Sisters. When they were putting mascara on their legs. I knew they were putting on their make-up. They sent me for a trowel

Re Ugly Sisters: Always complaining their shaving water's not hot

Work up from comic not knowing who wrote the poem he is reciting.
John sat in the gallery. He had no fear of falls.
Though his head was in the gallery, His feet were in the stalls
Who was that? Longfellow

How can you be so stupid?
I get up very early

All the boys undo their belts and braces, all the girls make their own arrangements

Three watches
This is a Frost watch. It only works Fridays, Saturdays and Sundays
This is a government watch. It's time it was wound up.
This is my potato clock. Potato clock? Etc Get up at eight a clock.
How do you tell the time? Ask a policeman

Show me the Sheriff and I'll show you a coward
I'm the Sheriff
I'm a coward

I'll train you to be a robber
Shall I be a train robber?

Animal, vegetable or Mr Wilson?

He can't help smiling, he swallowed a banana sideways

In some counting or paying situation – two Guiness for guineas

(To man about to touch her breast)
Take your palm off my olive

British Railways watch. It strikes every year.

Are you a married man?
No I'm one of the bachelors
You look like one of the Monkees
(After feeling business) I think he's one of the Searchers

What did the gas meter say to the shilling?
I'm glad you dropped in because I was just going out

Birds called Oh-My-Bum-Bums
They have no legs. When they land on the ground they cry "Oh my bum bum"

What are you doing down there?

I've got my nose stuck in a hole in the floor

I am the new girl
You look like the old one done up

I'm going tossing in Russian. (singing) Kiwi, Cherry Blossom, Nugget
That's not Russian
No, but it's Polish

I'm a fret worker. I work Mondays, and then I fret for the rest of the week

I'll commit suicide
You can't
I can. I've done it before and I'll do it again

Tadpole is a frog not yet
Tanner is a bob not yet

(to gorgeously dressed Dame) You must have won football pool

My solicitors are Carter Paterson.
Carter Paterson are not solicitors
Well they always handle my case

You're so bad tempered
I'm teething, I can't help it

So this is a British restaurant

The something of Magnesia

What shall we cook? One meat ball

You'll marry some nice girl
I don't want a nice girl. I want you

Own parking meter, take it out of car and put down

You shall be the favourite of my 16 wives. It says so in the marriage service
Four better, four worse etc

When I'm 69 I shall sit with all my grandchildren round me… you can't have grandchildren if you're not married. Ah, but I'll sit with all my g-children round me and tell them it's your fault they never happened.

Comic called to wings. "We're making too much noise. There's an old man in _____ who's very ill" (later) It's all right, the old cock's dead

Good morning
Good gracious

Orpheus in his Underpants

Two lines… Shakespeare
"Before I go to bed at night, I clean my teeth and make them bright." Milton

Pre-flabbergasted house

You wait till I get you by yourself
I am by myself
No you're not. I'm with you

What cooking good-looking?
Nothing spectacular, Dracula

I've searched every crook and nanny

He's got fifteen children
Fifteen children? He must be stork raving mad

I'd like to see all the beer at the bottom of the ocean
Are you a teetotaler?
No, a diver

(helping his mother) Re Turkey: I've plucked it and stuffed it. All she has to do is kill it.

Go inside (or something) and we'll be safe from the Frost
Yes and from Eamonn Andrews too

Russian dancer has seat concealed up back of coat, for sitting on to do Russian dance

You're a spy
No, my dad was a spy
Your dad was a spy?
My dad used to look after sheep etc. Yes, he was a shepherd's pie

Where's the Forth Bridge?
After the third one

Glean something from this?
I'll go and glean my shoes

I'll beat you to a jelly
What flavor?

I can see right up your nostrils

Have you ever been in love?
No, but I've felt round the edges

I'm the greatest wizard who ever wizzed
You know what a wizard is?
Yes, the inside of a chicken

I think you're disquisite

Pauper – Cinderella. She couldn't be a pauper, she could be a momma

I know a place where a woman wears nothing but a string of beads
Where's that?
Round her neck

The times I've taken you to the pictures in the four-pennies

I was brought up at Eton
You look to me as if you'd been eaten and brought up

Is it true you've kissed a hundred girls all told?
No, one kept her mouth shut

Post it to Vernons

I'm the fifth member of Scotland Yard's Big Four

Summons
Summons' going to get it in the neck

You must see my solicitors
I've seen 'em
They're a shocking sight, aren't they?

Stop, stop, this can't go on
What?
(holding up miniature shirt) This. It's too small

I'm going to sing "Until"
Until when?
Until I've finished

I'm going to sing Faust, then slow then Faust again

She's so skinny that when she sat on half a crown you could still see two shillings

(After sea or air trip) My stomach gets here tomorrow

I aint gotta pencil
Not good grammar. I have no pencil, he has no pencil etc
Well, who the hell's got all the pencils?

Twenty too. I was twenty and you were twenty too. I was not twenty two, I was twenty

Kill me and then I shall die

The umpteenth of Umptember

You've cut me to the quick and my quick cuts very quickly

I must have a long flowing train
Well there's one at Euston

What's a bachelor?
A man with no children to speak of

Aunty – Aunty Septic

To person with bum, bending over
I thought I recognized your face

When I was a boy there was no coal for a fire. My father sucked a peppermint and we all sat round his tongue

You're wicked, wicked, wicked
Three wickets down, they should be out by lunchtime

Re Queen
Give her an inch and she'll think that she's a ruler

I've got laryngitis
Laryngitis? Why aren't you sneering?
What for? It's not a secret

(after instant appearance by magic) What kept you?

What lies on the ocean bed and shivers?
A nervous wreck

I won't say you're pretty
And I won't say you're ugly
Oh
You're sort of in-between
Really?
Yes. Pretty ugly

What does a sixteen foot canary say?
(deep voice lowering over smaller person)
Who's a pretty boy then?

Well, I'm dehydrated

I'm a bum baliff
Well, it's a bum job, making all those holes in baby's chairs

He's like you, biscuits
Biscuits?
Yes, crackers

Forefathers. You had four fathers too.
Mother must have been a bit of a sport

Dame: If I did, three of them never came home

I was one of triplets
I remember the day I was born. My brother turned to me and said "Don't look now but you're being followed."

Those lips, those eyes, those nose

Spelling gag
Demisemiquaver. Each letter accompanied by a slap. "That was a comma" "no, no, that's wrong" "There's no M" Rubbing off slap

Re Dame: I'll spit in her shaving water

I'm a little stiff from Rugby
I think you're a big stiff from _____

I've ordered the dustcart
What do you mean the dustcart?
It's used to carrying rubbish

You know whisky is slow poison
I'm in no hurry

My friend's name is Mustapha
Every time he has a drink he says he must have another one

Thousands of requests from one or two people

Sausage – a steak that failed to pass his medical.

"Ah sweet mystery of life" conducted by well-known conductor U. R. Belching. "My little chipolata"

My doctor said I must have plenty of oxygen. So I have Oxo in the morning and Gin at night.

Do you know they've stopped all the buses at _____
Stopped all the buses? Why?
To let the people get off

Well I'll be nationalised!

Kate's twin sister – Duplicate

Is there anybody about?
Yes. Who? Us
Is there anybody else about?
Yes. Who? You

Girl: You can't expect me to sit on that dirty seat
Comic: It's a bit mucky isn't it?
(gets out vest from back of coat and puts it down for her on seat. Next time gets out pants)

Frying tonight notice hung on the Emperor during transfixion scene

Pease pudding and bangers

Sorry but I've just seen something awful
What?
You

I was in a trance once
I know. When are you coming out of it?

My grandfather was so crooked when he died they had to screw him into the ground

Who was the first footballer?
Moses, he dribbled down his beard

You look to me like a razor blade
Well, I'm Ever Ready

I can't talk to a fool
I can, carry on

Bet five pounds change into an Admiral of Fleet in thirty seconds. (Music and retire behind screen. Clothes thrown up, appear same on chord) He's in fancy dress

I was a contemporary of _____'s. He held me in the greatest contempt

(looking down shirt) The doctor told me to keep an eye on my stomach

Princey, you don't arf look smashing

I could love you till the cows come home (mooing off). Blimey, they're home early.

I want to be bound to you in deadly padlock
You'd better get a locksmith

We must find out where we are by studying local conditions.
The conditions in our local are awful

The time we were stranded in _____ and couldn't get back to England

Charles Boyer
More like his brother Life Buoyer

What's a flirt?
A person who goes round destroying the germs of love

Trouble with you is you're next to an idiot
You're telling me

I can see myself now when I was only a baby. I can hear the nurse saying "Buttons, sit up and have your eyes put in"

My parents don't know I do this sort of thing. They think I'm still in prison

The Borough Treasurer is learning music. He doesn't need to. He's good enough on the fiddle. When I called on him he was in the kitchen cooking the accounts… Jumble Sale where everyone brings along what they don't want. Last week several women brought along their husbands.

Prop gag
Putting prop at side of proscenium. Audience must shout out something when anyone tries to steal it. Get the audience to try shouting straight away (ref to those in bargain basement) Try one pinching business right away as soon as audience has tried out the shouting

I'm it
I'm that
What's that?
That's it

Short blackboard gag
King
Pig
Cobbler
5 Policeman
North Pole
South Pole

(after knock) Someone's knocking on the [illegible]

Kissy kissy
A Kissy Kissy Kissy (two light taps on cheek to block noises)
B repeats same business with hard knocks (different block) and knocks A over

Singing in the Rain
Comic or Dame singing this. Second Comic gets cape and sou'wester and puts them on her. Then watering can and steps which he mounts and are fixed to her back. Exit singing, B pouring water from can, A with umbrella up.

How about some cigarettes with tobacco tips?

It's not my knees shaking, it's the wind blowing up my trousers

Principal Boy to Comic: If you do that again, I'll take your head and throw it over there (noise) and I'll take your legs and throw them over there etc. Business build up with all parts of the body noises, and comments from comic. "What do you say to that?" "That's me all over."

(Enter with horn) I'm riding in my car. I've bought it on the instalment plan. I've paid one instalment and they gave me this. (into) What is the difference between that and that business with horn

Crisps. Don't take a blue one. I had blue one yesterday. It wasn't half salty

I know I'm no Robert Doughnut

Wonderful fags. They call them Vernons – four draws and you're away

What would you give to have hair my colour?
I don't know, what did you give?

A bit big for twelve aren't you?
They fed me on elephant's milk

Toasting bread by candle flame. Candle in bottle

When I see that Giant I'll get my nose between his teeth and I won't let go

I call my dog Ingersoll
Why?
He's a watch dog

What would you do it you had that? (clenched fist)
Wash it

I'll show you how to kiss
Put your lips together and suck

I worked in a factory making counterfeit half-crowns. I had to give it up. The money was no good.

(Underwear job. Underwear in pocket). Only thing left in pocket half a nicker

(singing) Pyjamas are coming down (three times)
Conductor: What's the name of this song?
The Lost Chord

Is it expensive? Yes, it says inside the box Woolworth 2/6d

Where do you live? My card (business ticket punched in puncher by comic)

Who are you shoving?
Here, where's your grammar? Not who are you shoving? Who are you a shoving of?

I'm going to marry the Squire and have a lot of little squirrels

Wedding build up with organ playing Rescue the Perishing

When were you born?
1066 BR
BR?
Before Rationing

Have you heard the latest, babies by wireless?
Where are you going?
To put my aerial down

Do you know they're going to pave all the streets of Birmingham with wooden blocks?
Where will they get all the wooden blocks from?

The Town Councillors are going to put their heads together

I think you're nice
I think you're nice
It's nice, isn't it?

Playing with the squirrels. The squirrels always play with me. They think I'm nuts.

Where did you learn to kiss like that?
I used to blow a bugle in the Boy Scouts

What are you bobbing up and down for?
I've just taken some medicine and I forgot to shake the bottle

Crew, shun
I never touch it
What?
Kruschen

Who was Lady Godiva?
She was a cyclist. She went round without a tyre

I'm upset. I'm put out.
When you're put out it's closing time

Where's the doctor?
Practising
I'll come back when he's perfect

East is East
And West is West
And North and South are irrelevant
Everyone knows you can milk a cow
But you can't mess about with an elephant

There was a girl with golden hair (lovely locks)
She curled it
And at night it curled up in a box
I knew a girl completely bald
Her head was bare
She painted rabbits all over her head
And everyone thought it was hare.

Comedy scene (Buttons and Dandini)
Buttons does girl getting ready to go out with young man. Mirror, tongue put out, lipstick business
Powder on face and under arms. Puts on woman's hat. "We're alone" (scratching bus) "We're not
alone" "You haven't any Flit on you, have you?" Sweet passion "I have a pound of aniseed balls" "I
said sweet passion not sweet ration" After line re biting "What do you think I am, a toffee apple?"
Into number "I'm bashful"

Interruption scene
Comic on to Principal Boy and Girl scene. Interposes self and gets kiss meant for girl. "Smell that"

gag and off. On again with new coat with car springs sticking out all over it. "This is my new spring coat." Exit. On wearing funny hat and carrying jug. "I'm going to milk the cow" "In that hat?" "No, in this jug" Fight builds up to I stepped into the ring and took off my dressing gown. A great roar went up from the crowd. "It did?" "Yes, I'd forgotten to put my pants on."

Are you going to say anything?
No, but I could be arrested for what I'm thinking

What are rich people? Only poor people with money

Cloak with hot water bottles sewn inside and telephone. Ring then answer telephone inside cloak

Build up re when we are married. "I shall put your slippers by the fire all ready for you. Then when you come in" "When I come in? Where have I been? "Well, you've been to work, aint you?"

Are you a new boy?
No, the old one reconditioned

There's trouble in the Baker's shop
What trouble?
One of the stale loaves has started to get fresh

Love scene with mop
Princess gives mop to Wishee to show him how to propose. "That is a girl" (called Lulu)
She's a bit skinny isn't she? She'll catch her death of cold
Say to her Darling I love you, kiss me
Oh I'm all embarrassed. Oh I can't (shy business) (Mop hits him. He kisses mop) She's been drinking Harpic (mop knocks him. Noise from drummer. Each time he advances on mop he trips. Two lines to say to mop he mucks up)
What are arms? Only legs higher up
Nobody loves Wishee (cries)
Sings "They'll never believe me" to mop
Exit crying with mop

Fight business
We'll toss for it. If it stays up you win, if it comes down I win. That's fair, isn't it? Fair business. We'll start when I say start and stop when I say stop. Fair business. A hits on start and stops on riposte

We've got our disguises on so we're disgizzled

A Remember the golden rule of heaven "Do unto others as you would have them do unto you"
B Remember the golden rule of Birmingham
A What's that?
B Do others before they do you

A I've sung it before the President
B The President of the United States?
A No, the President of the United Dairies

Revolver gag
Clicking business "Just a minute, there's a message coming through" Ticker tape comes out of weapon. What does it say? "The favourite got beaten" "I'll blow your brains out, both of them"

Sir Thomas Beecham and his fourteen pills

Cannibals? Well, there's no need to get in a stew

People think I'm crackers but I'm not. I'm only half crackers

I think you're the most beautiful woman in the world.
Do you really think that?
No, but I don't mind lying if it's going to get me anywhere

Say something soft and warm
Custard pie

I only know two words of Spanish
Manana – that means tomorrow. And pyjama – that means tonight

(Cannibal king) Coco! (end of gibberish sentence)
He wants a cup of cocoa

He thinks he's everyone around here but he's not. I'm somebody

Dame and Idle Jack
Jack about to commit suicide. Farewell speeches. Cook on, wants to watch. Will enjoy it more than pictures. Jack jumps off ship or quay and comes back feeling his bum. "The tide was out" "I'll take poison" "Oh I've got some poison" (Dame produces it out of suitcase) "I'll hang myself" "I'll blow my brains out" (Dame has rope and gun in suitcase) "I'll put my head in the gas oven" "You can't do that, I've got the meter" Jack is put off committing suicide.

Get aboard (comes in with plank, bangs it down)

Enter with enormous anchor
What do you think happened last week when we were all asleep? (produces little anchor from behind big one) We don't know yet if it's a little boy or a little girl

I got a piece of soap and washed myself ashore.
I swam ashore. I didn't know you swam?
Oh yes, I'm one of the best swimmers in England

I met a bull once but I made a noise like a cow and he came up and kissed me

Enter with barrel round tummy with tap
"lost all my clothes in the wreck and I've got to wear this"
Takes cup for drink from tap

(after kiss) You've been eating candy floss

Sh. There's someone looking at you.
Who?
Me

Three sacks flour etc. Have you got that down? (list of things – each one Have you got that down)

One pair of velveteen trousers. Have you got them down? Yes. Then pull them up again.

There was a fellow called Hardwick
Why by a hard ball got struck
Now there is writ on his tombstone
Hardwick, hard ball, hard luck

(when playing instrument)
What are you playing?
_____ At least that's what I'm blowing in. What comes out the other end is nothing to do with me.

I play the piano with my toes
What do you do with your hands?
Keep them over my ears. I can't bear the noise.

Comic knocks on the door then hides. Dame comes out. "I thought it was the milkman and he promised me." Comic indicates to audience not to tell Dame who knocked.
Dame: Oh yes it was
Aud: Oh no it wasn't
(Gag starts with comic knocking and Dame coming out and shaking powdered mat in his face)
Knocking on door, door opens, face appears, he knocks on Dame's face. Then he realises what it is. Dame chases him off with nap.

After fall on bum
"I've cut my throat"

It's Dirty Gerty from number thirty

Left and right gag
Go down there turn to left and then to right
Or in drilling routine or other situation
That's my left isn't it? That's right
Rept. ad lib and confuse comic

I've got a brother who's _____
And I've got a brother who's detained to give his Majesty pleasure

Sir _____ BA. Answered by _____ BF

I wish you were a statue and I was a pigeon
I don't get it
No but you would

Egg under cap. Tap with hammer and egg oozes out down face onto "magic carpet" strip placed there before.

Your toute ensemble is inadequate
I'm upset about that
What?
My two tonsils being in Harrogate

(Enter with pump) Where are you going?

I'm going to put the wind up the _____

Shake. Comic shakes literally.

I'll make love to you
You can't
Who can't? I've been to the pictures. Call me Gregory and I'll give you a peck.

Don't have to shout. I'm not blind.
How are you?
I'm very ill thank you

You know what rhubarb is? Celery with blood pressure

Get that sack of flour into the stores. Jack enters carrying long sack. He puts it down and it jumps into stores by itself. (person inside) What's the idea? That's like Mitchell and Butlers. Mitchell and Butlers? Well, it's full of hops.

You're late
I'll be later still tomorrow
Why?
I'm not coming

Wages owed six and eight. Given threepence.
What are six and eight? Fourteen
What's fourteen pence? One and two
What are one and two? Three
Three pence. There you are.

Explosive balloon like plum pudding

After magic fluence. The beer must be good round here. Hissing business with Rat. "Your turn"
Dame hisses at audience

Do you know Charlie Smith?
No, what's his name?
Jack Robinson

Chap bought farm twenty one miles long and three inches broad.
Was he eccentric?
No, narrow-minded

After non sequitur – answer is a train
I don't get it
No, you've missed it. You'll have to wait for another one

You work from seven till you're unconscious

Cook a Toad in the Hole
Well I can cook a Toad but I'm pretty sure I couldn't cook a Hole

Everyone's after me. Just because I'm pretty.

May I have a word?
Yes
Good. Which word shall I have?

(Sitting down on bench with girl)
That's right. Spread your parachute

Mother, I'm being got at

Dramatic farewell.
"Next week – East Lynne"

Dance the Sailors Drainpipe

Rat   (hypnotising Jack) Look into my eyes. What do you see?
Jack   Eyeballs
(work to)
Rat   Are you asleep?
Jack   With all that row going on? (Rat has been shouting)
Rat   (stabbing J with dagger) Do you feel anything?
Jack   No
Rat   Do you feel anything?
Jack   No
Rat   Do you feel anything?
Jack   Only that dagger
Rat   Walk towards me. Slowly, slowly, slow, slow
Jack   Quick quick slow

Any danger of any work?
I come from Manchester
What part?
All of me
You're abominable.
You don't even know what it means.
Oh yes I do. You have a field like this (biz) There's a bull in it, aeroplane overhead, drops bomb, bull sees bomb coming and swallows it. A bomb in a bull.

Put basket over comic, carry it off, comic still crouched underneath

Pull off pants, two eyes on pants

Ideal suitor
Five wheel scooter

You want her hand?
I want the rest of her as well

Nincompoop
I may be a nincom but I am <u>not</u> a poop
(spitting business wipes eye)

Self raising flower (flower presented shoots up)

Two horses. Must tell them apart.
Cut tails off, other one gets tail cut off
Cut mane off, other one gets mane off
Now how are you going to tell them apart
I've suddenly realised the black one's bigger than the white one

Three bears sitting on iceberg
Each tells story "I have a tale to tell"
"my tale is told etc" Little one says "My tail is told too"

Give her these (flowers from waistband)
Rich beyond the dreams of Edgbaston

Coat with springs attached to it
"This is my spring overcoat"

Ugly Sisters entrance
In pram, crying. Big jar of milk with tubes in pram. Baron puts tubes in their mouths. Milk goes down. They cry again.

Enter in sedan chair, walking behind. Carriers turn it round, showing trick. "It's better than walking"
Police: We've been following you.
Well there's nothing doing

Sawing wood with imaginary saw – sound effect
Opposite end falls off, sawdust pours out

What time is it? It's chocolate time
(Exit for two or three)
Hot chocolate, drinking chocolate
Hot chocolate, drinking chocolate

Business entrance
Head round flat. Arm from flat with hand round throat as though it is someone's hand. Enter in same position to show aud.

Comic entrance
Pulled on in laundry basket by kids

Ugly Sisters entrance
One enters in pram with hood up. Huge water container (glass) with milk in it and tube from it. Baby crying noise. "What does Baby want?" Puts tube in hood. Disapp of milk very quickly. Full sized Ugly Sister comes out of pram (no bottom to pram) Before this when baby crying noises "Oh shurrup" 2nd Ugly Sister walking business Push tummy – motor horn. Walk off with pram round middle.

Brief entrance
Enter with gun. Shoot with gun at picture of ship at sea. Ship sinks. Exit like soldier with drum taps.

Exit
The carriage awaits build up from footmen. Enter pram with "pig food only" written on it. Exit in pram pulled by footmen or comic

Tankard with froth. Blow off froth which is cotton wool.

Hanky business
Wishee gets audience to hold up hankies to show how much washing there is to be done

Jug Business
Pour water into it. Water comes out for A but beer for B

Entrance of Dame in Aladdin. In rickshaw pulled by coolie.

Stand like that
Leg up, elbow on knee, chin in knee. Kick over. Second time B does it to show C and gets kicked over himself.

Brief entrance or entrance
Enter with candle on head, lit up.
"I've gone lightheaded"

Horse and cart entrance
Enter in tip-up cart pulled by horse. Cart tips up when horse stops. Put horse in cart to get horse off.

Entrance
Comic enters on penny farthing with umbrella up. Goes up to flies (nearly) pulled by umbrella top.

Two enter and stick in a door, one carrying tin plates, when eventually they burst through, plates go all over the place.

Enter in tricycle cart with donkey riding tricycle, come out of cart when C has goldfish in bowl, introduces it to audience and tells it to say something. Gurgling noise through mike.

Long carpet rolled down for entrance of King. King enters as on end of carpet it is pulled up at the other end and King falls over.

Where are you going to?
I'm not going to, I'm coming from.

Pram hood up. Huge bottle of Guinness inside

Enter, knock on door, and exit

Shooting business at back of circle, several entrances with gun bell rings. Third time fails, long delay and business then bell rings eventually, congratters.

Enter with toy dog put through hoop and dog pulled off quickly on a string

Dame's Entrance

(Enter Dame with basket full of shopping)
Good afternoon, boys and girls. I've just been to Slough Market for my shopping and look what I've bought – Bangers (produces sausages) Christmas Pud (produces it) and here's a frying pan with a dried egg attached (shows pan with egg painted on it). Oh I've had a terrible time. The business was so crowded even the men were standing. And then to crown it all just as I reached here someone shouted "They're coming down" and they were. I hope you like my frock. It's an American frock. Yes, American. One Yank and it's off.

Ugly Sisters Entrance
Enter separately in two halves of car. When joined together this makes complete car, one in front, one in rear.

Entrances with little case. "Where're you going?" "I'm taking my case to court." Return with ladder. "They've turned me down. I'm taking steps to a higher court."

Coat-hanger from back of posh clothes

Dame enters, singing and dancing, is knocked over by procession of children, basket goes flying, last child, jumps over her deliberately. She picks herself up. "Don't laugh, don't laugh. They've ruined my chassis."

Enter on scooter with L on it

Enter bowlegged. "I've lost my horse. There was a horse under here this morning."

TV aerial on hat.

Ugly Sisters Entrance on tandem and back one falls off.

No reaction on horrid mask. On taking mask off and showing own face, double take, shriek and off.

I hate you, I hate you, I hate you. Three hates – that's twenty four.

Dame enters pursued by shower of vegetables and shouted abuse. "Well, that's one way of getting the vegetables."

Lights out. Headlight on. Lights up to discover comic riding bike with headlight alight.

Dame enters pushed on rag-and-bone barrow and marked as such.

Dame's Entrance
On bicycle. Food and veg for each member of orchestra. Sausages pulled out – "likes it by the yard," scraggy turkey

Umbrella gag
I'll put up my umbrella
But it's not raining
I'll soon fix that (exit with water spurting from stick of umbrella)

Comic entrance
Parcel brought on by kids. Comic puts head thro' paper on top. "Why did you come in a parcel?"

"It's cheaper than travelling by rail."

Comic enters on motorbike. Off & crash

Fitz Oh my greenhouse
Jack (re-entering) Did you think I'd smashed your greenhouse?
Fitz Yes
Jack Well I have

Gag for entrance
When the Mate comes on repeat everything he says. That makes him angry. Rehearsal. Do it when B and C take their hats off. Stop when they put hats on. Work entrance. "Hallo chaps" etc repeated. Coughing repeated. Etc. "You're a silly old sausage." "And so are you" "And you"

Bells on record. Dick enters. Separate entrance for cat. Bell theme in music. Cat steals something. When told to take it back throws it to Dick. Then chorus come on chasing cat. Cat mimes through love scene.

Youth, youth, mad youth (exit) (false exit)

I'm going
Where?
I'm going daft. Are you coming?

Enter on scooter, fall off.

King enters miserably in bath chair pushed by two chorus girls
Take the car back to the garage and milk it
Have you seen yourself this morning? Business with mirror
Is that me? (Shriek on looking in mirror) No it's me etc

Au revoir
Reservoir
Olive Oil (exit)

Enter holding umbrella which is up and flown from flies.

Enter to Volga Boat song pulling on line. At end of line is small live dog.

Enter on child's tricycle. "This is the answer to the parking problem." You want to watch out for the puddles otherwise it dampens your enthusiasm.
How do you like my clothes? Italian cut. Tailor said to me "What do you think of the cut?" I said it looks as if it had been cut with a meat axe. From Cleaver to Wearer.

Enter with bunch of flowers in pursuit of chorus girl. She exits, he follows, slap, he falls back onto stage. "I know. She's a Dairy Box girl." Takes her chocs. Same business. Falling onto stage.
"What happened?"
"She likes Black Magic."

Baron pushes on Ugly Sisters in pram with bottle of milk (large) and tubes. They cry. He puts tubes in their mouths. After this hitting business with bags. Into trio, Sisters dance with can-can skirts. Push Baron off in pram.

Entrance as dwarfs with shoes on knees.

What's your name?
Bicarbonate
Bicarbonate?
Yes, I'm one of the early settlers.

You stole my wife, you horse thief

Captain Napkin (Atkins)
Don't be wet

Chicken falls from roof after shooting business
Where did it come from?
Sainsbury's

Go to the devil
Any messages?

I'm going to kill you
If you do, I'll never speak to you again

Re old man with white hair
Just because there's snow on the roof doesn't mean to say there's no fire in the furnace.

What's that?
An owl
Who's 'owling?

It reminds me of when I was engaged…
Now you're just vacant

Robinson Boozer (Man Friday)

If he dieted a bit he might be out by lunchtime (Billy in stocks)

I call him Carpenter. He does odd jobs about the house. He has no nose.
How does he smell?
Terrible

When something does not work
"Can you come back next week?"

Whistle. Walking prop follows him off

Wonderful hat. Seventy years old. Did you make it yourself? Yes. One wet Friday.

On the way to the Corn Exchange
What for?
To exchange my corn for a bunion

Slave   If you give her the lamp she will become my mistress

Twankey   In that case I'll leave the lamp

Abanazar is made likeable and good. Sings "Today I love everybody" and exits in corny dance routine.

Dame and Fitzwarren
Dame as oriental dancer. Salaam, salaam
Fitz pulled up veil. Oh, false salaam.
Fitz sits first. Sitting down in front of a lady
Why don't you sit down? Haven't you got a seat?
Yes, but I've nowhere to put it.
Nero business fiddling (with saucepans as brassiere)
Don't do that. You'll break my brassiere
What do you wear that for? Two very good reasons
Face lifted. These aren't my cheeks. No? Those are my kneecaps

Go home and I'll be Squire and you'll be my Squiress
Build by "Squire" from Dame and "Squiress"
And all our children will be Squirts
Into comedy duet for exit with business for Fitz fiddling

(re umbrella) I got this in my stocking for Christmas. It was a very long stocking

Garridge
How common. You must say gar-age
What about sausage. No sausidge
All right, ask the kids

I heard you with my own two eyes

Two mugs. A has full mug, B empty. While A talking to C, B siphons beer from A's mug to his with umbrella

(Arrow in bum)
Did it hurt?
No, but it's given me a terrible headache

There's nothing I wouldn't do for you
There's nothing I wouldn't do for you
If we were married we could spend the rest of our lives doing nothing for each other

Why don't you kiss me on the back of the neck like you used to?
Why don't you wash the back of your neck like you used to?

I was flummoxed. I was really. My flum has never been so oxed

Dame asks Princess to read out washing list to her and she will check washing. Princess finds letter to her from Aladdin and reads from this. Dame thinking it is washing list
Blank it seems (blanket)
Hanker chiefly (handkerchief)
Stays in my heart (stays)
Charmer (pyjamas)

My heart pants (pants)
Over all (overall)
If you have a pain in your heart I have a counter pain (counterpane)
Brave front (dicky)
Letter draws to its close (drawers)
Letter draws to its close (drawers)
Dame   I'm very much obliged (exit Princess)

My complexion. Peaches and cream.
More like prunes and custard
I've head of Max Factor pancake. This is Macfisheries fishcake

Elastic – that most important item of woman's attire – at that price something will have to come down

Where have you been, what have you been doing and I don't believe it

You're 17, just on the threshold of life and I'm 33. That's the difference.

Letter from the butcher
What did he say?
What did he say? According to his letter I ought to be in his window

(When wealthy) Then I can wed my fair Princess
And I can have a Toni perm

I am a collector of antiques (puts arm on Dame's shoulder)

I want to give you a farewell present. A box of crackers.
I want to give you a farewell present. A bag of nuts.
Sarah, your crackers
Fitz, your nuts

Undressing scene
Skirts with one word on each of them. "England expects each man this day" Puts nighty on over stays and then gets stays off under nighty, saying to audience "I'll turn around" and doing so. Look for po, wanting to pee business. Takes nightcap out of bedside cupboard. Blowing candle out business eventually blows candle clean off table and out of door.

He cocked an eye at me. I cocked an eye at him. And we both stood there, cockeyed.

Sweet smell of old brewery
Lower your boom (sit down)
I was a fan dancer (build to) I fell on my fan
It was an electric fan

Dame wears as jacket pair of bloomers (white) round sleeves. When takes them off they are revealed as what they are.

I am a sorcerer
A flying sorcerer?

Nurse
The nappies I've changed in my time. Made a terrible mistake putting a nappie on a bald-headed father. (re nappies) I never forget a face

D   He's out
A   Out?
D   Well, you can't keep Aladdin (laughs) He's gone now (re husband)
A   Is he... (indicates heaven)
D   No, he's... (indicates hell)

Dr Who

Roses are red, violets are blue
A face like yours
Belongs in a zoo

He was drowned in bed.
Drowned in bed?
Yes, he fell through the mattress onto a spring

He first saw me bathing. He said I had a figure like Diana Dors. Then I realised what it was. I had my bathing costume over my water wings

Birdcage gag
Dame going to sleep constantly woken up by bird whistling in cage (spot on cage) Eventually Dame eats birds. Whistle business in inside, hiccupping

I think I'm going to scream (Does so) I've screamed

Where is Felixstowe?
On Felix foot

What is the staff of life? Bread
What comes after bread? Mice, cats, tom cats, kittens

Ee by gum, mum, my bum's num (Lancs accent)

This is my new Playtex girdle. It's killing me. It's my own fault. I should have taken it out of the tube

Dame   (to Aladdin's lines) I will not be wheedled. I will not be wheedled. I will not be wheedled.
Aladdin   Mummykins darling
Dame   I'm wheedled

Dame and Principal Girl
Mother you're an angel
On no I'm not – angels don't weigh twelve stone
Mother I must tell you that I had a beautiful dream last night
It's the new bread dear, don't worry
I dreamed about my Fairy Prince. He was so handsome
So was your father. And look at him now
I stretched out my arms to him and then – and then – he touched me
They all do dear, they all do. Your father touched me for thirty bob yesterday

(stretches out arms knocks Dame down) Mother are you all right?
If you've broken anything you'll pay for it
Mummy this is romance – love, life and laughter
That's what your father promised me
And what did you get?
You
Mother I must find him
You will, darling, you will
NUMBER Some day, somewhere (She throws violets from basket to audience during number. Dame enters with basket of vegetables singing tune to herself. Throws onions after, letting Girl smell them while they sing. Then carrots. Finally tangerines and big cabbage. Prep. To throw with drum roll then throws down aisle. Exit with eight bars hotted up chorus with Girl)

Dame mends Aladdin's pants
Tells Wishy to get stool and workbasket. Gets one, W keeps other, to and from business Aladdin bends across knee while Dame mends hole in his pants
Stop wobbling. You've got a nasty place there. How did you get this hole?
I slipped
Just like your father he was always slipping. Slipping (build up) – on day of marriage – slipped into the Crown for a quick one and I've never seen him from that day to this
(Song "Mighty like a rose" re-written to character and situation)

Genie makes flap come down and jewels are revealed as in jeweller's shop window on black velvet stands
"We've a gentleman in a green suit who provides us with everything"
Give him a million pounds Aladdin, I left my purse on the piano

I think I've split an infinitive

I'm so poor I can only just afford a television set
I'd make you rich
Rich? I could have a pound of bacon

Ironing with big iron (called away) then picks up iron which has red light inside. Pants are burned with big hole in seat.

Aladdin	He's come down from up above
Dame	(re trap) I thought he'd come up from down below. How do you do, Mr Green? My name is Abanazar
Dame	Have a banana?

He asked me to do the can-can. Then I remembered my knobbly knees and I said "I would if I could but I can't can't"
I said "Will you dance with me?"
He said "Certainly, Madam. I didn't come here entirely for pleasure."

I've just left my seat in the country.
I hope you had a good sit-down before you left.
Where is your country seat?
In his country trousers

Enter with flower pot with flower in it. Comic waters it with watering can. Flower stands up (on wire)

(after being tickled) You'll make me go all historical.

(taking chicken from basket) Here's a nice spring chicken (bounce it on the floor)

I'm so forgetful last night I put the retriever to bed and slept in a glass of water

(with carrots) I can't get these bananas ripe

If you've got a daughter about seventeen or eighteen you should really take them on one side and have a talk about the facts of life. My word you'd learn plenty

You must have a rotten old mother
I had a better mother than you have (from Dame to son)

(to audience) Did he pull an ugly face?
Anyone can pull an ugly face. I bet I can pull an uglier face than you can
Look at the start you've got

Enter with cat in cage
"These are my two pets, my cat and my canary."
Where's the canary?
Inside the cat

Enter with large bottle of Guinness. Wishee gives garments one by one to Twankey and Twankey gives each a perfunctory bang with iron. Enormous drawers – at least six feet. One pair of drawing room curtains. Whose are these? Mrs Braddocks. Trousers with hole in it. It must belong to a Liberal, he's lost his seat.

I'm chick (chic)
You look like an old hen at the moment

Cutting out pattern routine
Paper patterns rise in air with draught. "Close that window" Wishee shuts it. It flies open again. Patterns blow about. "Close that window" "Didn't I shut it?" (to audience) "I'll show you how to shut it" Does so and window flies open immediately. Get hammer and nail (large nail). When I nod my head, hit it. Hit with hammer on head. They nail the window shut. It opens again. They cut out pattern on floor. Garden shears for scissors. Piece cut out. It is put in Singer Sewing Machine. Must be oiled. Wishee gets finger stuck in oiling can. Twankey helps him and gets her finger stuck. Twankey: I told you to get rid of that. Opens window and throws mat out. Windows opens again – she shuts it afterwards – and mat flies back in her face. Twice. Wishee does it and ducks and mat flies overhead. First tries to get rid of it in corner but it is thrown back at once. They try on dress on dummy – pattern same colour as dress Dame is wearing. Dummy is on spring. Business springing it from one to other hitting on bum and in tummy. Take a bit off the bottom. Wishee tears bit off Dame's dress. D looks at model. "Take a bit more off." "You haven't taken enough yet" (goes on tearing till Dame is without dress at all) Exit

Genie   I can do the impossible
Dame   Can you get me a bottle of whiskey for three and six?

I'm a respectable girl and I defy you to prove it

Can you stand a shock?
Well, I've told you I'm a widow

(to Aladdin) You'll grow up to be a spiv. Stealing apples, disgraceful. Give us a bite.
Mother, you were young once
I was young twice
(sung with Aladdin over knee being mended)
"You're my everything"

Mother, this isn't you
Well who the devil is it?

Smoky Joe (after flash and smoke)

Talking to a girl? You'll be smoking next

I am the biggest pot in China
You said it

Tell me, is this the Palace?
It is
When does the big picture start?
Milord Ovaltiney
Where do they come from (re Dame etc)
Dame: The Co-op
Building palace business
The licences have been held up
(re Genie) It's only our old friend Cucumber
What's his name?
Mr Macmillan

I can see right into your heart
What do you think I'm wearing – a cellophane vest?
Careful of my built-up area

On the threshold of the year (cuddling)
You'll be on the threshold of a thick ear in a minute

We'll embark on the seas of life
Remember this is my maiden voyage
Love potion
Dame (drinking it) There's nothing in it
Take the cork out
A little toast
Through the lips and round the gums, look out stomach, here it comes
Take potion. Build up to leap on Emperor – tropical speech – Take me to Balham. We'll be married
etc organ will play "Rudolph the red-nosed reindeer" Kiss me as I've never been cussed before

(Spitting on hanky for washing again) You're not going to wash me in spit again?
Why not?
It always smells of Guinness

You've got what it takes
Oh have I? Well, you try taking it away from me

Picture on wall. "That was my late husband. The Town Crier. (tears spurt from eyes of picture)

Empty mirror for combing hair. Lights candle. Candle is at back of picture with black back. When candle removed, flame remains. Dame removes flame which turns out to be blackened end of candle.

He offered me tongue. I said no thanks. I realised where tongue comes from. A cow's mouth. I had an egg.

Let me take you through the perfumed garden
Page by page

I am a Moor
You're not going to sell me an Alamanac?
No a Moor
Oh parlez moi d'amour

Who is this woman?
Who called me a woman?
How do you do it?
How do I do what?

(after ripping noise)
There's a split in the cabinet

I was divorced
On what grounds?
On the recreation grounds

You're like something from a Fairy Tale Book
I know, Grimm

Draughts scene
B and C playing draughts. A watches. All is in silence. A gives silent advice, first to B, then to C, finally one of them wins with explosive remark.

Dame sewing red pants. "What are you sewing?" A pair of curtains for my back sitting room.

You know Beau Nash and Beau Brummel. He's like them.
What is he then?
Bow-legged

You must be very tired
I am tired. I've been breathing all day

Dame falls down on arm. It is fixed and so is shoulder. D has expression of agony.
Feed: Have you hurt yourself?
Dame: Oh no. No. It goes like this sometimes, especially when it gets broken.

Dame on bench gets finger in "nut hole" Holds up finger to make it better, gets finger of other hand stuck, same business

A new broom sweeps clean
A new broom may sweep clean, but an old broom knows all the blooming corners

I got caught in the one way traffic at _____ and I only had a two way stretch

If I live till next April I shall be 51
If I don't, I shall be 64

I have spoken
I have heard you

Guinness in cage. "What kind of bird is that?" (taking bottle out of cage and drinking from it) This is a swallow

Can we have tripe?
You can't have any tripe
Why?
We haven't got a television set

Run to the seaside and bring me back some Tide

(When someone is gorgeously dressed)
Have you been to _____'s sale?

His nose is cold. Otherwise I'd have given him a Bob Martins

He is alas no more (re Principal Boy)
He is more of a lass than I am (Dame)

(When Genie is on)
Strike me pink (pink spot)
Hot flush
Blow me down
Chase my Aunt Fanny (G starts to chase her)
It's the genie with the light brown hair

(looking out of window)
What a lovely view of the Lickies

You'll look like a million dollars
I feel like fourpence

(re Genie up through trap)
I wish he'd stayed down his drain

They're worth a King's ransom
Yes, we got 'em at the Bull Ring

(When Aladdin is over Twankey's knee)

Oh Aladdin how you have altered
(looking for nits in hair)
I told you not to go to _____

I don't know what he died of. Nothing serious anyway. I hope to live for another twenty or thirty years. I want to hear the end of Mrs Dale's Diary.

Song with audience
You'll all be kept in
I want it louder, beware of the consequences

(Couple kissing) Come unstuck. I thought you were doing voluntary overtime.

You sail there and then you sail here (build)
Oh Robinson, why do you Crusoe? (cruise so)

Yes Mother, here I are

I've worked my fingers to the bone, and what have I got?
You've got bony fingers

The Captain's been making overtures to me. You know what our overture is, don't you? It's that little bit of fiddling before the band starts to play.

I've got you under my eye
In one of those little bags?

To tell the truth I've had a slight touch of the wind.
Watch your heart. You know what the chiropodist told you.

Hot water bottle labelled Cold Feet

When I was a baby I was all pink and dimples.
Look at you now. All drink and pimples.

I'm a perfect gentleman
And I'm a perfect lady, and I defy you to prove it

Look where you've got your gun (to Dame)
He can see right up your barrel

I've been married twice before. It didn't take the first time.
My first husband, what a lover. He had everything. Spots, boils, pimples, the lot
I met him in a doorway. He said his name was Liberace and would I like to go up to his flat and see his candelabra.

In cinema, holding hands, I said your hand is frozen. A little boy said "He's moved two seats away, you're holding my iced lolly."

There were a hundred people at my wedding. If the wedding had been a week later there would have been a hundred and one.
My brother came out of the army.

The doctor said I might have sea air. My old man sat by my bed all night fanning me with a kipper.

We're the same age. I'd say you were about fifty.
You're twenty years out.
Seventy?
I've seen only twenty summers
That's all most of us have seen
Reckless young blood. More like a bloodless old wreck.
Beautiful baby, all pink and dimpled.
Look at you now, all drink and pimples

In stockingette outfit. My new frock. In the summer I wear it like this (as it is, short) In the winter I wear it like this (pulls it down for long)

(to children) Pull my skirts down. This cold rainy weather.

You are the Brigitte Bardot of _____
Oui oui
Second door on the left

I'm a good clean widow and I've got a packet of Daz to prove it

Dame: I used to bath in milk
Pasteurised?
No, Just up to here

I've come to raise the rent
Good. I can't

Does he use glasses (or do you use glasses?)
No, I always drink it out of the bottle

What's your name?
Glug glug
Glug glug?
Yes, my parents wanted to call me Gladys but the Vicar fell in the font.

Bread costume
Long loaf for muff (sandwich) Hat of elaborate bread loaf. Rolls on necklace. Stockinette dress. Rolls as earrings. Other comic has gag re Dame being well bred.

Dame examines face in shiny frying pan, singing Camay song
Comic: Pity she's been trod on, isn't it?

I'm so happy I could run into Woolworths and shout Marks and Spencers

Buffett
Boofey. The tea is silent.
Not when I drink it

King: They're awaiting your address
Dame: I see. 23 Edgware Rd (local)

Your father's getting old. He may not keep through another hot summer.

You'll split my infinitive

If only I had some banana skins I'd make myself some more shoes
What kind of shoes can you make out of banana skins?
Slippers

I knocked on monastery door and saw a monk with a frying pan. I said "Are you a friar?" He said "No, I'm a chipmunk."

My little boy is wonderful. He said DADA yesterday quite distinctly. He's only eleven.

Apple with water spouting out of the top

Like my hat
Round
No, not the one I wear on weekdays. The one I wear on Sundays
Square
Now what shape is the world?
Round on weekdays, square on Sundays

Now we'll do some harmonising. You know what harmonising is, don't you?
Yes. The stuff they put on the Christmas cake.

They used to call me the boy with the Sunday School face
Yes, and the Saturday night ideas

I want you for my wife
Silly. What would your wife do with me?

Are you sitting comfortably? Then we'll begin

You got the 11 plus didn't you?
Yes. I got 13

(revealing Scots knickers)
Those are my harvest festival bloomers.
All is safely gathered in

My grandad's birthday party. What a party.
He wasn't there. He died when he was 29.

What's a triangle?
A square with a bit missing

Bolt in cake in corsets

My perfume Evening in Paris
Smell mine. Half an hour in the Cattle Market

My husband grows things in the garden. His marrow. Up all night in frost and snow - build up. And in the morning there he was (just him and marrow etc). Frozen to the marrow.

You remember the day we had summer last year?

Have you tried the new Stork?
No thank you. I had enough trouble with the old one.

Put that woman down

He was so ugly I used to go with him rather than kiss him goodbye.

First time I saw him he was wearing suede shoes. One swayed this way and the other swayed that

Towel number - girls, to open Baths scene. Twankey enters with necklace of loofahs, and sponge tied on head.

We went in a field with a lot of cows. And I fell. I fell right in it. I went home and had a bath and came out in mushrooms.

I am a ghost. I want a bath.
It's extra for ghosts
Here's my visiting card (carrying tombstone)
"Here lies the body of Marjorie MacDougal
Who once had a bath
And slipped down the plughole."

Mat thrown out. Comes back
Comes back again, hits on bottom
Then out through window

Italian feed. Does he live-a here?
Yes he live-a here-a and he drinka pinta milka day

After Genie provides food
Thank you Mr Finefare

Who's your friend?
Hughie Greene

Key to Box 13 (on label) Room 504

My little cherry blossom
He takes me for a tin of boot polish

I can see what goes on in your heart
What do you think I'm wearing? A cellophane vest?

Love, build-up - it starts at tips of toes etc
Until you have a lovely glow all over
That's not love, that's fibrositis

Girls who trip the light fantastic
Shouldn't trust in cheap elastic

Hanky on elastic

Grab me while the sale's still on

I can't stop. I've got my liver in the oven

I went into a shop and said "Have you got any hot water bottles?" They said no sorry we haven't.
"Why don't you try Boots?" I said "I have but the water comes out of the lace holes."

Mop head used as powder puff

Shall we join the young people?
Why, are they coming apart?

I'm Cinderella's sister, Umbrella

The warm applause
The what?
The warm applause
I thought you said you'd torn your drawers

I've got an ache for the ballet. Yes, I've got an ache for the ballet. I've got a ballet ache.

Nine buttons on your nightgown, but you can only fasten eight

I'm five foot two with my shoes on
I'm six foot six with my umbrella up
I noticed you were a bit bumpy round the Bahamas

I've kept my figure
You had to. No one wanted it.

In the springtime of my life
If that's the springtime she must have had a terrible winter

Where would she get a dress like that?
C and A I should think

I don't think I've had the pleasure
I don't think you ever will

C and A's
C and A's?
Yes, coats and hats

(re menace) Look, Inspector Barlow has turned up

(re gorgeous costume) You look like Woolworth's waiting for someone to open
(ditto) Your Premium Bonds have come up at last

You'll look a little lovelier each day with fabulous Nescafe

After B has urged her to look.
"I'm looking, I'm looking, I'm looking. You'll have my eyeballs on the floor in a minute."

I know what you're thinking
Why don't you go then?

Kippers and custard don't mix
(sung) If you should go across the sea to Ireland
And find you're eating pork chops on the way
Oh, what's the use of eating all those pork chops
If you're going to lose the lot in Galway Bay

How many boy friends have you had?
Three
Only three?
On no, I'm telling lies. 82. I forgot that fortnight at Butlins

(re flowers) They're out of the ordinary
They're out of the dustbin

Walking through the woods with a Prince. Anything might happen. I hope it does.

Chicken pie. Big pie and chicken springs up from middle of pastry. Cock crows. "I'm not eating that. It looks fowl.

Shoes make scrunching sound. "I can't understand it. They told me they were Hush Puppies.
Shoes make squeaking sound. B says "They're asking for Kennomeat"
Shoes squeak as A goes out

Re dress. It's my religious one
"Lo and behold"

Clothes up. Clothes up the other way
C puts bucket under dress when she has raised skirts over bum

Boom boom boom
Esso Blue

How it takes me back to my youth
Careful dear. Those long journeys are very tiring

Shall we dance? (bus)
Why dance?

Shirt. Belongs to a golfer.
It's a shirt with eighteen holes

An example of warmhearted womanhood
Come to Godfrey Winn

You polluted old perisher

You do me wrong
Well, you're not going to do me wrong, I can tell you

Is your price above rubies?
I don't know, what does Ruby charge?

I want to go somewhere where no-one will ever find me
Try BBC2

You silly old royal sausage

There's plenty more fish in the sea
But my bait's not as fresh as it was

It must have been black magic
Black Magic! I'll never doubt their commercials again

He has four wives and four hundred porcupines

He was always ailing. He thought he had a hole in the heart. Then he found out it was a polo mint in his vest pocket

You're FOB
You mean FAB. Fabulous
No I mean FOB. Falling out behind

My name's _____ I expect you know yours
(to audience) Are you shy?

(When he has hands in pockets) Pockets! (from audience)
If the Squire sees me with hands in pockets he always gives me a clump round the ear. You don't want him to give me a clump round the ear, do you?

One verse re plumber coming in and girl in bath
She screamed and grabbed the bath mat
And so she met her fate
The mat had welcome on it
Now she's a plumber's mate

Show him you're naval
(Comic exposes navel)

I come from a long line of sailors. My father was a smelling salt. A smelling salt? Yes, a sailor who didn't use deodorant

Help me or it'll be (throat cutting business)
They start throat cutting business, then say together "We'll help you"

How old are you?

Around thirty. Eh? Second time around

Throw your chest out
Well you asked for it
(Dame throws out brassiere and bounces it)
It's a living bra

I'm making cakes for tea. Would you prefer a maid of honour or a Blue Tart?

You've got something that other women haven't got.
Yes, and I'm going to keep it

How old are you?
I'm not going to tell you
If you were going down a country lane and you saw a worm, would you stop and pick it up?
No
Well you're no chicken

Do you like gardening? (produces self-raising flour)
Do you like drinking? (or anyone here like drinking)
Like a pint? (produces pint of milk)
Smokers here? Anyone fond of a smoke? (smoked kipper)
Jewellery? (Eighteen carrot necklace)

You are Fitzwarren?
(looking round) I hope so. I had breakfast this morning

Who am I?
You're the boss. Who am I?
You're nothing
You've got a fine job
What's that?
Boss over nothing

(re Dame) She's in there, creating
Creating hats?
No, creating hell

Bottle
It's the liquid truth. Smell that and you tell the truth.
Paraffin
That's the truth

Wanted - a dressing table by a lady with wooden drawers.
I bet she picks up a few splinters

(after something over eyes)
I thought there'd been a power cut

I once did a good trick
What was that?
I turned a horse into a field

Where's your grammar?
She's playing Bingo

After eating fish, smells fish. Fish fingers

Wee Willie Fraser
Found his Dad's electric razor
Now Willie's arms that once were hairy
Now are bald, and so's the canary

Re three people - Snap, Crackle and Pop

You ought to eat Maltesers, the chocolate with the less fattening centres

Oh look a little cockroach. Would you like to go to heaven when you die little cockroach?
(squashing it with foot) Well, go then (wipes foot on Dame's skirt)

To the royal antechamber
I'm going to the royal chamber to see Aunty

Chord please maestro. Large white cord. Then bad chord.

A wants dumplings. B making long pastry says No, Roly Poly
B How can you have Roly Poly when you've got dumplings?
A (cutting long pastry into slices) There you are. Dumplings.

He gave me thirty lashes with the cat
Thirty lashes with the cat?
Yes, the cat was in hospital for a week

Echo gag
If I say radish I repeat (echoed by girl's voice)
Hullo, hullo. Where are you?
You hoo. Typhoo.
Boom boom boom. Esso Blue
I know where I can get a bottle of whisky etc

These are the Virgin Islands
Thank Gawd I'm in good company

(Life belt) What's that?
My Colgate ring of confidence

Re Friday: It's chocolate time
Don't say brown, say Hovis

(running round on tiptoe)
What are you doing?
I'm doing an impression of the Salvation Army
The Salvation Army?
Yes, I'm saving souls

Say something Spanish
Onions

Why can't penguins fly?
Because they're biscuits

Football routine
You have to guess which team it is
Sou'wester and brolly. Manchester
Bosom stuck out. Chester
With bit of coal. Colchester
Two babies. Oldham
Changing them from arm to arm. Alteringham
Also with babies. Motherwell
Brassiere - they're not a football team, they're supporters

Doing pools
Have you got your homes down
Yes I've got my homes down
Have you got your aways down
Yes I've got my aways down
Have you got your draws down
Yes I've got my drawers down

Waiter routine
(to waitress) What have you got on?
(re menu) I'll have that with chips
You can't have that
Why not?
It's the manager
(to waitress) Have you got pig's feet?
No, it's my corns
It's bean soup
I know what it's been. I want to know what it is now.
Syringe (after soup business) syringes plant. Collapses, says Mackesons. Plant jumps up again
This pigeon pie has got some wood in it.
Hullo wood pigeon
This routine done with waiter and waitress, waitress is an old nippy with bad feet. Calls Charlie
outside door each time. Waiter comes out, door hits face.
Cabaret done by same two

I'm a sandwich, I'm a sandwich
If you're a sandwich, why are you talking?
I'm a tongue sandwich

Hullo cock
Don't call me cock. My name's Roach
Hullo Cockroach

Where's Liverpool
On the Mersey

Where's Brussels?
On the sprouts

Look Carruthers, the natives are setting fire to a missionary
Holy Smoke

You've all heard of Lorna Doone? This is her sister Nothin' Doone

Welcome to our shores
What shores?
Mine's a brandy

Wrestling business twist nose
(through nose) I suppose you think that's funny

...to a connoisseur
You filthy swine

Stand by. A slaps B on shoulder. B slaps C. C falls R

Playing football with Squire's hat

Elvis the pelvis? Well I'm Sidney the Kidney

That's my watch dog
What does it watch?
Television

Hi (Robert Mitchum walk and imitation)
What's all that?
I'm being romantic
I thought you had the wind

Come, let us flee to the west
I've got fleas in my vest

Hits one. Another falls down
Hits one. Three fall down

A coughs
What's that?
A toad in the hole

Hot Dog Machine
To make hot dogs. First thing is we must have a hot dog. They get live dog put in machine. Turn handle, out come sausages. Tiger Rag during?

Jack and Jill went up the hill
Something to eat to get
Jack sat on a razor blade
Gillette

My dog. I call him carpenter
Carpenter? Why?
He made a bolt for the door

My dog. I call him fruit salts
Fruit salts. Why?
Enos

We shall be filthy rich
We're filthy now

Give us a niss
(B kisses A)
Not a kiss, a niss

Strike a match
Al lights come up

Hold up hoop, round face. Cough through it. Whooping Cough

Enter with large silver container
Brought you the largest container in the world
The Hope diamond
No. A Double Diamond (giant bottle inside)

One does disappearing trick with egg. Other spits out ping pong ball at stooge

Put your right hand like that and your right knee like that. Comfortable? yes (kicks over)

Blackboard gag
123
456
789
A points to number with pointer. B has to guess which. A points to one number then slides pointer to another, so B gets it wrong. "You just missed it" "I wasn't cheating. Oh no I wasn't" (to audience) So A wins money. A goes. B does it to C. "I think he's cheating" (to audience) "Did you see him cheat?" So B wins money. A comes back. They decide to fix him. A will tap B on the shoulder to give him cue. Gets number right. A was he cheating? Re member of audience. "She's got glasses. She can't see well." "Has she got glasses?" "Well she will have in a minute" This re someone in audience who says one is cheating. "You call me a cheat once more and see what happens" "Cheat" "Nothing happens" A does it again, turns flap number down to it shows nought. B has trouble signalling with pointer and jabs C who says "Ooh" "Correct"

We're a couple of big nickers

You can't be as daft as you look
Oh yes I am

I'll have middle and leg
(having drunk from cricket bat with panel in it)
That was a foul
So was that drink

(drinks again from handle)

We're from Cornwall where the clotted cream comes from.
I'm the cream.
I'm the clot.

You do the job or else
Who's Else?

I have a friend called Isaiah
Isaiah? Why is he called Isaiah?
One eye's 'igher than the the other

Take the paper off and eat it (after B is eating it with paper on)
Take the paper off and eat it? Right. (takes off paper and eats that)

Would you like a bit of chocolate
Is it Cadbury's?
Yes
Well I won't bother then

He's rough and ready
Rough and ready?
Well, his father was rough...

There was a soldier, a Scottish soldier
Oh how he did perspire
The night his kilt caught fire

You were sixteen before you knew about girls
You were eighteen before you knew you weren't one

I went out last night with a girl with a wooden leg
With her I could not linger
How did you know she had a wooden leg?
I got a splinter in my finger

Go to the devil
Any message?

I promise you something else Fairy. I'll always use your soap

Go and get some pepper
Red pepper or white pepper?
Neither. Toilet pepper

I'll be a real prince and you'll be a real princess and we'll put our names down for a council house

They can't cook me. I went to Harrow
What difference does that make?
It means I can't be eaten

Re cannibals
We're surrounded by Liquorice Allsorts

Cannibal King: Me bridge that gap with ____ snack

I know a place where a woman wears nothing but a string of beads
Where's that?
Around her neck

I'm going to feed my parrot
What are you going to give it?
Polyfilla

You'll be Mrs Buttons. We'll be Mr and Mrs Buttons and we'll have a lot of little zippers

Could you go for me?
Can't you go for yourself?

What are you wearing that lemon in your ear for?
I said what are you wearing that lemon in your ear for?
I can't hear you. I've got a lemon in my ear
What do you wear it for?
Well you've heard of a hearing aid. This is a lemonade

On the night you proposed on your face there was such a look of ecstasy
That wasn't ecstasy. You were standing on my foot.

There's a terrible draught coming from somewhere
I don't know where it's coming from, but I know where it's going to

I wouldn't have the nerve to speak to an ogre
I've spoken to dozens of 'em
When?
Every time I pay my Income Tax

My Pedro. My ____
My goodness. My Guinness

Queen cries
King brings out small umbrella

He wouldn't hurry for a Murray Mint

Get this down (all aperients) Got that lot down?
Yes
Well, the best of luck to you

Take my hand
(false hand which comes off)

Browned off
Don't say brown. Say Hovis

Re seal on document
Oh look. A jam tart

I'll very likely do you

What's the time?
It's chocolate time

She lives in Coronation Street, next to _____

You can be Mrs Buttons and we'll have a lot of zip fasteners

The Fizz of Magnesia

Long du Maurier
What have you got there?
A long player

I shall make you a major domo
Major what?
Domo
Domo adds whiteness to cleanness and brightness

You couple of Tetley's teabags

Three canaries on perches in cages. One on upper perch, one on middle perch, one on lower perch.
Who owned the cage?
Bottom one. The other two were on higher perches

I'm in a proper pickle. I feel like an onion

You cast me aside like a withered bloom
More like a wrinkled walnut

(small suitcase) What's this? Kildare's last case

Forest build-up
Now we're listening to the Archers
Alan a Dale and his wife Mrs Dale

Oh my Norman forefathers! Would that I had your Norman wisdom

Christmas! It was different when I was a boy. Dad used to go out in the back yard and fire off his gun and say Santa Claus had shot himself

Taking snuff. 3 times, nostril, nostril and over shoulder. Squeaking noise from drummer

My moods are like the weather. When it's mild, I'm mild. When it's brisk, I'm brisk
Thank heavens it's not wet and windy

Your teeth are like petals

Rose petals?
No, bicycle petals

I used to think a rump steak was a shooting stick

Dancing routine
Monkey will show Bill how to dance. Bill will copy steps. Monkey does various different dances all modern and jazzy. Each time Bill does same little dance with blocks from drummer to Pop goes the Weasel. Monkey (dancer) mimes "Square" Shrugs and does his dance. From this they both go into Sunny Side of the Street dance

What have you got in that bucket
Horse manure
What are you going to do with it
Put it on my rhubarb
Funny, I usually put custard on mine

Where is dinner?
There's fish and chips in the conservatory
Fish and chips served in the conservatory?
No in the News of the World

My father occupied the musical chair at Oxford. He was very well connected
My father occupied the electric chair at Sing-Sing. He was very well connected too

Tray dropped and slid under hoop skirt. Comic has to crawl under and find it. Biz
It was dark under there

Who do you think you are? James Bond?
I'm 00784569
What's that?
Premium Bond

Waiter routine
Are you the waiter? Yes. Well wait there till I get back
What would you like to eat?
Food
How much for gravy, bread, water? We don't charge - each time
I'll have three plates of gravy, two loaves of bread and a bucket of water
Waiter pushes him and he falls over with table
Can you speak French?
Fluently
French for an apple. Pomme
French for two apples? Pom Pom
Crate of apples. Pom pom di pom pom. Pom pom
Soup syphoned back in pump when customer does not like it
So hungry I could eat a horse
Sorry we've only got the doovers
Have you got a wild duck
We've got a tame one I could aggravate
Any tripe
Fred, switch on the television set

I mean special tripe
Turn on the commercials

Enter in laundry basket, pulled by children. Puts down rope ladder. "That's me, that's the basket. Don't get them mixed up." re corsets. I hope they haven't starched them. They starched them last week. I was walking about like this. Bedsocks stiff, make noise when thrown down. "Sitting room curtains" pair of bloomers. "She's made a bloomer there." BB Brigitte Bardot? No. Mrs Braddock. Trousers with hole in seat. Someone's been dancing cheek to cheek

Rocker and cooking routine
Cook and comic. Comic feeling sick. Don't like it when we go over these hills. Nearly sick in cook's cooking bowl, cook takes it away in time. Sick out of porthole, comes away with fish in mouth. Comic asking for cook for apology. "I apologise?" (angrily) "Thank you" Ironing board with iron on stage as well as kitchen table with usual props. Cook re iron. Wet your finger and test it. Comic spits on finger, keeps missing. I keep missing it. Lick it. Comic licks iron, flash, burns tongue. Drink some water. Comic does so. Put some water on your tongue. Spits it out at cook, cook keeps talking, comic keeps spitting. Comic puts iron on cook's hand. Speaking tube (hose pipe) Tell them to send up a little water, Water out of hose. Comic assisting with pastry throws it on floor, trying to make a bang. Look at the state of this table. Filthy. Cook cleans table with pastry. It goes on floor. There's fluff on the duff. Comic goes back to ironing, big pair of pants. I don't know whose these are, but he ain't half got a big head. Ironing all over, on bum, crutch etc. They're mine. No they're not, they're St Michael's. It says so inside. Comic irons pastry instead of trousers in trousers shape. Haven't they shrunk? Elastic sausages round cook's neck. They keep popping up in dish. Hold it down. Pastry put on top. One sausage or another keeps popping up and down. Get hammer. When I nod my head, hit it. Comic hits cook. Then hammering down round edge of pastry. Hits cook's fingers. Cook gets pastry on mouth. Comic removes it. Cook has lost teeth. Into Rocker and Water effect.

Drummer Routine
Bass drum, cymbal, one stick. Seat with hole in it. Spike that comes up through hole. Boxing glove that comes out. Iron weight that comes down on head. All worked by hand lever, or foot lever on other side of post. Learning to play drums. First time puts in bang or cymbal gets weight then spike. Comic in agony. Stooge says "smile." Later "You're asking for an anesthetic." Next time hits cymbal he gets boxing glove. Falls over. "Don't worry, it's only blood." "It was right on the beat." "It was right on the bonce." Re weight. "It's only iron." Spike and head next time. Try and see the point. All three effects. "now you're getting it." "I'm getting it all right." "Tiger Rag" Everything goes.

Supper Routine – Dame and Sheriff
Nappy folded and put round his neck.
Menu cleaned off.
Soup pumped from bucket into plate with bicycle pump.
I want some splash (for drink) Dame gets soda siphon.
"Shall I?" (to audience)
Shampoo
Is that bird high? (thrown up and shot)
College pudding on plate. "A very small pudding." "It's a very small college. What college is it? (after munching it) Eton.
Everything on table picked up in cloth. Saves washing up. Could be hammered with hammer.

Tricks
Ball and two cups. Both on floor. Ball put under one. Get it under other. Magic words. Ball is now under other (does not show this). Really difficult thing to do is to get back under first. Magic

words. Now back under first c up. Shows. Drum roll.

Indian Rope Trick. Two small lengths of cord. Put in bag. Will come out tied. Hold behind (both bits). Let audience examine bag. Give to MD but before he can show to audience "That's enough." (This before putting rope behind him) Backache gag to hands behind him. Audience can think he is tying them, he can fool them refusing to show bits still separate after this. Magic words. Come out tied. Brings out packet of Tide.

Tricks

Cloak and bucket. Bucket disappears. No one will ever know how that trick was done. Exit showing bucket hanging on hook on back of dress.

Bit of wood (long) Sawing business Other end falls off.

Bottle of beer, upended on something (fixed)

Undressing

Each pair of pants a different colour. Stick no Bills. Shorty nightdress.

Duck pie routine

Baron and Buttons. Baron with huge lump of dough and open cook book labelled Bob Martin's Cook Book. Buttons enters puts hand on dough. Baron hits hand with wooden spoon. Flour. Buttons gets a flower. Bag of flour. Buttons gets it. Bung it in. Buttons bungs bag of flour into basin. Time. Clock. Bung it in. Sausages. Buttons re-enters with long string of sausages slung over shoulders. During dialogue sausages are pulled off on string. Duck. I want a real live dead duck. Buttons gets revolver, shoots one way. Duck falls down the other way. Playing bagpipe with duck. Duck in basin. At this point second interruption – dog and hoop. Toy dog about to jump through hoop, pulled off from other side by string. First one has been tin teapot and cups on tray bal;anced on pole, tray is fixed and crockery on wires to tray. Egg on frying pan onto picture. Third interruption see-saw. A and B. A is going to do jump on see-saw and somersault, but a section of see-saw breaks off when he jumps on it. Buttons holding pastry, it falls down (drooping). It's alive. Shoot at pastry with revolver. Drummer starts duel with own revolver. Buttons is shot. I'll chop his cymbals off. Pastry balls. Playing tennis with cotton wool balls that look like pastry balls. Knocking balls into audience. About to throw huge lump of dough into audience, put it down front of Baron's trousers instead. Meanwhile C and D have come on with basin apparently full of pastry balls but has bits of paper which they throw into audience.

Egg routine

Dames sees box of eggs on table. Breaks two in bowl to show they are real. Rest are dummies. Puts two down front. Feels self. Four behind in pants. One under hat. B and C enter, she must rehearse the adagio dance. I can't, I'm too fragile. You don't want to drop a clanger. That's not the only thing I may drop. Throw yourself into it. Dance. Big bang – reaction. Walk carefully. Bang in right breast. Holds out dress, looks down to see if eggs are all right. Ole. Just misses banging right breast. Smells where eggs were. B tries to kick her in dance, she runs away. Falls over. Gets up slowly with everything smashed. Bang on head finally.

Sticks gag

Two people. Whatever I say you've got to answer sticks. Game with bet on it. Are you ready? Yes. Lost. Are you ready? Sticks. I nearly caught you that time, didn't I? You did and all. Lost. Which would you rather have, the money or the sticks. B picks up money. You've got them.

Baths routine

Vizier on with huge bandaged foot. Mind my foot. Wishy trips over it passing twice. Then hits it with stick. It's all imagination. Hits it all over leg with stick till Vizier falls over.

I want a bath neither too hot nor too cold.

Would you like a bit of lemon in it?

On my foot

Put your foot in your pocket. (very small towel) These things are sent to dry us.

Dame: I only use Dreft

Dreft? Why?

It keeps everything soft and fluffy.

Lights out. Turn the lights on. Girl seen undressing in shadowgraph. (lights up). Turn the lights out again. (lights out) Dame undressing in shadowgraph. Big comb business Taking off clothes. Two baths on stage with Dame and Emperor.

Shooting business

A with gun asks B if is long-sighted. Can you see two miles? Details of what can see, build up. Through lattice window can see edge of great bell. A shoots. Bell from back of circle. Repeat with bet. Should be slightly different direction (other side of circle). Same business through lattice window edge of bell in church steeple. Fires, pause. A about to walk off leaving B with his tuppence. After delay bell rings. A collects tuppence then says I've got my own tuppence back.

Bomb gag

Dame, Comic, Man, King

D	I've just heard the six o'clock news and they say Edgbaston's declared war on Erdington
C	Good morning, good morning, good morning
D	Who it this hoi polloi? We know him not

(wraps scarf rolund neck with flourish and hits Muddles. Drum noises)

C	Don't do that
K	You know what I've called for
D	The empties I suppose

(Scarf business)

C	I said don't do that
K	I want my pocket money. You promised to pay me at the end of the month.
D	But I didn't say which month did I? (laughs)
C	And you didn't say which end (laughs) (Scarf) I said don't do that or you'll be sorry
K	You didn't pay me last month or the month before that or the month before that (Claps hands on each month. Other two imitate him)
D	And if I'm not mistaken, the month before that (tries to clap hands, falls, is picked up by Comic by seat)
D	I wish you'd cut your nails
M	(entering large parcel) There's a parcel here for one of you folks
All	It's for me, it's for me
D	Ladies first, it's for me
M	And there's ten shillings to pay
D/K	It's for him (exit)
C	All right, I'll be a sport (gives money to man who exits) A parcel for me, I wonder what it is. And there's a note with it. Dear Sir, You have been selected to place the enclosed bomb (reaction) beneath the witches cave. Failure means certain death. You are in no danger carrying it around as it only explodes when you put it down. Signed The Black Hand Gang. Oh what am I going to do?
K	(entering) I want to be happy etc
C	Hullo Kingy, many happy returns of the day
K	It's not my birthday
C	Oh yes it is, but you don't know it. There's a present for you.
K	It's very kind of you. But I don't know if I should take it. The Queen might not like it
C	Oh I assure you she'd be delighted. There you are. There's a note with it. Bye bye. Oh by the

	way you are an ambitious man aren't you?
K	Oh I am. One of these days I'm going to be a big noise
C	He is
K	One of these days I'm going right to the top
C	You are
K	I'll be seeing you
C	I don't think you will
K	(reads note) What a dirty trick. I must get rid of it (calls Dame) This parcel was for you all the time
D	I knew it. I wouldn't be surprised if this was from Humphrey Bogart
K	Have you ever heard the little birdies singing in the trees and seen the angels flying about in the sky?
D	Not since I signed the pledge
K	It won't be long now
D	Au revoir
K	Oh no my dear, not au revoir. Goodbye (exit)
D	(reads note) Tries to put parcel down (orchestra yell - She offers it to audience – Comic enters) Aha
C	Aha
D	Come to Queenie
C	Oh no I won't
D	Queenie wants her little Muddley Puddley Wuddley
C	Queenie's not going to have her little Muddley Puddley Wuddley
D	(throwing it to him) There's a parcel for you
C	(throwing it back) I don't want it (parcel thrown from one to other. Dame does splits receiving it. C helps her up, pulls up her skirt)
C	Someone doesn't use Persil
D	What on earth shall I do with it?
C	You'll have to carry it round for the rest of your life
D	I bet you I won't
C	I bet you you will. I bet you my hat to your dress you will.
D	All right, wait a minute while I get my dress off. Here hold this (he takes it)
C	On no you don't (runs off)

(D throws it after him. Explosion. Boots come on, on lines, chasing Dame or Muddles runs across in long pants with seat on fire)

Drilling gags
Comic enters late with long pole with Union Jack on end. Pole brought on getting longer and longer.
Driller One two
Comic Buckle my shoe
Driller Left, left, as if you were riding a bicycle (All imitate this. Wishy does freewheeling business) What are you doing?
Wishy I'm freewheeling
Driller Right turn (to W who has turned left) I said right turn
Wishy I'm left-handed

Shaving routine
Barbers chair. Muddles and two others waiting on trick bench. King gets into chair while Muddles is putting hat on bench. Fight starts in which others join in. Dame rolls up sleeves gets into middle of it with heads down and stops it
D   If there's any fighting in my kitchen I'm going to be in it. Get up or I'll kick you up (to

prostrate one) Who was first?

Others   Muddles was first (All sit down, M in chair, D turns away)

K   I'm first and what's more I can fight (pushes M back on others on trick bench)

D   You can what?

K   I can fight

D   Why didn't you say that before? (pushing him hard into chair) Sit down, you're next

M   What about me?

D   The trouble is he can fight. Can you fight?

M   No I can't fight

D   That's all I want to know. Siddown (hits him. He falls back on others on trick bench) Coming in here upsetting me like this. For two pins I'd do you. (rushes at M but is caught by K. Others get up. M falls off trick bench)

(K sits down in chair. D pulls sheet tight. He yells. D gets lather on brush, drops it on floor, picks it up and puts it back on brush.)

M   (to others) It's my opinion they found more work for the men

(D goes over to him belligerently. Puts bit of lather on nose, replaces it on brush)

D   Who found more work for the men?

M   The government

D   Oh the government. That's all right. But if I thought you were talking about me I'd dash your brains out (makes to hit.   Others get up. M falls off trick bench)

(Big man enters singing Girls and Boys and dances round. Others join in going round chair)

D   Do you want a shave?

BM   No, I don't want a shave, I want to be reduced (Singing starts again, Dame ushers him into reducing Chamber and turns handle from Cold to Very Hot)

D   Tell me when he's been in there ten minutes

K   Will that reduce him?

D   Reduce him? It'll paralyse him

(D puts lather all over K's face scattering lather everywhere. He gets real razor (blunted) and uses wrong side. Strops it and strops it again on sole of shoe. Takes hair from head business with noise. Shaves with business)

M   I'm fed up

D   (pointing with razor across K) You're fed up? I'm fed up? (everyone frightened. K holds D's shaking hand with razor, flicking of soap onto others with razor)

M   That's enough. I'm off. (all make for door)

D   (barring way) Siddown (they go back to seat, cowed) You'll all get your turn (to M) You're next (K has tiptoed to door, D whistles to him)Hey, come back (D attacks shaving vigorously. K yells. She gets on his knees and hacks away. They all gather round to restrain her)

M   What have you done to the man?

D   Never mind the man. Look for his ear (They all look for ear, clapped back on by D when found)

(Squeezing water from sponge onto his face. Hitting cheek hard with sponge.)

K   What are you doing?

D   There are one or two here I didn't get off, so I'm shoving 'em in

(squirts powder on K from bulb – horn noise – K blows powder up in cloud. Covers face with towel and twists nose. Ratchet)

D   Now I'm going to shave the back of your neck. You'll have to take this back stud out

K   That's not a back stud, it's a wart

Others   Kingy's got a wart

K   You'll have a wart yourself one of these days

(Dame cuts it off. Yell from K. She holds it up, tosses, heads it, kicks it – noises then holds it again)

D   You're quite right. It was a wart

(Explosion off and flash from R Chamber)
M   Your majesty, what about the man in the Reducing Chamber?
D   Let him out, give him air
(She opens door. Very small man comes out in big man's hat and clothes)
Blackout

Court routine
Emperor on throne. Two policemen with naps. Wishy takes wrong position and Emperor shows him, then W sits on throne saying Drunk and Disorderly, Take him away, Chop off his napper, Next case etc. Dame on with hat made of frying pan with egg, bacon, sausage on it
E   Take the dock
D   Thanks very much. It'll come in very handy for my ducks (takes it off)
E   No, no. I want you in the dock
D   What do you think I am, the Queen Mary?

Party routine
Dumb waiter with glasses and jug. Pouring various drinks from jug of water yet they come out different colours in glasses for beer, milk etc. Jelly down dress of Dame. Have a cracker, have some nuts (these held out, put back before anyone has chance). Whisky and splash?
Where's the splash?
Syphon in to enquirer's face. Comic searches D's clothes for jelly. Conjurer gag – One of his tricks. Comic uses umbrella to siphon off crème de menthe drink from D's glass into his own and drinks it.
He's drunk your crème de menthe
That's not crème de menthe, that's Cascara (or some terrible drink)
(C spits it out. Flash)

Rocker scene
Two bunks one over the other with ladder at the side. Dame on, undresses – puts hat out of porthole and everything she takes off goes out of porthole. On pants she has L, Cross Here, Fox tails on front of one pair, two heads crossed over crack on rear. Not Frying tonight. Eyelashes off into mug with flopping noise. Wig off showing bald head. Nightcap and dress on, gets into bunk, waving goodnight to audience. A comes in finds D in the bunk. Scream. Chase. While D looks out of door, A slips in and into bunk. D gets into same bunk and A rolls out underneath it. A climbs to top bunk, almost comes through – bottom of bunk comes right out. Jack enters finds Dame. J and D go round and round in (turning) door. J gets in lower and D finds J in, they get in together lying with feet meeting. Pulling clothes business Fish comes in through window. Pillow falls down and clanks. Rocker starts. Green light on it.

Shop scene gags
(To customer) Have a seat (puts chair for customer then takes it away so customer falls down – chair without seat) That chair's got no seat in it (sitting down) It has now (Customer takes bale of cloth and exits after distracting Jack by pointing to something else) I want some shot silk (showing bale with holes in it) I shot it myself this morning One customer took a whole roll this morning. I'll do the same (takes roll and exits)

Trying on routine
D trying on various comedy hats. Each one does not go with dress. Wants hat of same material. Comic takes big scissors goes behind her, produces hat which suits. As she goes off we see large bit cut out of back of her dress and utility marks on her pants.

Cooking routine
(radio on for cooking talk)
Salt (Epsom Salts – a running certainty on packet)
Flour (calls for flour into blower. Flour out and on face)
What did you say? Business with radio voice
Vim into it. Big bowl. Scramble – dance in bowl which is on floor (during exit of comics radio is changed to talk on gym class)
Toss the ball (dough) from one to other
(dough business wiping floor etc)
All lie down on it. Stretch

Rubber boot routine
Stooge enters and wants pair of rubber boots. Comic takes his shoes off, bites laces to get them off. Squeezing etc. Socks with holes in them. I want some waders. I thought you said rubber boots etc Well why don't you make up your mind? I want a Wellington. Together – altogether. Those up there. They're gumboots. Little Girl and Mother enter. LG wants ballet shoes. Tongue put out by comic to LG. 6 and 7 eighths. I want them with… blocks. She wants them with… blocks. She'll get a thick ear in a minute. C gets sizes and orders mixed. Getting boots down with long pole. Knocks stooge off chair with pole. Puts ballet shoes on man with toes upside down on his heels. Smelling feet business Pulling S along floor to child and away. Clench your toes. Can't get Wellington off child's foot. Don't do that, you'll take the polish off. Tries to pull boot off in vain. Knocks Mother's hat off in vain. Oy Septic (LG has running red nose) Holds child upside down, then pulls on floor, lifts by leg. Don't smile to S, knocks S off seat. Wrestling business with LG her legs over his head. Throttling business Bell. LG and C to chairs, fanned by M and S. Bell again. Back to wrestling. Mother pulled in too. Three pull together. Stooge behind comic. Stooge pushing comic business Sudden pull and fall. Rat enters up trap immediately.

Cooking Routine (5)
Cooking Toad in the Hole (see other gag). Philip Harben cod to teach them. He leans forward on table confidentially so do A and B imitating him. He and A come back. A tells B Time to get up. Three bowls. Flour. Water. A uses siphon. Mix it up with a spoon. Singing business for mixing. C puts flour under arms. Throw flour over shoulder. Birthday for Harben. Shake hands with A who has filthy floury wet hands. Bit of dough over, thrown across Harben from C to A. Harben tastes it. A spits into it. Piece of pastry thrown into audience. Baking tins produced. Make a hole in the centre. C does this with winding twisty. Pull away flour, off floor and off feet. Harben shows them some movement with fingers in pastry. All doing it. Don't put your dirty fingers in my duff. Business Wipe Harben's face with dough. Chicken for filling. Bagpipe gag. Sausages for filling. Elastic. Pull and fall. Sausages in duff, tie in knot. New dough for cover (prepared). On floor. Brush with broom. Knead the dough. Skip. Fur round neck. Flatiron on dough. Jump on it, flatten it with bum on floor. Spread the dough over the top. Hat for Harben. Bend round head like period headdress. Hammer round edges with hammer. Hit thumb with hammer. I saw you do that. Don't do it maliciously like that but lightheartedly like that. Banging dough down harder and harder. Wiping table and floor with it. Getting shoes stuck in it. Put it in oven. Get plates down. Not that like that (breaking one) like that etc (from dresser). One plate does not break so they drop iron on it on floor. Climb up dresser to get at china on top. Plates thrown down from top. Explosion from oven. Steam. Oven goes up with comics both clinging to it.

Crusoe. Comics put in pot wheeled on with fire underneath. A first (Dame) vegetable and condiments in. Then B I didn't know we were going to have mixed bathing. Singing business C I swear to tell the whole truth. Three sing as pot is carried off for cooking. Re-enter when saved all carrying various vegetables.

Crate gag

Enormous heavy looking crate on dockside scene. Mate told to get it aboard. With Dame he gets long rope for her from flies and for himself rope with hook with what looks like round iron weight. Get that crate on board. Order repeated, eventually Mate to no-one. Got to sling it. Banging on head with weight, pushing weight to and fro. Like that gag. Dame pulls but Mate is hooked to crate. Crate up (hollow) comes down on Mate's foot. Jump to it, show a leg and look alive (Captain on for this) Mate crushed under crate. Child emerges as Mate.

Under the Sea

Whittington and Cat on raft. (Silk held and rustled for sea) A in barrel paddling. B with pack hiking. C on bicycle with sails

Counting up to Nine (*2nd* version)

A and B bet. A makes them come to ten, B to nine. B to C. C makes them come to eleven. Ask kids what it comes to. Bet. B makes kids count with him, last time it comes up eight (picks up hats at eight)

Globes of Fate

Demon on with six balloons, gives them to Dame and Co. Globes of Fate. If you tell a lie, think a wicked thought, do a dirty deed, globe will burst. When all three are burst I will come for you and drag you down to the bowels of the earth where you will sizzle like a sausage.
Go and put your trousers on (as Demon exits)
Repeat prohibition. Life's not worth living is it? Woolworths, Dame served behind counter. She denies it and says she was Manageress. (One bursts) See what happens when you tell a lie? I never tell lies (One of Comic's bursts) They do it selves. Girl comes on. We were not even married (One of each goes). Seeing two gone Comic starts to cry. Hit each other with balloons. I never touched her. (last one gone) Down down down. Demon with one of them off. Girl comes on and winks. Comic bursts own last balloon. Move over, I'm coming down.

George Washington story

GW who never told a lie
Why was he dumb?
No, he was American
Did he discover America?
No, Columbus discovered America
Well who lost it?
One day...
Which day?
It was Friday
Oh that's different
Different to what?
Different to Saturday. Which Friday was it?
1st fri
His father was sitting in bed reading
What was he reading?
The Sunday Pictorial
On a Friday?
They published it early that week
Orchard...
What's an orchard?
A place where people orch
Well you orch to know

Apples on the trees
What sort of apples?
Rosy red apples
On the first Friday after Christmas?
They were preserved apples. They grew on the trees in tins
They can do anything in America.
Do you believe in early closing times?
Well shut up
... ...
Were you there?
No
Then how do you know all this?
Because it's history
I thought you said it was GW's tree
Open the gates, peter. Someone's coming up

Short Bucket gag
Dame throws bucket off one side of ship. It comes back. Feed explains that she has thrown it into the wind. Demonstrates by throwing other side. Dame throws other side and gets it back. Feed says sudden change of wind. Dame throws other way runs across deck to avoid it coming back and gets it from other side

It's half past bedtime

Dough scene with dog
Music: Roll along covered wagon, roll along. Long roll of dough hanging over end of table. D to dog Hands off. Dame spits on hands before rolling again. Dog plays with end that hangs down. It's a bit long isn't it? There's room this end. Takes hanging end, joins to other end. Sneezes into dough, wipes nose with one end. Snake charmer music and business with long roll, swing round neck like tibbit, bit comes off and goes in corner. Take it to my room and put it under the bed with... the other rubbish. Dog takes it away in basin.

Balloon scene
Gas bag hanging in front, established. Enormous binoculars, Shouting to attract attention. B stamps. A Don't do that. The people underneath will complain. That's ballast. Don't use that language Shows ballast bag of sand. Thrown out. Crash of broken glass. You don't want to fall out. You're not insured. Radio got out and clipped on rail of basket. They talk to it. How do we find out where we are? Look over the rail you fathead. Don't you dare speak to me like that (hits radio). Oh (three times). Hits – tum, tum ti tum tum. Radio cries Oh oh. I'll give you such a clout in a minute. Radio: Get out of it. Gas bag lit, Dame almost falls out and wig blows off revealing bald head.

Hoop dance
All comics as little boys and little girls. Dame in centre dressed in gym clothes. With music that stops constantly while they hold pose (like Pizzicato). Dame gets stuck with hoop between legs. Group round hoops in centre. Two get hoopp round nexk. DSame drops hoop. Picks up hoop, falls down. All go round hoop. Can't get apart. Exchanging hoops between two of them. Skipping with hoops.

Sticks gag
Three sticks held up. Bet. Answer sticks to whatever I say
Are you ready?
Yes

You've lost (another bet)
Are you ready?
Sticks
I nearly caught you didn't I?
Yes (same again)
Are you ready?
Sticks
...etc
Which would you rather have, the money or the sticks?
Sticks (other exits with money)

Custard song
Song sung by A ending Give me custard. B comes on and gives him custard in face on cue. C comes on so A and B try to do it to C. Fond of singing. Fond of singing about food? A gets custard ready. C starts about boiled beef and carrots. They dance and A falls into custard. They get C to sing custard song. But B returns and falls into custard. I slipped. Splashing gag. Again, C sings last line twice. I've forgotten it. Gets words wrong. Give custard to you. No, to you. Oh to me. When he does it right both A and B have custard, C ducks and A and B give it to each other.

Money gag
A has money that B and C want. He thrusts fistfuls of notes under their noses. It falls on floor. C surreptitiously takes some, puts it under his hat. B does conjuring trick. Gets money. Makes it disappear under arm. Reappears it under C's hat.

Rocker scene with routine
Tessie and Dame discovered one over other in bunks
I feel horrible
You look horrible
I know what sailors mean when they say heave ho
The cheerful sailor passes. What's for supper?
Pork and trifle
Second cheerful sailor passes. What do you suggest?
Soup. Is soup good?
Oh yes, I always say easy down, easy up
They get out of bunks and go into
Numbers routine
A produces board to cheer them up. Little game. It has following numbers on it
12345
67890
A bets them he can tell number without looking. They bet. B points to number. A asks Is it odd or even? Is it between 2 and 4? It's 3. A wins bet. There are no flies on me. No, but we can see where they've been. Good, isn't it? Running gag for winner. B does it to A. I'm touching it, I'm touching it. Is it between 5 and 7? No. Is it between 1 and 3? Yes. B gets it by C hitting her. Both say Good, isn't it. They do it again. It is 7 this time. I'm touching it, I'm touching it. Some line re Bristol. What's Bristol on? Severn. Seven. Good isn't it? Double stakes. This time A touches 0. I'm touching it. C kicks B. Oh. Take money and hoppit. Good isn't it?

Mop drill gag
One had mop with no tassels on it at all. Business. It has terrible smell. Each smells it in turn. All throw over shoulders. One two three catch, mop thrown to and fro. One about to hit driller with mop, driller turns, so comic turns to start mopping bus, knocks away mop from another who is leaning on it and he falls over. End with very long pole with tiny flag on for march off.

Tea gags
Tea urn with tap and cups and saucers.
Putting mop in urn then washing floor with it.
Then getting tea from urn to give to someone
While doing this sneeze into sugar. B drinks tea, then spits it out at someone else
Who's been mucking about with me urn
Customer wants sausage roll
Comic takes roll, blows through it, then blows on sausage. Puts sausage in roll, throws it onto plate, plate breaks into bits. Too much tea. Throw some in face from cup. Pair of ear-rings? Well these are soused ear-rings? Reading the tea leaves in cup. Fortune telling.

Drum gag
A is going to recite. Can you recite? Splashing gag. B told to stand in corner. Cannon to right of them. (timps) He's good isn't he?
Cannon to left of them
(timps) The cannon's still on the right
…volleyed and thundered
I thought we were going to have a storm
Then cymbal splash. Dinner is served
We'll have that again
I haven't had the fish yet
Rode the four hundred. B: Five hundred
Band: Six hundred
B Sold to Joe for six hundred
During gag B bends down, drum bang, he jumps
They've got me. They always said they'd get me in the end
Long-pouring pot
There we are dear, just half a cup
How many lumps of sugar? Fourteen
Emptying basin in. Have the lot

The Bells of St Marys
Two comics, two extras
Right turn, Quick march. Timpani thumps for exit each time
No 2 plays to missing person each time. They come back looking very forlorn
First extra sings wrong note
Second goes into hot number for no reason
No 2 does Double Diamond
3rd time slow
No 2 goes round so as not to be in place of missing person
They swivel round, back to back. No 2 ending up as before
Last time out no 2 goes round in circle just before exit
No 1 gets hold of him keeps him going out first
After shot no 2 comes back. She missed me

Nurse routine
Let me examine your chest
A hairy chest. Yes I got shot in one leg and dandruff set in
Whole hairy chest is pulled out. Becomes woofenpoof
Huge hypodermic
You're not going to stick that in my arm

Who said anything about your arm? Bend over. I'll check your oil at the same time

School routine
You should have been at school at 9.30
Why? What happened?
Huge bun eaten. Ooh, a currant
Put that away
(eating) I am putting it away
Stuffs bit of bun in neighbour's ear
Let's take General Knowledge
Three comics stand up and salute
Who are you saluting?
General Knowledge
Tom cats kittens verbal routine
(to one who wants to go to lav: You can stay behind after school and fill the inkwells)
Cricket with bun and napo. Nurse runs, then sits down on bench and falls

Undressing
Alarm clock wound up for hours with effect. These alarm clocks, you have to wind them up fro eight days.
Long long glove on one hand. Very short glove on other
Sack dress with King Edwards on one side. King Kong on other

Brokers men routine
Ugly Sisters entertaining Vicar. Cinderella serving. Brokers keep taking chairs away just as people are going to sit down on them. Trolley for tea wheeled in. Tea pot taken below by one of Brokers men sitting concealed under curtain below trolley. Cinders sent for another one. Vicar in big chair. One BM puts arms through holes in chair and they become Vicar's arms. Business while he is having tea, eating and drinking etc. Strawberries and cream. Cream in Vicar's hat. He goes not to put it on at first, but gets or is given tea cosy by mistake. When he does put it on it has hole in top so cream squirts straight up.

Comic's opening routine
When I count three you all yell your names
I never heard a flipping word
They do it again
Tell Mums and Dads to join in. Take a deep breath
You should see your eyeballs popping
(name calling) There's a boy there yelling Shirley
Take that toffee out of your mouth Madam. You'll spit it down the woman's neck in front
Turn to person on your right and give them a nudge
Turn to person on your left. Do you like the look of them?
If very posh, say How do you do?
Into number with repeated words Having Fun plus handclaps

Haunted House routine
Pounding very hard bed. Pillow that chinks with metal inside. Flit used on bed. Hat put on cabinet top, goes inside. Appears on wall in two different places successively. Candle put on wall disappears and reappears elsewhere. Long candle goes up and down. Flat behind bed goes up and Demon appears in red glow laughing about getting them down below. Then snow scene in blue light, snow descends on them and sheet is whisked up to ceiling. Clock turns into a demon's face and tongue comes out and licks head. Handkerchief to mop face turns into whiffenpoof with business. Drawer

taken out becomes ladder, when used to go up wall all rungs straighten twice but go back when looked at by climber. A disappears into wall and reappears behind prison bars.

Car routine
Horn
Self starter
Colonel Bogey played on Ice Cream chimes
Don't kick it. You won't start it by kicking it. (it then starts)
Check water
Exhaust. Seat goes up in air with comic on it (US)
I've never been so elated
Door falls off on foot
After something on bum. You've ruined me future
Explosion and smoke
Back seat shoots over and out with US on it

Flaps
Score board by window for chalking up hits. Double in and out. Both on revolve door. Snap

Wishes routine
Comic gets all wishes granted by fairy. Only to say the word. Rain. Snow. Fog. Blow. (Sailors wish it would blow) These all happen by accident as he says word. Wishes for pie (to feed) I wish you'd put a sock in it. Feed: (taking sock from pie) There's no need, there's one in it already

Dough scene
Big squeezy thing (for icing cakes) squirt some on other comic
Wash him clean with soda siphon
Nothing better than an egg (break one on his hand)
Always wipe off with soda siphon
Milk from jug poured down trousers front
Flour emptied over head
Black treacle. A produces it then sits in it on table "into battle" finish. Trousers come off

Partridge in a Pear Tree parody
Row of comics and others behind washing machines
The first day of Christmas my true love sent to me etc
The first day of Christmas I saw on TV…
so many washing machines, so many drip drip shirts (Dame washing them) two rubber gloves, and a clock that makes the tea. Include one packet of Daz. Each are produced as mentioned. Eventually porter comes on with trolley of packets. (Get actual number to write parody from)

Villain comes on to recite poem. Comic gets them to hiss him and appears between tabs with last line written on card for audience to say "Why don't you belt up, you silly old goat" Comic persuades him to do it again. This time he sees comic holding card up and chases him off.

Conjuring gag
A places box on B's head. Puts pill in B's mouth. Is going to transfer pill from mouth to box, which he had shown to audience as empty
B talks with pill in mouth
Abra Cadabra A takes pill from box with flourish
B says "What about this?" producing pill in mouth again, having previously disappeared it

Mind-reading act

A introduces B as greatest mind-reader in world. Few gags – There's man down here with a brown hat. What colour has he on? Etc Build to A giving phone directory to one of audience asking him to name page he chooses. B will say first name on top column. Works perfectly. Second time B says doesn't know. C emerges from behind curtain with directory saying that page is missing from his copy

Water gag

A on stage. B (deadpan stooge) comes on with water can. Holds hand up and waits. A goes to him, turns can upside down, no water comes out. Then slaps face. B throws water from can over A's face and exits. (Query: has B meanwhile gone off and returned with full can or different can?) C with fat stomach comes on. A prods it and gets water in face from C. A persuades B to prod C's stomach, little driblets of water come out in B's face in response to B's prods. A fills mouth with water to give B the lot, keeps laughing and spilling it on ground. Eventually B gives A lot from own mouth.

Wuffenpuff gag

PB comes on with long cage covered with cloth. A present for Dame, wuffenpuff. Dame opens door to look at it, and it flies off (this done near wings). Ask children to call out if they see it wuffenpuff practise this. Dame and PB sit down for tea, table DC with two cups, pot and two loaves. Wuff appears URC down
Wuff appears ULC for longer. Dame turns to it, hits at it but too late. (signal is when chair is banged down hard)
Wuff appears URC again longer. Hit with bread too late
The fastest wuffenpuff I've ever seen
Appears over door. Too late both hit at it with bread. It resumes further along over door. Both hit at it. Round set Dame hits at next hole it will appear shouting Come out, come out, come out. PB hits Dame on bottom with bread
Don't do that, you're bashing my brains out
Sit down for tea again. Clock ticks noisily, pendulum swings
Quiet there. Tea pouring ad infinitum
Quiet there. Say when, for tea. Each Quiet there, clock stops
Clock goes round and round on wall for finish
Cuckoo business possible or wuffen comes out of clock?

Balloon dance (three handed)

To Pizzicato
On first pompom they pat balloons onto ground and catch them again. Comic does not catch
On second pom pom comic's balloon goes in air
When he gets it he breaks it, has to get another
In section following they toss to and fro, comic's goes right out of sight. Bouncing on breast
Bouncing on bum on pom pom, motor horn
Middle section, twist round wrists, passing as bodies pass. Break. One of breasts (balloon) breaks. He adjusts with one breast in middle of chest.
Also somewhere crawling underneath with balloon between

Whitewashing scene

Board and trestles DR. With coloured stiff whitewash in three buckets. One separate white whitewash also stiff. One separate white liquid whitewash. One large bath of liquid yellow whitewash at bottom of ladder UL. B (comic) puring liquid white from one bucket to another. A not touched. B pours it into bucket with no bottom. A fetches another bucket. This has pee hole through which whitewash comes out. A holds this to himself. A mops up. B goes up ladder and holds it to self up there. Then from pee hole whitewash goes into A's hat, then over A's feet.

They start on paper. Paper keeps rolling together again. We've got to take it by surprise. Splashes whitewash on it, goes on A's hat. They do some flicking at each other. You're pasting it on the wrong side. B whitewashes underside of trestle with brush. He goes up steps holding paper in front of him, stepping in paper as he goes up and tearing it, so only has small piece at top which he puts on wall. B Give me a little bit of paper with a large bit of paste on it. A provides this (stiff whitewash). B Shall I? He slips on ladder and gets it on own face. Coming down B slips and puts foot in bath of yellow. Then trying to get out sits down in bath. Trying to get out again he squelches – boating movement. A rubs his behind with paper. They go to trestle and work up the sploshing business with mixing different colours. Down front. Say Ah gives it him in mouth. Pile on head. Puts hat on top of whitewash on head, pull down. Hat with hole in top so comes out in spurt of toothpaste like ribbon when hat pulled down. Bucket with the lot in put on head. Sliding in yellow.

Cooking routine
12 dozen new laid eggs. Crate of eggs dropped.
Sack of nuts (nuts and bolts?)
Something to darken the pudding. Coal scuttle emptied into it
Date (calendar leaves off wall)
Beat dough. Anvil chorus
Stretch dough – Volga boatmen

Cake-making routine
A and B. A says Take four eggs (eggs put out). Beat them. (Smash with hammer) Then throw egg into audience. Flour in tin. Poring flour all over self. Put flour in tin into oven. Take it out. Large pink cake there, all wobbly. B falls in it. A laughs, back to audience. Leaning against dresser. B lifts A's shirt and puts cake down his back. Putting on head. Pushing down on head. Down front. Posing A in statue position, hand to chin, leg up. Put cake into up lifted hand. Kick A's foot. Take two more cakes, clap hands together with them as though playing cymbals. Put big one on head, so around neck like collar. Light candle on it. Band plays happy birthday. B blows out candle

After finding ghost in bed
I've just had a funny experience in my bed
Rings bell and goes up. Tells B to ring bell. A in bed. Bed folds right up into wall
Chest of drawers in adjoin ning room. When you pull drawer out on one side it goes in other side etc As A puts something in B pulls drawer out other side and A's thing goes on floor. When A pushes drawer in it comes out other side hitting B on bottom. Are you having trouble with your drawers? Etc Clock is wrong. A puts it right. It whirls round to wrong. He puts it right again, it whirls round and round several with sound effects.

Cake routine
Coloured cakes on shelves of dresser. Large wedding cake on top. Table DR. Three eggs. Beat them. Comic beats 'em with mallet. Get one of eggs. Let me have it. (eggs thrown at him) Flour. Flour thrown over stooge. Stir the mixture. What with? Oh, use your head. Comic puts bowl on head upside down, moves bowl around. Gets cake, falls down on it, gets foot stuck in it. Stooge laughs, leaning on dresser, bend down. Comic lifts shirt, exposing bare back, puts two cakes together and puts them down back of trousers. Stooge gives it to comic on face. Comic retaliates down front. Cake in flower pot with plate is put on comic's head, plate removed and cake pulled down over his head, wet going over him. Wedding cake put on his head, picture of bridge comes down in front of him.

Cream in the cake
A B C D. Bowl of cream. Tray of cream pies. D (King) with huge cake with cream on top. A preparing cream flicks on B. B puts cream on A in retaliation. Work L to R but D nearby chucking

it misses it each time. Finally falls in face in own cream cake.

The Fiddle Inn
The Fiddle Inn? Is that a good inn?
No, it's a vile inn

Captain Catskin (Atkins)
I beg your pudding

(seasick business) It's a beautiful nite. The moon will be up soon.
Blimey, don't tell me that's got to come up too

Just you and me and thirty sailors?
Are you afraid?
I can't wait

Enter with lav chain
I just pulled this and the palace flew out of my hand

Karate business A lot of grunts and movement . Villain give him slight slap on face (or just blows)
and comic falls down

King: You can have half a crown. (taking crown in half) Half a crown for you, half a crown for me

The Giant will have you shot at dawn
He can't do that. I don't get up till tea-time

I've been making money. I've been playing snap with a bloke that stutters

I've got a marvellous date tonight with a redhead. She's wonderful. No hair. Just a red head.

Fish fingers
I didn't know fish had fingers

Sound of music and gay laughter – lyrical build up. I've always wanted to go to Butlins

Water routine
Comics dying of thirst, ask audience to tell them if they see any water. Friday goes by at back with
two cans on pole, marked Water. Then returns with large teapot on head. Oh I wish we had some
beer. MF goes by with barrel marked Light Ale. All lying down. Friday enters with watering can,
sprinkles flowers then sprinkles them. They revive.

My Prince
My Princess
My goodness
My Guinness (with glass of real Guinness)

I've got the finest voice in the country
It sounds horrible indoors but it's all right in the country

Bringing down tiny word sheet for audience. That's what binoculars are for

Two comics dressed as schoolgirls with hockey sticks
Do you know what that is? (stick)
No, but it's bent (Try to straighten)
One shows other what bully up is
A knocks B's stick flying. B falls down
B cries Smile for sister
Do it again. B insists on this and same thing happens
Another thing you mustn't do is raise the stick above your shoulder. If you hit anyone, hit them from there, like that (hits B hard on knee with stick)
Into number

This is a Pawn ticket. You can't go to the Ball with that
No I go to three balls with that

Two eyes on pants. Bend down with back to audience. B puts hat on face on A's pants

Snogging in wood

I'll give you a prize from the Walls of China (build up)
Eventually – large ice cream cornet

Phrases in Chinese
This means Help, my … is caught in the spin drier
In Chinese restaurant. That cheese is too strong. It's eating the cheese roll
I think I've swallowed the chopsticks

Name: I Ping
I Ping? You Pong
Counting gag with rickshaw man. How many miles. How old. Where do you live? My sister lives at. How old you say your grandfather is?

An example of proud dependable good-hearted womanhood
Come in, Godfrey Winn

Am I addressing Widow Twankey?
You look as if you were undressing Widow Twankey

Long lost sister from the Orient
Something re full back for the Arsenal

Aladdin called after well-known oil heater

No more Hue and Cry
That's not coming off is it? What?
My favourite programme – Hugh and I

You are his brother. He had a head pointed at the top just like you.

Laundry gags
Kelly, Which Kelly? Kelly from the Isle of Man

(Curse) You'll post your coupons just too late to win your Treble Chance

Counting gag
Comic owes feed £4 18s. That's 58s. No 98s. Counting out notes, one two three etc
How old are you? 10. 10, 11, 12 etc
How long do you want to live? Till I'm 58. 58, 59, 60 etc
How old is your Grannie? 95. 95, 96, 97 etc
Thank you. Exit Comic

I love going to balls don't you?
No, I went to three balls last week
If you bought a ticket for £1, 1 and 4d, where would you be going to?
I don't know
Then what did you buy the ticket for?

I saw a nasty accident. A Teddy Boy was running to catch a bus and he caught his foot in his pocket

In a bus a fat man sat on my sausages. The trouble I had putting all that meat back in my sausages

Old man said I've had all me teeth taken out and television put in

I'm a Whitbread basher (tummy). This is what's called brewer's goitre

Bless your little cotton socks

Index

(This index does not include the appendices)

Lightning Source UK Ltd.
Milton Keynes UK
UKOW042116150113

204932UK00001B/184/P